ONE

The Invasion

Hitler launched his campaign of military conquests by attacking Poland. In August 1939 he told his generals that he would concoct a "propaganda reason" for the invasion, the plausibility of which should not concern them in the least. Declaring that the victors write the history books, he encouraged the commanders to close their "hearts to pity" and to "act brutally." Eighty million people, he explained, needed their Lebensraum. He had written in *Mein Kampf,* "The Reich must again set itself along the road of the Teutonic Knights of old. . . . And so we National Socialists . . . take up where we broke off six hundred years ago. We stop the endless German movement to the south and west, and turn our gaze towards the land in the East."[1]

In late August, Hitler ordered SS General Reinhard Heydrich, head of the Gestapo, to stage an attack on German units stationed on the border with Poland, a mission requiring disguise and subterfuge. To create a provocation, Heydrich and Heinrich Himmler, head of the SS, obtained 150 Polish uniforms from Admiral Wilhelm Canaris, the head of the Abwehr (military counterintelligence agency). Dressed in these uniforms, SS soldiers assaulted the broadcasting station at Gleiwitz on 31 August. Heydrich then ordered several concentration camp inmates from Sachsenhausen murdered and dressed in the stolen Polish uniforms. The SS offered the bodies at the Gleiwitz station as proof for foreign journalists that Poland had attacked Germany. Consequently, Hitler ordered the invasion of Poland without declaring war. He knew he had to have a reason to attack other than imperialism, and this provided him with an excuse. "Actual proof of Polish attacks is essential," Heydrich said, "both for the foreign press and for German propaganda."[2]

On 1 September, as his legions swarmed across the border, Hitler announced on the radio: "The Polish state has refused the peaceful settlement of relations which I desired and has appealed to arms. Germans in Poland are persecuted with bloody terror. A series of violations of the frontier, intolerable to a great power, prove that Poland is no longer willing to respect the frontier of the Reich. In order to put an end to this lunacy I have no choice other than to meet force with force; the German Army will fight for the honor and rights of a new-born Germany." He mentioned fourteen border incidents by the Poles that had left the Germans no recourse but to return fire.[3]

That day, Karin Tiche, a twenty-year-old unmarried Pole and the daughter of a Jewish mother and a Christian father, walked onto her balcony in Warsaw. Observing two airplanes performing strange acrobatic turns in the air, she yelled for her mother to come see how their men were training for war. Then the aircraft fired their guns, and suddenly one fell from the sky engulfed in flames. The victorious plane, she now saw, had Nazi markings. The Polish government immediately announced on the radio that the Germans had started a border conflict that the Poles would readily win. "They told us this while they moved our government to the south of Poland, away from Warsaw," Tiche says, "and we would soon find out that it was not just a border dispute but a full-scale invasion and that we were losing everywhere." Hitler's anti-Polish rhetoric and military maneuvers on their border had led many Poles to expect war, but when it came it surprised everyone.[4]

To many Germans the attack seemed wholly justified. The Versailles Treaty had forced Germany to give up territory to Poland, a country created, in part, as a result of Germany's defeat in World War I. The Allies appropriated other German territory as well and parceled it out to neighboring countries. Germans were shocked that the Allies separated East Prussia from Germany proper by the Polish Corridor, which led to the Baltic Sea at the free city of Danzig. They were enraged at Poland for accepting territories that it had no apparent historical claim to and that it had not conquered militarily. Writing in 1920, General Hans von Seeckt, head of the Reichswehr, declared Poland "Germany's mortal enemy," one that had to be destroyed. In the mid-1920s, 90 percent of Germans felt similarly. By the 1930s, the "overwhelming majority" of the Wehrmacht's officer corps supported launching an attack on Poland.[5]

Hitler's invasion of Poland in 1939 also met with the enthusiastic approbation of the German population. The Evangelical Church in Germany issued an official appeal a day after the attack "for Germans to support the invasion to 'recover German blood' for the fatherland," and the Catholic hierarchy encouraged and admonished "Catholic soldiers, in obedience to the führer, to do their duty and to be ready to sacrifice their lives." Many religious newspapers claimed that Germans were simply fighting for essential Lebensraum. As the American journalist William Shirer wrote on 20 September while living in Berlin, "I have still to find a German, even among those who don't like the regime, who sees anything wrong in the German destruction of Poland."[6]

Hitler used overwhelming force to conquer Poland. On 1 September, one and a half million German troops crossed into the country, backed by two thousand planes. Wehrmacht soldiers sliced through the widening gaps of an unprepared and poorly equipped Polish army stationed along the border with Germany. Poland had two million men under arms, but they were outmatched by the motorized, highly trained, and disciplined Germans. Despite their passionate defense, the Poles would not last long.[7]

As Germany swallowed up Austria, Czechoslovakia, and Poland in 1938 and 1939, thousands of Jews tried to escape the Nazi juggernaut. Many sold their belongings to purchase passage out of Europe, and some abandoned their families altogether. Few of them reached freedom. After Germany crossed Poland's border, the U.S. government received pleas from its own citizens to help relatives trapped in Europe, thousands of whom flooded American embassies and consulates in Europe with petitions for visas. Most cries for help went unanswered. The American government was too busy with social issues, such as the massive unemployment resulting from the Great Depression, and too intent on maintaining diplomatic neutrality to involve itself with refugee problems. Anti-Jewish sentiment in the United States, moreover, peaked in the late thirties, worsening an already difficult situation for Jews suffering under Hitler.[8]

In 1938, one poll claimed that 58 percent of Americans believed that the Jews were partly if not fully responsible for Nazi persecution. Many Americans simply did not see the Jews' plight as their own. As the "arch foe of immigration liberalization," Senator Robert Reynolds of North Carolina said, "Why should we give up those blessings to those not so fortunate? . . . Let Europe take care of its own people."[9]

When President Roosevelt heard of the Nazi invasion, he exclaimed, "It has come at last. God help us all." In his fireside chat on 3 September 1939, he said that he wanted to keep America neutral but that he could not ask his fellow Americans to remain neutral in thought: "Even a neutral cannot be asked to close its mind or conscience." Roosevelt knew he would have to aid the Allies in order to defeat Germany but would need to determine when and how to do so. American military intervention would ultimately be triggered not by human rights violations but by the threat posed to democracy and the Western world.[10]

Many in Poland, as well as in the United States, looked to the Allies to take quick action against Hitler. Chaim Kaplan, a distinguished Hebrew school principal in Warsaw, wrote that he hoped the Allies would stick to their word and not leave Poland to the mercy of the Germans as they had left Czechoslovakia.[11] But it seemed that a timorous world would indeed let Germany roll over the helpless Polish nation. Although France and Britain mobilized and deployed their forces in the West, they did not invade Germany. Would they ever act? The only country that could help Poland in the East was the Soviet Union, but the USSR was bound to Hitler by the Nazi-Soviet Non-Aggression Pact signed in August 1939. In fact, Stalin was also bent on Poland's destruction and hoped to gain vast amounts of land after its imminent defeat.

With the blitzkrieg preventing most Polish Jews from fleeing, worried family members in the United States wrote the American government for help in getting their relatives out from under Hitler. They had good reason for concern, because Hitler did not waste time starting his killing of "inferior people." Almost immediately after the invasion, the SS began to liquidate undesirable elements of the population, including Jews, Communists, Polish nobility, clergy, and intelligentsia.[12]

Most of the 3.3 million Jews in Poland in 1939, one-third of them in poverty, would perish in the Holocaust. Having as yet no organized plan of genocide, the Germans initially killed Polish Gentiles with the same frequency as they did Jews, focusing especially on the Polish elite. "There was no way of knowing in 1939 that Hitler would be murdering us by the millions in a few years. No one would ever have thought this back then," observes Tiche. "The nation of Beethoven, Bach, and Goethe murdering people like they did was unthinkable." Historian Nora Levin writes that even in the summer of 1940, no one, not even Polish Jews, could have foreseen the full extent of atrocity under the Nazis.[13] Many observed acts of persecution and isolated murders, but the systematic gassing of millions lay beyond the human imagination.

Hitler had given ample indication of his intentions, but few had taken him seriously. En route to Poland, German troops traveled in railcars emblazoned with large-nosed caricatures captioned "We're off to Poland—to thrash the Jews." Moreover, Hitler had proclaimed in a major address in January 1939 that "if international monied Jewry within Europe and beyond again succeeds in casting the peoples into a world war, the result will not be the Bolshevization of the globe and a victory for Jewry, but the annihilation of the Jewish race in Europe." Hitler aimed not only to reclaim lost territory and pride but also to begin his eradication of inferior people, including Slavs and Jews. He had written about such racial discrimination and world conquest in *Mein Kampf,* but few who read the volume took him seriously. William Shirer notes, "Whatever other accusations can be made against Adolf Hitler, no one can accuse him of not putting down in writing exactly the kind of Germany he intended to make if ever he came to power, and the kind of world he meant to create by armed German conquest." Shirer observes correctly that although Hitler mentioned his plans, only when he started to put them in action did people begin to realize his true intentions, and even then, many of the crimes he committed were still unbelievable in 1939.[14]

A tiny minority saw the coming storm. Chaim Kaplan, who had heard Hitler speak on the radio in January 1939, wrote in his diary on 1 September that no Jew under Hitler's rule had any hope. "Hitler, may his name be blotted out," Kaplan recorded, "threatened in one of his speeches that if war comes the Jews of Europe will be exterminated. . . . Our hearts tremble at the future. . . . What will be our destiny?" On 10 September, Kaplan again referred to the speech and questioned why God had allowed Hitler to subject the Jews to such cruelty. Wondering if they had sinned more than others to war-

Reich Labor Service personnel en route to Poland in railcars emblazoned with large-nosed caricatures captioned "We're off to Poland—to thrash the Jews" (United States Holocaust Memorial Museum Archive of Photographs)

rant this punishment, he concluded that they were "more disgraced than any people!"[15]

Poland in 1939 was a strange land for the German invaders, especially with its large Hasidic Jewish communities. In Eastern Europe, many religious Jews spent their days in yeshivas, advanced academies for Talmud study, or *shtiblekh,* small houses of prayer. Many Polish Jews lived in shtetls or small ghetto enclaves that were often no more than clusters of dilapidated shacks and the requisite synagogue and house of study. Since most Wehrmacht soldiers enjoyed relative prosperity and led secular lives, they were shocked at how tens of thousands of ultrareligious Hasidic Ostjuden, as Eastern European Jews were pejoratively called, lived. The Ostjuden appeared strange with their long beards and *peyes* (side locks), and the skullcaps, *gartlekh* (fancy silk belts), and long dark coats reminiscent of seventeenth-century Polish aristocracy and intelligentsia. The Germans, unable to understand how these Jews earned a living since they prayed and studied all day, regarded them as lazy. Even German Jewish soldiers stationed in the East during World War I had expressed disgust at the appearance, habits, and living conditions of the Ostjuden.[16]

For decades before Hitler, many German Jews felt that the poor, culturally backward, and "dirty" Ostjuden gave the typically well-educated and cultured German Jews a bad name. A few German Jews helped the Ostjuden philanthropically, but by and large they rejected any feelings of kinship. The Ostjuden lived in anachronistic ghettos and learned only "Polish Talmudic barbarism," as contrasted with refined German *Bildung* (education). To self-regarding German Jews, they observed an irrational, mystical, and superstitious religion that no longer had a place in a world based on reason and scientific knowledge. The Ostjuden, in turn, felt that their heretical German brothers had abandoned *Yiddishkeit* (Jewishness) by shaving off their beards, adopting modern ways, and not keeping the Sabbath holy.[17]

Many assimilated German Jews regarded Hitler's antisemitism as a reaction to the culture of the Ostjuden. Perhaps some German Jews felt as they did because the Ostjuden represented a part of themselves they wanted to deny. They knew that at one time their ancestors resembled the Ostjuden they condemned. That painful fact prompted many to reject their Ostjuden brethren with disdain and arrogance.[18] Ostjuden simply represented all that they had fought to distance themselves from in their secularized, modern lifestyles. It is hardly surprising that most German Christians, too, perceived them as primitive. As a result, German Jews were even more concerned that they not be associated with such an unpopular group.

In the first days after the invasion, the Germans randomly destroyed hundreds of synagogues and murdered hundreds of Jews. At Czestochowa alone, they shot 180 Jews. In the village of Widawa,

Waffen-SS soldiers cutting off an elderly Polish Jew's beard (YIVO and United
States Holocaust Memorial Museum)

they burned Rabbi Abraham Mordechai Morocco alive when he refused to destroy the sacred writings. On 8 September, they herded
200 Jews into Widawa's synagogue, locked the doors, and set the
building on fire. Other German soldiers took pleasure in hanging
Jews from street lamps and watching them struggle with the rope
as they suffocated. During the first two months of the occupation,
the Germans killed at least 7,000 Polish Jews and forced the living
into harsh labor and sudden "resettlement." Although there was as
yet no organized plan of genocide, it became obvious that the Jews
did not have a future under the Nazis.[19]

Many Polish Jews felt helpless. Hasidic Jews, in particular, had
dedicated their whole lives to learning Torah, the five books of
Moses, and did not know how to use weapons or to fight. Germans
often expressed shock at how passively these Jews accepted persecution, but they also grudgingly admired their dedication to God.
When the Nazis torched a synagogue, it was not uncommon for Jews
to run through gunfire into burning buildings to rescue the holy

scrolls. Many willingly died doing so because they considered life meaningless without the Torah.[20]

The atrocities against Polish Jews were so shocking that eventually even a few members of the German armed forces protested. General Johannes Blaskowitz of the Wehrmacht complained to Hitler that "this state of affairs undermines order and discipline. . . . It is necessary to forbid summary executions forthwith. The German army is not here to give its support to a band of assassins."[21] He further argued that the atrocities would have a horrible effect on the German people because "unlimited brutalization and moral depravity [would spread] . . . like an epidemic through the most valuable German human material. If the high officials of the SS continue to call for violence and brutality, brutal men will soon reign supreme." Hitler ignored Blaskowitz's complaints. Even the notorious General Walther von Reichenau did not approve of the SS actions. Hitler continued to disregard these misgivings, declaring that one cannot "wage war with Salvation Army methods."[22]

Wilhelm Canaris, head of the Abwehr, tried to influence those in power to remove SS units from Poland to end a situation he believed disgraced the German people. He had experienced problems with the SS over authority throughout the 1930s, and now he regarded their involvement in domestic matters in Poland as encroaching on his territory of operations. Also, Canaris disapproved of wholesale murder. In response, Hitler asserted that "our struggle cannot be measured in terms of legality or illegality. Our methods must conform to our principles. We must prevent a new Polish intelligentsia taking power and cleanse the Greater Reich of Jewish and Polish riffraff." He told his generals the SS would intensify its work. As relations between the Wehrmacht and the SS deteriorated, Hitler removed the SS and police from military authority on 17 October. On 19 October, he decreed that by 25 October the military administration of Poland would be replaced by civilian rule—that is, the SS and the Nazi government.[23]

In retaliation for Germany's invasion, the Poles committed atrocities of their own. Fearing a fifth column, Polish officials gathered between ten thousand and fifteen thousand ethnic Germans for deportation to centers in the middle of the country. During these actions, many Poles became enraged and murdered thousands of these Germans. The worst massacre occurred on 3 September at Bromberg, where Poles murdered more than a thousand Germans. Since the Nazis conquered territory so quickly, they soon discovered the mass graves, which the SS men promptly used to justify their own, far vaster crimes.[24]

On 3 September, France and Britain declared war on Germany. When the news reached Hitler, he "sat immobile gazing before him." He had not expected the Allies to respond, especially on behalf of a "pathetic" nation like Poland. Although he feared a two-front war, an Allied attack in the west never materialized. Anglo-French actions were limited to blockading ports on the North and Baltic seas, conducting scattered air operations, and fortifying the western frontier with Germany. Initially, celebrations took place throughout Poland, and Warsaw was adorned with French and British flags, but soon the Poles realized their putative friends Britain and France would not act. Colonel Jozef Beck, Poland's foreign minister, informed the French that his nation felt betrayed. Even though back in May General Maurice Gamelin, commander in chief of the French army, had promised General Tadeusz Kasprzycki, Poland's war minister, that "as soon as the main German effort against Poland begins, France will launch an offensive against Germany with the main bodies of her forces," when the attack came, Gamelin did nothing. The French had no desire to undertake an offensive against a country that had demonstrated such "frightening destructive capabilities" in its campaign against Poland. The French feared German military might, although Germany's western borders were very lightly defended. The British also worried about Hitler's new form of warfare and the possibility of an all-out air attack on London. The West, in effect, deserted Poland.[25]

"We are left abandoned and the shadow of death encircles us," wrote Chaim Kaplan. Germany had only a few divisions on its western border, and had the Allies attacked they would have forced the Wehrmacht to withdraw a considerable number of its forces from the East to meet the assault. Practically all of Germany's planes were in Poland, and most of its tanks were engaged in the East. General Alfred Jodl, chief of Wehrmacht operations, wrote after the war that "if in 1939 we were not defeated, it was only because about 110 French and English divisions, which during our war against Poland faced twenty-three divisions in the West, remained completely inactive." The actual breakdown was seventy-six Allied divisions facing thirty-two German.[26] Even so, the Allies heavily outnumbered the Germans. The governments of France and Britain were led by men who had experienced the senseless bloodshed of World War I and wanted to avoid large land battles that might again turn into murderous trench warfare.

Had the Allies honored their commitment to attack Germany once Hitler invaded Poland, the war might have taken a different course. As it happened, France and Britain delayed for nine months until Germany attacked France in May 1940. In the United States, Senator William Borah of Idaho termed the inaction of the French and British the "phony war," while the Germans called it the *Sitzkrieg* (sitting war).[27]

After the Nazis invaded Poland, it became evident that they were focused on the Jews, even though SS units killed large numbers of Gentiles as well. Many Polish Jews tried to pass themselves off as "Aryans" or joined partisan groups to survive.[28] Others tried to escape the Nazis, but only a small number succeeded. Most needed assistance in order to flee, but few received such support. There was one remarkable exception.

It was at this point that the U.S. government, seemingly indifferent to the plight of European Jewry, cooperated with some of the highest ranking officers and politicians in the Third Reich to carry out one of the most spectacular rescues of the war. The plan relied upon, of all people, Abwehr personnel. These German soldiers received orders to find, protect, and then escort the ultra-Orthodox Lubavitcher Rebbe Joseph Isaac Schneersohn out of war-torn Warsaw and to send him on to the United States. This daring operation required elaborate effort on the part of Abwehr agents and American officials and lawyers. These unlikely allies came together to rescue a most unusual victim. As the rescue plot crystallized, many wondered if he could possibly survive Hitler's inferno. Time was running out for him.

TWO

The Lubavitchers and Their Rebbe

The religious dynasty of Hasidic Jews called Lubavitchers originated in Lubavitch, Byelorussia, in the late eighteenth century. Hasidism itself began with the Baal Shem Tov (Master of the Good Name), who mobilized Eastern European Jewry in response to decades of persecution and poverty and to the trauma inflicted by the messianic crusade of a charismatic figure named Sabbetai Zvi.

Zvi entered on the scene with Europe still recovering from the aftereffects of the Thirty Years' War (1618–48), a time when many people were yearning for a better future. Zvi tapped into their fears and desires, with devastating results. Although himself unstable, he could mesmerize audiences with his pronouncements of the coming kingdom of God. Believing he was on a sacred mission, he traveled to the Promised Land from Eastern Europe to launch his self-described crusade. While in Gaza, in the Holy Land, in 1665, he proclaimed that he was the Messiah, and many there supported him, saying they had seen visions proving his declaration. As stories about him spread throughout Europe, the Middle East, and Africa, thousands proclaimed that God's reign on earth had commenced. According to some sources, Zvi's message captured the imaginations of a large percentage of European Jews. Emboldened, Zvi and a group of fervent followers traveled to Turkey to ask the sultan to surrender his throne. When the sultan learned of Zvi's mission, he presented Zvi and his followers with a counterproposal: convert to Islam or die. Zvi and many of his followers chose the former. News of his conversion and betrayal of Judaism devastated Jewish communities around the world. Their Messiah had turned out to be a charlatan.

In the end, although Zvi's false crusade demoralized Eastern European Jews, it encouraged them to seek a personal relationship with the divine. They hungered for a legitimate movement that would raise their spirits and connect them with God. Hasidism filled these needs, and the Baal Shem Tov was its leader.

The Baal Shem Tov (or Besht, the acronym by which he is known) was born in 1698. His life, according to Lubavitch legend, started out like the life of Isaac. An angel visited his elderly parents and told them that God was going to grant them a child. Just as God had blessed Sarah and Abraham, the angel explained, he would bless them with a son who would take the Lord's message to mankind. The Besht's disciples described his ability to perform miracles, even as a young child. By the 1730s, he had gathered a following who were later known as the Hasidim, or "pious ones."[1] Although the traditional Jewish leadership (the Mitnagdim) opposed the Besht's movement, considering it a possible second Zvi crusade, it won the loyalty of hundreds of thousands of eager followers.

The Besht taught that the essence of Judaism is the fusion of scholarship and personal transformation. The Jewish people of his time were polarized by a deep rift between scholars and lay people, between knowledge and behavior. The Besht said that the experience of studying the Torah and the Talmud could not be compartmentalized and needed to extend into every aspect of life. He taught that the Torah was a holistic experience that should not only engage the mind but also inspire the heart and the soul. As a brilliant and original teacher, he revealed new layers of understanding in traditional biblical texts. Using the traditional teachings of Jewish mysticism, known collectively as the Kabala, the Besht explained the spiritual and psychological dimension of every Torah verse, every Talmudic law, every mitzvah. In the eyes of his disciples, he revealed the vibrant soul of the ancient Torah and gave it dynamic meaning and new life. Although many of the stories surrounding the Besht are "possibly (or probably) completely fictitious," according to the historian Avrum Ehrlich, they took on a life of their own and have become "the basis of Hasidic custom, theology, and tradition."

The Besht's teachings promoted a mystical and religious fervor among the uneducated, impoverished Jews of Eastern Europe. Torah scholars recognized in his teachings the sacred truths passed on through the generations; the Besht was continuing this tradition by revealing to all people the inherent godliness of their souls and their lives. His philosophy fulfilled a spiritual need by teaching that each Jew was sacred and special to God and should serve the Lord with love and joy, with music and dance, and with prayer and passion. God could be found in nature, in work, in good deeds, and in daily living, for everything contained the spark of the Divine; everyone had access to God. Contrary to what the Jewish establishment taught, even laypeople and non-scholars could learn about and discover God in their lives. Although the Besht encouraged the study of Torah, he also taught that one should look for God in the physical earth; refining and spiritualizing one's own life could help refine and spiritualize the world. He urged his followers to realize that deeds could hasten the coming of the Messiah, who would usher in a harmonious world free of disease, war, and suffering. Such a Messiah would create a world suffused with spirituality, "filled with Divine knowledge as the waters cover the sea."[2]

When the Besht died, in 1760, he was succeeded by one of his students, Dov Ber of Mezritch, known as the Magid. The Magid is regarded as the educator of the largest class of Hasidic leaders and is considered the "supreme mystic, saint, and scholar who, by virtue of his reputed discipleship with the [Besht] became a legitimate interpreter of the new techniques of Hasidism." Upon the Magid's death in 1773, the movement separated into around thirty sects throughout Eastern Europe. His disciples, known as tzaddiks, or enlightened, righteous leaders, continued the Baal Shem Tov's work of educating all Jews in the ways of God. Many of the splinter groups took their names from the birthplaces, headquarters, or grave sites of their leaders. The Lubavitchers, named for the Byelorussian town that was the headquarters of the movement, were one such group. Their founder was Schneur Zalman of Liadi (1745–1812).

More than other Hasidic groups, the Lubavitchers emphasized learning as well as worship. Like most other Hasidim, however, they believed that their Rebbe and their unique philosophy, Chabad, were incomparable. Chabad is an acronym of the Hebrew words *Chochmah, Binah, Da'at,* meaning wisdom, understanding, and knowledge, the three levels of divine emanation in the Kabala. Chabad demanded of its followers comprehension, understanding, and appreciation of the message of Judaism and Jewish mysticism. Questioning, debating, and contemplating the ideas of Judaism and Hasidism are intrinsic to the Lubavitch system. According to their doctrine, Lubavitchers should strive to eliminate ego and vanity from their lives and cultivate a spirit of brotherly love and mutual assistance. If one is in touch with his divine soul, the founder of Chabad wrote, he automatically falls in love with every single Jew, since all are "fragments of God." Schneur Zalman wrote in his book *Tanya* that he ardently believed in such spiritual growth and that Jews should strive to do everything in their power to connect with God, to realize the purpose of existence. Although messianism had been a constant theme of Judaism for two thousand years, the Chabad movement emphasized the importance of yearning for the coming of the Messiah and the actions that could be taken to hasten his arrival.[3] One contemporary of Schneur Zalman wrote of his book,

"With the *Tanya*, the Israelites will go forth to meet the Messiah." Tzaddiks like Schneur Zalman often took the title of "Rebbe," a variation of the word *rabbi*, meaning "my teacher" or "my master." As each generation's Rebbe is the master and guiding force of his sect, the title is given to heads of Hasidic dynasties.

When Napoleon invaded Russia in 1812, Schneur Zalman opposed the French and fled Liadi with sixty wagons full of household goods and numerous followers. Rebbe Zalman said he would rather die than live under Napoleon. In the course of his flight, he died. After the Russians finally forced the French out of their country, the czar did not forget the Lubavitchers' loyalty, and the government's oppression eased. Rebbe Zalman had had no special devotion to the czar or to Russia, but simply supported his homeland for fear that Napoleon's "enlightenment" would secularize Russian Jewry and destroy the foundations of divine-based morality. That was a bigger threat than continued persecution under the czar. Over the next 120 years, Chabad experienced ups and downs and suffered splinter factions, with several leaders competing for the position of Rebbe. Despite the hardships it remained a vibrant Jewish community and a guiding light for many Russian Jews. At the start of the twentieth century, the Lubavitch movement, owing to its outreach efforts, had tens of thousands of adherents throughout Europe and America.

By World War II, six generations of Schneersohns, descendants of Schneur Zalman, had guided the Lubavitch, or Chabad, movement. In 1939, the sixth Lubavitcher Rebbe, Joseph Isaac Schneersohn, led the movement and was widely considered the unofficial leader of all Russian Jews. Most Lubavitchers believed their Rebbe was endowed with mystical powers and regarded him as the Moses and possibly the *Moshiach* (Messiah) of their generation. According to Jewish theology, each generation of Jews is thought to have a potential Messiah—the Lubavitchers just believe that if there is to be a Messiah, he will be their Rebbe. Many believe that because a tzaddik has succeeded in transforming his ego to allow his inner divine soul to pervade his entire consciousness, he is "without sin" and God blesses him with the *Ruach Hakodesh,* the Holy Spirit.[4] Elie Wiesel writes of the tzaddik: "He is what can be, what man wants to be, he is the chosen one who is refused nothing, in heaven or on earth. God is angry? He can make him smile. God is severe? He can induce him to leniency."[5] His followers assume he knows intellectually and feels emotionally the physical and spiritual needs of every Jew and recognizes how to connect each to God. As a result, he has a special role as intermediary between God and people. Moreover, his followers believe the Rebbe is able to feel the pain of those persecuted and to suffer with them. "I feel each individual's hardships, and know more or less each individual's pain and suffering," Rebbe Schneersohn wrote. "Each one of you is close to my heart, and each man's distress strikes deep." In other words, the Rebbe's relationship to his followers is emotionally deep and intimate. Rebbe Schneersohn described the love a Rebbe has for his followers as stronger than what a parent feels for a child. As for the follower, he or she should say: "Rebbe, I am yours; I dedicate myself to you completely. It's only that the smart little fellow, who is wise to do evil—the Evil Inclination— is trying to fool me and ensnare me into a sack. Basically, that's not what I want. I'm yours. I want to be as I ought to be. Rebbe, have pity on me: take me out of where I am, and set me up where I ought to be!"[6]

For the Lubavitchers, the Rebbe is not only a human being but also a prophetic leader worthy of total submission. Although there are many rabbis, there is only one Rebbe in the Chabad community. Elie Wiesel writes: "In Hasidism, the Rebbe by virtue of the strength he incarnates and the majesty he evokes . . . represents the father figure par excellence: someone good yet strict, charitable yet severe, tolerant with others but inflexible with himself. In other words, a singular human being in whom all attributes converge and in whom all contradictions are resolved." Chabad philosophy teaches that contradictions and paradoxes are innate to life itself, indeed to

God himself; consequently, it might be added to Wiesel's observation that, for Lubavitchers, the Rebbe is the paradigm of not only how to resolve but also how to embrace the paradoxes of one's life and use them as a catalyst for deeper growth. Most Lubavitchers, if not all, also believe that Rebbes, once dead, are closer to God in heaven, and thus many ask deceased Rebbes to intercede with God on their behalf.[7]

Born in Lubavitch in 1880, Rebbe Joseph Isaac Schneersohn assumed leadership of Chabad Hasidism in 1920. Although the Rebbe cherished and supported all sects of Judaism based on the Torah, he believed that Chabad, which fuses the rational and mystical streams of Torah into a unified, comprehensive program for life, captured Judaism in its full majesty and depth. Regarding the Reform and Conservative movements, he made a clear distinction between their individual members and the general groups. Every Jew, regardless of affiliation, the Rebbe taught, was as Jewish as Moses himself. But he felt that any reformations of Jewish law and tradition (according to his Halachic definitions) were historical errors and would increase assimilation in subsequent generations. Once the Torah laws were changed, there would be no way to stop the downward spiral toward complacency and total alienation. Chabad is not unique in these views. Most Orthodox Jews, especially Hasidic ones, hold that the beliefs and practices of Reform and Conservative Jews are at odds with Judaism's core tenets.[8]

According to the Rebbe, Chabad philosophy gave Jews an opportunity to experience the full richness of Judaism, to "suck the marrow" out of the Torah and its way of life. As the Rebbe said, "The ethical teachings and guidance in the service of G-d which are to be found in *Chassidus* are intended for all Jews, not only for Chassidim. *Every* Jew ought to listen closely to the voice of G-d which has been revealed through our forefathers, the Rebbes." The teaching "unfolded through our Rebbes and their tens of thousands of chassidim" could help nonreligious souls "see and hear the plain truth

Joseph Isaac Schneersohn, the sixth Lubavitcher Rebbe (1880–1950), at his desk in Brooklyn, 1949 (Eliezer Zaklikovsky)

about the life of man in This World." Through the study of Chassidus, the "divine level of wisdom," one drew "down the revelation of G-dliness in This World."[9]

From the outset, Rebbe Schneersohn's life seemed shrouded in mystery, again much like the biblical story of Isaac. In the late 1870s many Lubavitchers had feared the end of the Schneersohn dynasty, since the fifth Rebbe had no children and his wife, Sara, had given up hope. According to Chabad sources, one night after crying herself to sleep she had a dream in which three men revealed to her that she would have a son. One of them told her, "Don't cry, my daughter.

I promise that this year you will give birth to a son—but with the following condition: immediately after *Yom Tov* [festival], you must give eighteen rubles of your money to *tzedakah* [charity]." The other men nodded in agreement. Then the three blessed Sara and left. Sara soon became pregnant with the only child she would bear. The Schneersohn family had practiced a tradition of interfamily marriage among cousins that strengthened a network of alliances for future leaders. Avrum Ehrlich writes that the inbreeding was so widespread "it can be seen as obsessive. The high degree of apparent infertility and other irregularities in the family might be linked to these practices." Since Joseph's parents were first cousins, his birth could also be seen as a genetic miracle.[10]

Joseph's father, Shalom Dovber, the fifth Lubavitcher Rebbe (1860–1920), trained Joseph as his successor. He deeply loved all Jews but viewed as "God's enemies" Jewish atheists, Jewish socialists, and all other Jews who did not believe in God's commandments; the large number involved with the Communist Party, notoriously hostile to religion, particularly worried him. He spent hours teaching his son and his followers how to defend the movement from such people and to inspire Jews in ways that would not be diluted by forces of assimilation. He trained them to be "'soldiers in the Rebbe's army' who would fight 'without concessions or compromise' to ensure that true Judaism would survive. Their struggle would pave the way for the coming of the Messiah."[11]

At an early age, Joseph regarded his father as endowed with unique powers to know the truth before a person spoke and to tell if someone was hiding information from him. Often, during prayers, his father would burst into tears from the emotion he felt for his God. Knowing that he would follow in his father's footsteps, young Joseph assumed the burden of expectation placed on him. At the age of eleven, for example, when his father was ill, he took it on himself to go to the grave of his ancestors and ask his forebears to take "pity [on] and arouse heaven's mercies" for his father. He returned to his father's bedside to find him recovered. "It was clear to me," he later said, "that it was my prayer at the resting place of my holy forebears that had aroused G-d's loving kindness and compassion." From his youth on, he had great confidence in his spiritual abilities.[12]

It was also at the age of eleven, in late 1891, that Joseph first got into trouble with the law for defending his fellow Jews. Witnessing a Gentile Russian policeman mistreating a Jew, Joseph attacked the Russian. The authorities arrested him for the assault but quickly released him. The future Rebbe was not afraid to take action against injustice and to inflict physical harm on the perpetrator.[13]

In 1893, Shalom Dovber told Joseph that just as Abraham, honoring his covenant with God, had bound up his son Isaac, he now felt called to do something similar. He had to bind Joseph to the mission of dedicating his life to the Jewish people.[14] Two years later, the fifteen-year-old Joseph became his father's secretary, helping to answer letters and organize the distribution of literature, food, and clothes. He gladly spent time with his father doing these tasks. In addition to his work, he continued to pray and study with great passion. His father often reminded him that he was "a natural-born *chassid*, and that I must bear this in mind while I eat, talk, pray and study."[15]

In 1897, Joseph married his cousin Nehamah Dinah, the daughter of Abraham Schneersohn, a prominent rabbi in the Russian city of Krishinev.[16] They would soon have three daughters. Joseph became the manager of Chabad schools and one of the principal agents of his father's leadership. In 1904, with the outbreak of the Russo-Japanese War, he, his father, and others led a campaign to provide Passover matzos for Jewish soldiers in the czar's army. After the war, his father sent him to Germany and Holland to persuade politicians there to intercede on behalf of persecuted Russian Jewry. Both father and son spoke out vigorously against the czar's mistreatment of Jews, which could often turn deadly when the czar turned a blind eye, for example, during the pogroms of 1905 and 1906. During

World War I, Joseph and his father were able to secure the exemption of Lubavitcher rabbis from serving at the front by aggressively petitioning the czar's ministers. He was raised, in other words, in an environment of political activism despite dangerous times.

Joseph succeeded his father as Rebbe on his father's death, in 1920. The dying man asked him to risk his life for the sake of heaven, the Torah, and the preservation of Judaism. Having worked at his father's side for over three decades, he did not need the admonition.[17]

The new Rebbe, with his chest-length red beard, looked wise beyond his years. He had fiery blue eyes and, though a grown man, moved with the energy of a teenager. He spent much of his day meeting with people, hearing their problems, and giving them advice. In addition, he answered countless letters from followers who lived too far away to visit. Every month, he gave a few sermons to his cohorts, analyzing the struggles of the human condition from the Torah perspective. Hundreds of thousands in Russia and throughout the world looked to him as their leader.

After the October Revolution of 1917, when Russia fell into chaos and civil war, Rebbe Schneersohn devoted himself against overwhelming odds to rehabilitating the Jewish community and its religious life in Russia. Under the Communists, Russia continued to oppress the Jews, who lived in constant fear of persecution, disease, and poverty. Russian peasants, jealous of the Jews' success in banking and business and obsessed with the idea of them as parasites on society, conducted pogroms that left several Hasidic communities devastated. Two million Eastern European Jews, many of them afraid for their lives, emigrated to the United States in the late 1800s and early 1900s.

The Communists outlawed religious education, and the Yevsektzia, the Jewish section of the Communist Party, went beyond the law to persecute religious Jews, including the Lubavitchers. Many Lubavitcher leaders were arrested on trumped-up charges of counterrevolutionary activities; in 1920, the Rebbe himself was arrested. Immediately, Jewish families throughout the United States urged members of the government to intervene on behalf of the Rebbe and an international movement worthy of preservation. Thanks to the intervention of such prominent Americans as Senator Robert F. Wagner of New York and Senator William Borah of Idaho, head of the Foreign Relations Committee, the Rebbe was eventually released.[18] Because the Soviet Union strove for international acceptance, once American politicians stepped in, it could not ignore their requests without undesirable consequences. Borah in particular was one of the U.S. officials who wanted to recognize the Soviets in the international community, and thus the Russians could not afford to dismiss him.

The Soviets had shut hundreds of synagogues and Jewish schools, so the Rebbe was forced to work clandestinely. He supported the "underground education of five thousand children" and dispatched emissaries to all parts of Russia to rebuild Jewish life. During the next two decades, the Rebbe and his followers opened around six hundred schools throughout the Soviet Union. The Rebbe believed that Jewish education was the single most important guarantor of Jewish survival.[19] He also decided to set up schools in Poland. Communist hostility toward religion, he felt, made the Soviet Union no longer a safe home for his movement, and a few years later he would found the main Lubavitcher yeshiva in Otwock, near Warsaw. Despite considerable antisemitism, since World War I Warsaw had become the leading center for Jews in Poland and, some would argue, a chief center for Jewish studies and Hasidism the world over.[20]

The Rebbe spent much of his time helping his persecuted brethren in the USSR between 1920 and 1927. The departure of most Jewish leaders had created a vacuum that the Rebbe quickly filled. He became head of the rabbinical council for Russian Jewry, and most people soon recognized him as the leader of Russian Jews. He received tens of thousands dollars from the Joint Distribution

Committee in America, a Jewish humanitarian aid organization, to support his cultural work. Although he did a lot of good with these funds, he was criticized for "showing partiality toward Lubavitch institutions" and not distributing the money equally among the various religious sects he oversaw as head of the rabbinical council, seeming to focus on Lubavitchers instead of on Jews in general.[21] The Rebbe strongly denied these accusations. The Yevsektzia did not care about his focus; it simply disapproved of his receiving funds to conduct religious activities. Because of its campaign against him, he was imprisoned in the USSR repeatedly throughout the early 1920s, each time eventually being released, since there was no evidence to prove his anti-Communist activities. He would immediately resume his work helping other Jews. He believed he was a "true soldier for God," and his activities almost cost him his life on several occasions, but supportive friends and foreign politicians protected him.

In 1927, he was arrested for operation of an underground yeshiva and embezzlement. This detention would prove his most challenging struggle yet, as it carried a sentence of death. When the police came for him, his mother, Sara, pleaded with them to take her instead and spare her only son, "who responds to others in their hour of distress. . . . Woe unto us, my dear departed husband! . . . They are taking our son, Yosef Yitzchak—your only son who sacrifices himself for others." The Rebbe gathered several items to take with him, including many religious books. When asked what his followers should do, he told his son-in-law Rabbi Samarius Gourary, "First let emissaries be sent to the graves of my father and my ancestors, in Rostov, Lubavitch, Nyezin, and Haditz to inform them of my plight. Also, ask all of the *chassidim* to recite Psalms during the first days."[22] The police then took him away.

In prison, the authorities beat him horribly during their interrogations. According to Lubavitcher sources, one waved a gun in his face and said, "This little toy has made many a man change his mind." The Rebbe replied, "That little toy can intimidate only the kind of man who lives in only this world and indulges in worldly passions. Because I have only one God and two worlds, I am not impressed by your little toy." Despite his defiance, he was frightened when he heard other prisoners being taken outside the cell block at night and shot. Nonetheless, he kept his composure. When ordered to denounce his religion, the Rebbe told his interrogators, "I have already declared that I will not abandon my principles. No man or demon has been born, nor will be born that will make me budge even slightly." When he refused to stand when guards entered his cell, he was beaten. In the moments when he had some time to think, he thought about his family and wondered if the authorities had harmed them or his precious manuscripts in any way.[23]

The manuscripts were necessary to continue Chabad. The survival of Judaism through the generations was due to the preservation of the books of Torah; for centuries, Jews had always gone to the greatest lengths to preserve the writings of the great masters, and the Rebbe continued this sacred tradition. He felt he was not only the continuation of a movement that had gone on for one and a half centuries but the embodiment of all its leaders and spiritual power. When asked his age, the Rebbe responded, "A hundred and fifty years old." He viewed his life as a reincarnation of the lives of all the Rebbes since the beginning of the movement and referred to them in the present tense. Such conviction must have given him strength to endure this trial.[24]

While the Rebbe was in prison, future his son-in-law Rabbi Menachem Mendel Schneerson risked his life frantically destroying incriminating papers documenting the Rebbe's illegal religious activities in the Soviet Union.[25] Several others, including his other son-in-law, Rabbi Samarius Gourary, also did all they could to protect him.

When the authorities took away his tefillin (the phylacteries worn during morning prayers), prayer shawl, and religious books, Schneersohn went on a hunger strike. Without his tefillin and his books, he could not pray or study properly. Remarkably, three days later his possessions were returned—for reasons that remain unknown. Equally remarkable was his guards' relatively benign treatment, considering that he brazenly called his interrogator an "ignoramus" and a "vile creature." And as if things were not already difficult, he refused to eat the unkosher prison food. He depended on his family to deliver food to him.[26]

In addition to the hundreds of people led by his sons-in-law who were working for his rescue, a number of leaders around the world pressured the Soviets to free him. They included Chief Rabbi Abraham Isaac Kook of Palestine; Rabbis Israel Hildesheimer and Leo Baeck of Germany; the Union of Orthodox Rabbis in the United States; Chabad of America and Canada; and Mordechai Dubin, a wealthy member of the Latvian parliament and of Agudah (or Agudath Israel), an anti-Zionist organization made up chiefly of Orthodox Jews. Under its president, Hyman Kramer, U.S. Chabad published numerous articles and announcements in newspapers to muster diplomatic support. Its legal counsel, Sam Kramer, worked tirelessly with the politicians. Lawyers Fred and Oscar Rabinovitz, sons of Rabbi Dovid Rabinovitz, a fervent follower of the Rebbe's, secured an appointment with Supreme Court Justice Louis Brandeis, who approached several government officials, including Senators Borah and Wagner. Borah and Wagner requested that the Soviet officials release the Rebbe. President Calvin Coolidge also eventually asked them to free him.[27]

Under this pressure, the Soviets released Schneersohn from the notorious Spalerka prison in Leningrad and sent him into exile in Kostrama in the Urals of eastern Russia. The Rebbe told his followers: "We must proclaim openly and before all, that any matter affecting the Jewish religion, Torah, and its *mitzvot* and customs is not subject to the coercion of others. No one can impose his belief upon us, nor coerce us to conduct ourselves contrary to our beliefs. It is our solemn and sacred task to cry out and state with the ancient steadfastness of the Jewish people—with courage derived from thousands of years of self-sacrifice: 'Touch not My anointed [the Jewish people] nor attempt to do evil to my prophets.' . . . We must remember that imprisonment and hard labor are only of this physical world and of brief duration, while Torah, *mitzvot,* and the Jewish people are eternal." His defiance of the Soviet Union and his successful release made him well known throughout the Jewish world.[28]

Commenting on the Rebbe's time in prison, Menachem Mendel Schneerson later said of his father-in-law: "This stance of heroic self-sacrifice in the face of great peril was an all-pervasive quality that characterized all of the Rebbe's activities, even prior to his arrest for the promulgation of Torah and the strengthening of Judaism in that land. . . . Fulfillment of Torah and its commands was in the manner of 'hewn letters,' intrinsic to the essence of his identity. Therefore, his self-sacrifice was not a function of intellectual deliberation as to whether an action was obligatory or desirable. His response to existential challenge occurred naturally, because his service of G-d was the very core of his own existence."[29] The Rebbe viewed all good deeds as actions of God. He interpreted his liberations, including the political favors he received, as God's will.

Others did not have people of influence to intercede on their behalf. Many Jewish leaders died in Siberian gulags, where the Soviets worked them to death, and some died before firing squads. Often the Rebbe sent his students to Russia as emissaries, knowing full well they might die. Almost like a military officer, the Rebbe knew he would take casualties, but he regarded them as necessary in the battle for the spiritual welfare of all Jews.[30] The Rebbe disliked the Communists and cursed the Soviet authorities, saying that if they harmed Torah scholars "may they be left without hands." In risking death to serve his people, he was doing what Chabad leaders before him had done. All the previous Rebbes had been thrown in jail or placed under house arrest at some point. The founder of Chabad, Schneur Zalman, had received a death sentence and spent fifty-three days in prison in St. Petersburg; his release is celebrated by Lubavitchers as the Festival of Liberation. The sixth Rebbe believed that Rebbe Zalman's liberation was a "spiritual matter" of the forces of good triumphing over evil and "an episode that ultimately brought about a distinctive turn of good fortune upon the entire House of Israel." He even felt that Zalman had willed the whole event to create good out of what appeared to be evil, since tzaddiks rule "over all material matters."[31] His own imprisonment must therefore have had profound meaning for him as well.

In 1927, soon after ordering him into exile, the Soviets forced the Rebbe to emigrate. They wanted him to leave immediately, but he refused, demanding to take his possessions, especially his sacred manuscripts and books, with him; his library had become part of the movement's spiritual reservoir of information. The authorities relented and allowed him to take it. Needing a considerable sum of money to emigrate to Latvia with his goods and family, the Rebbe enlisted the help of the executive head of American Chabad, Rabbi Israel Jacobson.

Chabad in the United States had grown into a strong organization by 1927. When, in the early twenties, the Rebbe had asked for volunteers to go to America and set up a platform to help Lubavitchers immigrate to the United States, Israel Jacobson had been the only one to raise his hand. Many thought him crazy to want to leave the Rebbe, but Jacobson felt called to help the future of Chabad. He arrived from Poland in 1925 with his wife and three daughters, bringing the Rebbe's blessing with him. The Rebbe knew the Jews' days in the Soviet Union, and even in Poland, were numbered, and he believed the United States offered the best future home for their movement. In New York City, Jacobson initially had a difficult time earning a living but eventually found work as a rabbi and Torah teacher. Soon Jacobson was also raising money for the Rebbe. By 1927, he was sending thousands of dollars overseas each year to support the Rebbe's activities. As the Communist regime's economic

Israel Jacobson, the executive head of Chabad in the United States, with his wife, Shaina, and their daughters, Rachel, Chaya Sarah, and Chava (Eliezer Zaklikovsky)

policies resulted in the confiscation of most of Chabad's resources, America became almost the sole supplier of funds for the Rebbe's movement.[32]

On receiving the Rebbe's appeal, Jacobson met with Lubavitchers Sam and Avraham Kramer and Rabbi Menachem Mendel Leib Lokshin and asked them to quickly raise four thousand dollars. They debated the possibility of raising that much money in such a short time. Jacobson insisted it could be done. The Kramers were convinced that Jacobson just didn't understand business, so Jacobson turned to Lokshin, who met privately with Sam and persuaded him and Avraham, his brother, to come up with the funds. Proving their resourcefulness, they did, and Jacobson wired the money to the Rebbe. The Rebbe immediately left Russia with six followers and his whole family plus his possessions and large library. Everything together occupied four train cars. Two days later, the Rebbe's party arrived in Riga, Latvia.[33]

Once in Riga, he began to transfer his vast library to Poland. With the help of Mordechai Dubin, he and his family became Latvian citizens.[34] It was a sad day when he realized he would probably never return to Russia, but he knew God's work was taking him elsewhere. In fact, he did not return, but he had several representatives within the USSR to encourage the Lubavitchers there and address their needs. If a community needed clothes, food, or prayer books, he made sure it got them, and he continued to build a network of underground schools.[35]

In 1929, the Rebbe traveled to Palestine and the United States and, according to media sources, talked to thousands of Jews at hundreds of gatherings to raise funds for the movement. He also wanted to explore the possibility of bringing Chabad's headquarters to the States. When, accompanied by Mordechai Dubin and Samarius Gourary, he set foot on American soil on 17 September to start his ten-month tour of the United States, he was greeted by six hundred Orthodox rabbis and thousands of Jews on Pier A in New York and hailed as a Jewish hero. The city police commissioner welcomed him on behalf of the mayor and provided a motorcycle escort. Because his reputation as a great spiritual leader had circulated, the authorities took him seriously. He was especially touched by his warm reception, as he was still in a "state of shock" about the Arab pogroms against Jews in Palestine that had broken out after he left the Holy Land. Asked about the events, he would cry. "The blood-spilling attacks on Jews which broke out one day after my departure from there

Two New York City policemen escort Rebbe Joseph Isaac Schneersohn off the SS *France* as he arrives in America on 17 September 1929 on a ten-month goodwill tour. Hundreds of people showed up to see him. During his stay, he would meet several prominent politicians, among them President Hoover. (Author's collection)

have utterly devastated me," he said, "and I have still not recovered from the blow."[36] In spite of his sorrow, he was "very happy to step upon this glorious country of freedom, liberty, and opportunity for all, irrespective of race, color, and creed," he told the crowd. "May the Almighty bless this great country that has been a refuge for our Jewish people."[37]

Needing some time alone, the Rebbe retired to a quiet room to pray and study his religious books. After a few days of rest, he turned

In July 1930 Rebbe Joseph Isaac Schneersohn met President Hoover. He was accompanied by (left to right) Oscar Rabinovitz, a lawyer for Chabad; H. Fogelman, vice president of Chabad; Hyman Kramer, president of Chabad in the United States; and his son-in-law Rabbi Samarius Gourary, Chabad's foreign secretary. (Eliezer Zaklikovsky)

his attention to generating support for persecuted Jews under the Soviets. The two million Jews living under Stalin, he said, faced both economic and religious starvation. Unless more funds were raised for them, they would be poor in body and poor in spirit, deprived not only of food and clothing but of Torah study and instruction.

Despite the Depression, the Rebbe collected tens of thousands of dollars. In Chicago alone, according to Lubavitcher sources, he raised thirty thousand dollars. Speaking at Jewish gatherings, he campaigned as well for building more yeshivas and synagogues throughout the United States and Europe. Since he had been Rebbe for only nine years, he also used his time to verify his credentials.

A breakaway group in the United States under the leadership of one of his teachers had turned against him, and it was important that he prove to all that he was indeed the legitimate head of Chabad. With Samarius Gourary and Hyman Kramer, president of U.S. Chabad, he met a number of American dignitaries, including President Herbert Hoover and Justice Brandeis.[38]

On his return to Europe, the Rebbe continued his work in Poland, where he had moved from Latvia. By 1935 his yeshiva in Poland had become internationally known for its Orthodox teaching of Chabad philosophy, the Torah, and the Talmud. Throughout the 1930s, he urged Jews everywhere to repent their sinful ways and become more observant so that God would not punish them but rather bless them. If they did, the Messiah would come sooner.[39] In 1936, after living two years in Warsaw, Schneersohn moved to the resort town of Otwock, thirty miles south of the capital, where the fresh country air was better for his health.[40]

At age fifty-six, the Rebbe had already suffered a heart attack and a stroke. He was also ill with multiple sclerosis, which affected his speech and his ability to walk. Although he could stand on his own, he had to be helped in and out of cars and up from chairs. His teenage grandson Barry Gourary was often at his side to assist him.[41] The Rebbe's mind, however, was still sharp, and he did his best not to let the disease restrict his activities, which sometimes included smoking more than a pack of cigarettes a day. At five foot eight and over two hundred pounds, he did not cut an impressive figure. Yet Lubavitchers and admirers throughout the world thought him a spiritual giant.

THREE

Poland Under the Germans

Early on 1 September 1939, a hot Friday morning, many of the yeshiva students in Otwock awoke to the sound of explosions. No one knew what was going on. Only several hours later did they learn that Hitler had invaded Poland. "It was like thunder," wrote Joseph Wineberg, then a student. The horrors of war quickly made their way to Otwock. The Chabad orphanage there took a direct hit that killed ten children during the first bombardment. Another bomb struck the house where the Rebbe, his mother, one of his secretaries, Haskell Feigin, and many others, including Israel Jacobson's daughter and son-in-law, lived. No one was injured.[1]

As soon as the yeshiva students realized what was happening, they ran to the Rebbe for advice. Gazing at his students with his clear blue eyes and stroking his red beard, he asked the six Americans to leave immediately for neighboring Latvia. "Do not be afraid of the bombs," he told them. "Every bomb has an address, and your address is not on any of them."[2] Rabbi Shmuel Fox remembered the Rebbe as also saying, "God will protect you wherever you will be and He will not let any harm be done to you."[3] After offering this encouragement, the Rebbe gave Rabbi Meir Greenberg, one of his departing students, a message for his Latvian friend Mordechai Dubin. He asked Dubin to do everything possible before it was too late to bring him and his family to Latvia, since they were Latvian citizens.[4] He also advised several of his remaining students to try to make their way to Vilna, in Lithuania. Before night came, heavy blackout curtains were placed over the windows in the Rebbe's house, and makeshift gas masks of cotton soaked in soda water were prepared in case the Nazis returned. Rabbi Samarius Gourary described the mood that Sabbath night well: "The chandeliers hung unlit, shivering in the eerie atmosphere."[5] The future was uncertain for all.

Late that night, the six American students, among them Meir Greenberg and Mordechai Dov Altein, left for the American consulate in Warsaw. Upon arrival, they were brusquely turned away. The consulate claimed it could not help them. The students believed the consulate denied them help because they were Hasidic Jews.[6] The following day, all six left Warsaw by train for Riga. A journey that should have taken twelve hours instead took them twelve days. The Rebbe relaxed only when he received news that they had arrived safely. Once in Latvia, Rabbi Greenberg delivered the Rebbe's message to Dubin and then, a few days later, boarded a ship for the United States along with the others.[7]

Although most of the young Polish yeshiva students should have been in the army, only one of the Rebbe's students, Hirsch Kotlarsky, had been deemed physically fit to serve. "Most of the other students," Kotlarsky says, "were not physically fit because of all the Torah study. I was of strong build and as a result I was drafted into the cavalry." According to the records, no Lubavitchers volunteered for military service. Most felt that God would save them, though they feared the authorities would draft them. Like other ultrareligious Jews, the Lubavitchers did not believe it an honor to fight for the country where they lived. On the contrary, they believed one should do everything one can to focus on Torah study and God, and war definitely does not help in these pursuits. Even a few years later, according to a survivor of the Warsaw Ghetto uprising of 1943, the remaining young Hasidic Jews refused to take up arms and fight and instead gave themselves over to prayer. "We, Jews, not having any sword at all, do not possess even this thin ray of hope," the Rebbe's newspaper declared, "and our fate does not depend at all upon anything material but is entirely reliant upon the heavenly mercy." War, the Rebbe said, was the "greatest insanity."[8]

Although many tried to convince the Rebbe to leave, he wanted to stay with his family and followers: "A Jewish Shepherd does not leave his flock alone especially in times of crisis."[9] There were obvious signs that he was not safe. The Polish government had started moving south from Warsaw, intending, if Poland lost the war, to slip across the border to Romania, and the Polish high command, too, announced its plan to evacuate, causing much panic among the population. If the government and the military were leaving Warsaw, many felt, the Rebbe should depart as well. Citing the verse "I [the Almighty] am with him [the Jewish people] in times of misfortune," the Rebbe stayed.[10]

Late on 4 September, realizing it was growing dangerous in Otwock, he changed his mind and went to Warsaw with his family and a group of students in the hope of traveling on from there to Riga. The Rebbe felt terrible forsaking thousands of his fellow Jews, but he knew that only from Riga could he conduct rescue operations.[11] Tears streaming down his face, he told those who remained behind, "Be well, everyone, and accept upon yourselves the yoke of Heaven. The king guards his subjects, and you, Jewish children, may Hashem [God] guard you wherever you will be, and us, wherever we will be." The Latvian consulate in Warsaw had sent a private car with foreign license plates for the Rebbe's thirty-mile trip to the capital. He took the most valuable Lubavitcher manuscripts, regretting that he could not take his "household effects and the entire Library," which numbered some forty thousand texts.[12]

Mutilated bodies, dead horses, and the charred remains of buildings littered the road to Warsaw. The Luftwaffe continued to rain explosives on the highways leading to the burning capital, targeting civilians trying to escape.[13] One witness described helpless Poles having to hide repeatedly in the ditches and gutters from "Death on Wings."[14] Black plumes of smoke rose high on the western horizon as the Germans moved closer to Warsaw. Weary Polish soldiers and frightened citizens in search of protection and food hurried toward the capital in the vain hope of outrunning the Wehrmacht. The constant attacks of Stuka bombers with their high-pitched sirens unnerved them as the sky and earth welded together in chaos. General Wladyslaw Anders witnessed a Stuka pilot diving down on a group of children: "As he dropped his bombs and fired his machine guns, the children scattered like sparrows. The airplane disappeared as quickly as it had come, but on the field some crumpled and lifeless bundles of bright clothing remained. The nature of the new war was already clear." Besides attacking refugees, Luftwaffe pilots also "brazenly attacked Red Cross aid stations." Hitler claimed his planes struck military targets only, but the reality was different. In fact, as he later acknowledged, they were bombing Polish cities to show the civilians the "pointlessness of their resistance."[15]

The journey to Warsaw seemed interminable, but Rebbe Schneersohn assured his family and followers that they had nothing to fear. "God will provide safety to all of us," he told them, explaining that his father, Shalom Dovber, was interceding for them in heaven.[16] His faith calmed the group.

Although the Germans had not yet closed in, the atmosphere in Warsaw was already that of a city under siege. Reaching a Jewish neighborhood in the north of Warsaw, Schneersohn decided to remain there to help his students escape to neutral countries with his yeshiva's precious documents. Recognizing the danger, he himself would have left, but the Nazis had bombed the train station and no trains were leaving for Riga. Many yeshiva students, though,

The Warsaw train station on 2 November 1939, after it was bombed (United
States National Archives)

were departing on foot for Vilna; the border with Lithuania would
be closed by the Soviets in November. By then, around twenty-five
hundred Orthodox yeshiva students and numerous rabbis, many of
them Lubavitchers, had managed to reach Vilna from Poland.[17] Unable to walk far, the Rebbe could not escape this way. Trapped in
Warsaw, he stayed at the home of Rabbi Herschel Gurari on Bonifraterska Street, a dark apartment building in a remote area populated
by a group of Lubavitcher Jews. To enter the Rebbe's new neighborhood was to step back three hundred years. The men wore tradi-

German soldiers and Polish citizens view the destruction of Warsaw from its outskirts (United States Holocaust Memorial Museum Archive of Photographs)

tional black caftans and large fur hats; the women dressed modestly, covered their heads with wigs and scarves, and avoided eye contact with men.

By the time the Rebbe reached this part of Warsaw, few people dared to leave their homes. Germany, he quickly learned, had already taken large sections of the country. If he wanted to escape, he had to hurry because the German Fourth Panzer Division had advanced to the western outskirts of the city.[18]

The "enemy is at the gates, and he sends his angels of death to proclaim his coming," wrote Chaim Kaplan. On 8 September, Joseph Wineberg described the chaotic crowds in Warsaw "running through the streets . . . crying and wailing" during bomb attacks. His brother suggested they attempt to escape the city; he had seen a way and wanted to seize the opportunity. Wineberg told his brother that they should put on tefillin and say their prayers instead and ask God for guidance. His brother agreed, and they prayed. Later, they learned that the Germans had ambushed those who had tried to flee the city using the route they would have taken. Wineberg felt God had saved them. When he asked the Rebbe if they should attempt to flee nevertheless, Schneerson replied, "If there is a sure way to escape, then escape, but if not, then we must trust that Hashem will take care of us."[19]

According to Lubavitchers, the suffering of the Warsaw Jews grieved the Rebbe. His bright eyes grew dull as he busied himself with prayers. Like Rabbi Wineberg, many came to ask his advice. When they were not talking with the Rebbe, Wineberg observed, they were reciting the Psalms and "shedding tears, beseeching G-d to save them." In this climate, the Rebbe told his followers one morning that in his sleep his father had visited him and declared that they should "fall at Hashem's feet and ask for mercy because Hashem will respect such a plea."[20]

As soon as Hitler attacked, the Polish civil authorities had instructed the population through newspapers and radio addresses to dig trenches and build barricades and defense works. Jews came out in droves to help defend the city, even on the Sabbath. But the Lubavitchers did not join them. Most believed the best way for them to help was to pray constantly and keep the Sabbath and other rituals sacred. The Polish police resented their intransigence and rounded up many Lubavitchers from their homes, gave them a "generous helping of deadly lashes and beatings," then forced them to go on work details.[21]

Thousands of refugees were entering the city each day. On 9 September, the commander of the Warsaw garrison issued an order to the troops, including those who had retreated there: "We have occupied positions from which there is no retreat. At this outpost we must die to the last soldier." By 11 September, thousands more terrified people flooded the already packed city.[22] The consequences were disastrous: when the Luftwaffe and army bombarded the city, they killed multitudes of innocent civilians who had no place to hide.

Many of his followers urged the Rebbe to move to the Latvian consulate, which had shown its support for him as a distinguished citizen. They feared the Nazis would target Jewish neighborhoods like the one they were living in. The consul general invited the Rebbe to come, but he was unable to, because city authorities had blocked off the streets.

On 12 September, the severest bombing of his sector of the city occurred, and he took refuge in a cellar. Forty people suddenly occupied a room built for no more than twenty. The air became thick with the smell of bodies that had endured two weeks of war without bathing and rest. Long, sleepless nights and warm, nerve-racking days had pushed the cowering occupants to the limits of human endurance. Late that afternoon, the cellar began to tremble from the explosions and air raid sirens blared throughout the city. Warsaw's streets erupted in flames. Tall buildings collapsed on their inhabitants, crushing some and burying others alive. As Schneersohn and the others looked to heaven through the dark ceiling, they feared that the cellar walls, "like the walls at Jericho," would fall down on them.[23] As dust from cracking brick and cement filled the room, many darted out and took refuge in a building nearby.

The Rebbe had instructed several students to carry some of his most prized books with them during the attacks. But in the chaos many of the students forgot to take the manuscripts when running down to cellars or out of burning buildings. As a result, several books were lost in the bombardments, causing him much distress.[24] Despite everything, he continued to prepare for Rosh HaShana, the Jewish New Year, on 14 September. He would not let a war interrupt his religious observances. Right before the celebration, air raid sirens sounded throughout the city, followed by silence. Slowly the roar of hundreds of approaching planes echoed through the streets. As the bombs fell, several hit the Rebbe's home and the structure

Poles look through the ruins of a section of Warsaw destroyed by the Germans. The German bombardment killed close to forty thousand civilians and severely damaged 25 percent of the city. (Jerzy Tomaszewski and United States Holocaust Memorial Museum Archive of Photographs)

erupted in flames. Remarkably, he escaped the building to another part of the city and continued with the ceremony.

Rosh HaShana represented a "time of trial and judgment" for people to take stock of their "fulfillment of the Torah and its *mitzvot*." During Rosh HaShana, the Rebbe emphasized, a person "takes account of the fact that [in the Heavenly Court] the prosecuting angels . . . bring to mind and verify the existence of all the sins . . . he was guilty of in the course of the year, and demand that he be sentenced to harsh . . . punishment. He further considers that if at this time he truthfully regrets his past, this will alter things for him."[25] The Jewish New Year now took on a new significance and many searched their hearts, as the Rebbe urged, to find what they had done to cause this misfortune. According to the Rebbe's philosophy, when bad things happened, God was in essence telling the Jews they needed to repair their physical and spiritual behavior to counteract the negative events around them.

As Rosh HaShana began, according to Rabbi Samarius Gourary, a thousand Jews went to the Rebbe's new quarters. They gathered in the streets, in the courtyard, and in the building. They all wanted to be close to the Rebbe. To those urging him to move, at least to a non-Jewish area of the city, he explained, "My children are drowning, our brethren are in the greatest danger, and you want me to separate myself from them, hiding in another neighborhood? No, I will stay with the other hundreds and thousands of Jews, and my lot will be theirs." Rabbi Gourary himself had a chance to leave with his wife and son, but they all refused to abandon the Rebbe.[26]

During the two days of Rosh HaShana, German planes bombed the Jewish section of Warsaw without mercy, and air raid shelters in basements often became mass graves. The Rebbe offered his followers the consolation that, although they had had a bitter Rosh Ha-Shana, God would make it sweet for them. In other words, the trials they were enduring brought them closer to God.[27]

As buildings were destroyed, the Rebbe had to move from house to house. His multiple sclerosis meant that his followers often had to carry him, but they considered it an honor to touch the Rebbe and bring him to safety. During one attack, an explosion threw him from one side of a courtyard to the other. Remarkably, he was uninjured and just asked for his things to be gathered and for help in finding shelter. His eighty-year-old mother, who was also wheelchair bound and almost deaf, had to be carried throughout on a stretcher.[28]

The Rebbe had his students carry his prayer shawl and the Baal Shem Tov's prayer book wherever he traveled. Despite the hardships, he continued to study the Torah. On 14 September, when the Rebbe's house was bombed and a wall in a nearby room collapsed, he sat at his desk studying his Torah while the place was showered with pieces of shrapnel.[29] As the air attack continued, Wineberg and a few others

Drawing by a "half Jewish" German soldier, Gerd Grimm, of a Polish town being attacked in 1939 (Author's collection)

took the Rebbe's mother to safety. In her new location, she realized she had forgotten her glasses and asked Wineberg to return to the building to find them so she could read her prayer book. He had to jump over several bodies and run around fires to get back to the old home. There he found the glasses in a room full of Jews engaged in prayer. When he returned to Sara and gave her the glasses, she asked about the situation. He explained that all who had remained were praying and that things had calmed down. "Oh, I missed witnessing a *bracha*," she said, referring to the blessing of witnessing acts of piousness.[30]

As the bombs rained down during the next attack, the air around the Rebbe's dwelling became filled with a strange gray substance. Fearing the worst, some screamed hysterically, "Gas. Oh no, gas!" The Rebbe's daughter Chana, the wife of Samarius Gourary, disregarding her safety, doused a cotton rag in soda water and placed it over her father's mouth to protect him from the fumes.[31] After a few moments, everyone realized the gray substance was only thick dust kicked up by the bombing. They were safe for the moment. As the bombers flew away, the survivors thanked God for sparing their lives yet again and emerged from the basement.

They were greeted by the terrible screams of helpless people trapped in burning buildings. The rank smell of burning flesh smarted in their nostrils and they could hear the shouts of the elderly mixed with the squeals of babies.[32] People scurried through the streets, some carrying infants in bundles and others running in groups, but all in a state of terror. As the tired, scared Lubavitchers witnessed this horror, smoke and fire engulfed their building. The Rebbe and his followers looked up into the sky to see the sun disappear behind a wall of fiery smoke. Yet, amazingly, they remained alive.

His followers thought that, if they remained close to the Rebbe, they would not be killed. They did not want to tempt fate by staying in the streets, however, so the Rebbe and a group of about twenty Jews rushed into a building spared from the destruction. The Rebbe led them in the Shema: "Hear, O Israel! The Lord is our God, the Lord is One." As they recited their ancient Hebrew litanies, the whole building vibrated under concussions from another attack; projectiles of earth, metal, and fire splattered their area.[33] Hearts pounded and breathing became heavy and rapid. But the death they expected passed them by, and the bombs stopped falling. Schneersohn and his group had survived another day.

Others were not so lucky. When the Rebbe heard that a building across the street had collapsed, burying many inside, he asked his students to dig out the victims. Most of those pulled out of the ruins were dead. They found a dead woman clutching her crushed baby girl; the child still had her thumb in her mouth. While they busied themselves with this task, several more bombs hit in the area, sending shrapnel and broken concrete and brick through the air.[34]

When it was clear that the bombers had gone and that there were no further planes coming, his followers transferred the Rebbe to the home of publisher and philanthropist Zalman Shmotkin, where they thought he would be safer. The date was probably 15 September. They found a wagon, put the Rebbe and some of his loved ones on it, and transported them through the city. As they made their way through the streets, burning debris often landed on the wagon, only to be immediately removed by a zealous follower. Mangled, bleeding corpses lay on the streets, on the sidewalks, and in courtyards, and the rank smells of excrement, decaying bodies, and burned buildings filled the air.[35]

The horror of war brought the Jews of Warsaw together in terror. One day the Rebbe, assisted by others, traveled along the ghetto's edge, where he mingled with secular Jews. "Some of the people had beards and side curls, others were clean shaven," he said. "Some of the women wore wigs; others did not cover their hair at all. Despite their differences, everyone was united by fear and despair."[36]

The Lubavitchers feared not only Nazi bombs but also secret enemies among their neighbors. As soon as the attacks started, "Nazi provocateurs," according to Samarius Gourary, would dress up like Hasidic Jews and sneak into the Jewish parts of the city to murder them. Using terrorist tactics, they would throw boxes of dynamite in homes or areas where they felt they could kill the most people and then quickly escape.[37]

On 16 September, the German planes came again. "The Nazis targeted the Jewish neighborhood of Warsaw," Wineberg claims. When encouraged to escape, he remembers, the Rebbe slammed his cane on the ground, saying, "We will remain and he [Hitler] will escape."

Yet for all his bravado, the bombs and incendiaries fell and his home caught fire. Several of his followers carried him down a flight of stairs in his wheelchair and out of the burning building. His mother somehow became separated from the Rebbe, and Wineberg recalls her bewailing her fate and "crying, calling out, 'Why should my son have to suffer like this?'" The Rebbe, placid, reportedly had his students recite a passage from the Midrash. When they made a mistake, he corrected them.[38]

The predicament the Rebbe found himself in was soon to get worse. On 17 September, the Russians invaded Poland from the east, justifying the violation of their treaties with Poland by declaring that the country no longer existed.[39] The Non-Aggression Pact that Stalin and Hitler had signed on 23 August had given them the security to carve up Poland without becoming alarmed by each other's actions. Hitler would take western Poland, and Stalin would take eastern Poland. Before the war, the dictators had agreed on how much of Poland each would occupy. Although Stalin claimed the Soviet Union had to intervene "to protect its fraternal Byelorussian and Ukrainian population," he did so purely for imperialistic reasons. When Germany started the war, Stalin was slow to become involved, having just concluded a small war in August with Japan on his eastern border and not knowing how well the Wehrmacht would perform. Stalin realized that Germany's blitzkrieg strategy was overwhelming Poland and he knew he had to invade soon to claim his portion. Hitler, probably to divert international criticism, also encouraged Stalin to strike. Poland had expected Germany to attack, but the Soviet invasion shocked the Polish high command. It was just a matter of days before Poland would indeed cease to exist.[40]

Commenting on Poland's tragedy, Winston Churchill stated the world "has watched the vain struggle of the Polish nation against overwhelming odds with profound sympathy and admires their valor." On 20 September, the London BBC sent a message of sympathy to Warsaw on its Polish news service. The Poles, however, wanted more than hollow words from the British. They wanted military action. The mayor of Warsaw, Stefan Starzynski, responded to the broadcast: "When will the effective help of Great Britain and France come to relieve us from this terrible situation? We are waiting for it."[41] Although British and French forces fought at sea and in the air, they did not mount a ground war against Germany. In the absence of such an assault, most of the German land forces could focus on the battles in Poland. Poland would die alone.

The news of the Soviet invasion alarmed the Lubavitchers. They feared that once the Soviets got their hands on the Rebbe again, no amount of international support would suffice to save him amid the fog of war. Finally, in late September, he agreed to leave Warsaw. He wavered, though, between wanting to be with his flock and saving his life, which would separate him from his people. According to Wineberg, for several days the Rebbe had even refused to believe war had broken out. As Wineberg points out, even though Noah had built the ark, it took the rains to get him to believe God's prophecy and board it. But just as the Rebbe began to plan his escape, the Wehrmacht encircled the city. Its perpetual bombing made leaving impossible. Nazi propaganda films capture Hitler watching through binoculars as the city burns. He turns to his military advisers, laughs, then returns his gaze to the deadly effects of the Luftwaffe's bombs.[42]

Even as Warsaw was in its death throes, the Rebbe and thousands of Orthodox Jews continued their observance of the High Holy Days, especially the most sacred of all, Yom Kippur, the Day of Atonement. On 22 September, the evening of Yom Kippur, when they could have been looking for food or trying to find an escape route, the Lubavitchers instead turned their attention to God. If Jews performed the rites required during Rosh HaShanah and Yom Kippur correctly and with the right heart, the Rebbe taught, angels would be created. Good deeds on earth are often actually performed by angels from heaven responding to the faithful acts of Jews; if he was going to be

Hitler reviews his victorious troops in the streets of Warsaw on 5 October 1939 (United States National Archives)

rescued, the Rebbe would need angels, because "all missions which are related to the material world are carried out by [them]."[43]

In Jewish areas already under German occupation, the holiday became an opportunity for persecution. The Germans closed synagogues and took the worshipers to army barracks, where they forced some to clean the floors and bathrooms with prayer shawls. Others they forced to march around pointlessly, shooting those who could not keep up the pace. They required the surviving Jews to bury their murdered compatriots—and even some who were not yet dead.[44] Yom Kippur, for many, turned into a Day of Death, not of Atonement.

The Rebbe did make one concession to the dangers encircling him and his followers. Before nightfall, the Rebbe's group blew the shofar early to give the sign that everyone could leave the service for shelter before the bombing started again. Mindful of what might await the crowd if bombs fell, he violated the traditional way of ending the service. In Jewish law, if life is at risk, violation of the law is sanctioned, indeed urged.

As the Holy Days drew to a close, the Rebbe blessed his followers, saying, "Good night, and may you always have happy occasions." But the holiday had brought no one joy. Kaplan observed that "mourning is on every face. As our prophet said, 'The whole head is sick and the whole heart faint.'"[45]

On 23 September, the Germans began moving formations no longer engaged in combat in Poland to Germany's western border, "where the French and British," Field Marshal Erich von Manstein later explained, "much to our surprise, had looked idly on as their Polish ally was being annihilated." That same day, German guns began shelling Warsaw in earnest. Hitler was growing impatient. On 25 September, he ordered intense bombing to force the city's capitulation. The Germans dropped more than five hundred tons of high explosives and seventy-two tons of incendiary bombs and directed heavy artillery fire at the city, which erupted into flames. The Rebbe lamented: "Houses burning, the piercing screams of the unfortunate victims, the terror-stricken people, especially the elderly, the women and children—all are beyond description." The previous day, the city had lost its electricity, gas, and water.[46] Along with the bombs, disease had begun to ravage the city.

The Lubavitchers discussed what they would do with the Rebbe when the Germans conquered the city. The Nazis did indeed search out and kill prominent rabbis and Jewish leaders, and they would consider the Rebbe a great prize. Whether his captors were Soviet or German, his demise seemed inevitable. The Lubavitchers' fears were not unfounded.[47]

The Rebbe escaped death several times during the final bombardment of Warsaw, leading many to believe, and surely reinforcing the Rebbe's sense, that a divine cloud was protecting him. On one occasion, he left a building just moments before it tumbled to the ground after a direct hit from bombers. It was probably during this intense bombardment that the Rebbe reportedly suffered shell shock. A Lubavitcher rabbi who is a scholar of Chabad disputes the claim, arguing that a man of the Rebbe's stature and spiritual maturity would have no such mental weaknesses.[48] Most Lubavitchers find it extremely difficult to assess their Rebbes critically. If their Rebbes show any weakness or make any mistakes, they will try to find a defensive explanation, usually theological. In this case, the Rebbe probably felt greater fear than he had even while in prison under the Soviets in 1927, and after the long hours of bombing and physical ordeal, he simply succumbed to fatigue. Noticing once that others had seen his hand start to tremble when a shell exploded close to him, the Rebbe said, "I am not frightened, but the blast causes the flesh to tremble."[49]

By now, his group was running out of supplies. The Rebbe would sometimes go days without anything to eat. Chaim Kaplan saw some people cutting meat from the rotting three-day-old carcass of a horse. Yet hunger was a mild torment compared with the death that surrounded them. "Every morning," Karin Tiche says, "you would go outside and the dead would be piled up along the streets and the living would busy themselves carrying the bodies off to quickly dug graves in parks and courtyards."[50]

Warsaw could no longer defend itself. On 26 September, General Juliusz Rommel, commander of the Warsaw army, sent representatives to the Germans to discuss surrender terms. On 28 September, Warsaw capitulated to the Nazis. A few days later, Kaplan wrote bitterly in his diary that Rommel "has made tens of thousands of people penniless and homeless; he has created widows and orphans without number." The Poles were enraged with their leaders; the Germans were ecstatic: when news of the surrender reached Germany, church bells tolled across the country to commemorate the Reich's victory in the East.[51]

"Beautiful Warsaw—city of royal glory, queen of cities—has been destroyed like Sodom and Gomorrah," wrote Kaplan. The German bombardment of Warsaw killed close to 40,000 civilians and severely damaged 25 percent of the city.[52] The Germans simply outmatched the Poles technically and strategically. By October, Germany emerged victorious from the campaign. The Wehrmacht suffered 16,000 dead and 32,000 wounded, whereas the Polish armed forces suffered 100,000 dead, including 6,000 Polish Jews, and 133,700 wounded. On 5 October, Hitler reviewed his victorious troops in Warsaw. Later, bursting with pride, he gave a speech before the Reichstag, declaring that "in all history there has scarcely been a comparable military achievement." He assailed Poland's leaders and justified his war against their "ridiculous State," warning of the dark future that awaited the vanquished nation.[53]

The war in Poland left the world stunned at how quickly Germany had conquered another country. No one had anticipated blitzkrieg warfare. The Germans had overwhelmed the Poles with three pincer movements—one from the north, from East Prussia, and two directly from the west, from Pomerania and Silesia—all headed straight for Warsaw. In less than a month, the Nazis had thrown their shadow over some twenty million additional people in Eastern Europe. Immediately, thousands pleaded with the American government to help them escape Nazism.[54] While the United States considered how it should react, Hitler established a murderous order in Poland.

The Nazis planned to turn Poland into a nation of serfs, as Slavs were good enough only to be slaves. And Polish Jews, of course, were even more despicable. Colonel Eduard Wagner, German quartermaster general, wrote on 9 September: "It is the Führer's and Goering's intention to destroy and exterminate the Polish nation. More than that cannot be even hinted at in writing." Many in Poland knew Jews had no future under Hitler. The country, Chaim Kaplan observed ironically in his diary, had fallen into the hands of the "sons of Ham," the people condemned by Noah to be Israel's slaves.[55]

The Nazis immediately put thousands of Poles to work clearing the destroyed capital of its rubble and dead. Throughout early October, they ran several soup kitchens in Warsaw to help feed the population. When Jews came, however, the army sent them away.[56] The Lubavitchers, with their conspicuous dress, were always recognized as Jews and thus were probably rarely able to get food at the distribution centers. Like other Warsaw Jews, they had to buy food on the black market, steal it if they could, and trade goods for it when and where possible.

It was obvious to all that Jews would be persecuted under Hitler's regime and that the Rebbe must be hidden. The building whose address Schneersohn had given to the Polish authorities when he arrived in Warsaw had been destroyed. His followers speculated that the Germans might believe the Rebbe was dead and not pursue him. They prayed that it would be so.[57]

FOUR

A Plan Takes Shape

While the Lubavitchers in Warsaw tried to stay alive and keep their Rebbe hidden, their American coreligionists pressed the U.S. government to help rescue him. Rabbi Israel Jacobson, then executive director of Chabad in America, felt lucky that he had been able to leave Poland a few days before the war began. Extremely close to the Rebbe, he feared for the leader's life. Jacobson obtained information about him through Rabbi Mordechai Chefetz, head of the Lubavitcher movement in Latvia. By telegraph, telephone, mail, and messengers, Chefetz himself received regular updates from Chaim Lieberman, Schneersohn's private secretary. How Lieberman kept information flowing from war-torn Poland remains somewhat mysterious, although he probably used messengers.

Lieberman escaped Warsaw on 21 September and arrived safely in Riga a few weeks later, having traveled largely on foot. Once he was gone, the flow of information about Schneersohn ebbed. "It is two weeks since I left Warsaw, and we in Riga are still unable to contact the Rebbe," he wrote. "The One Above alone knows what is happening to them there—pray that He protect them, and that we are reunited with them soon. It is impossible to describe the horrors of those first three weeks." A few days later, Lieberman reported to Jacobson that the Rebbe's situation in Warsaw was "horrible, unbelievably and indescribably horrible. In addition to the worry over the Rebbe's poor health, we know they are under the pressure of real terror, for the Germans are inflicting terrible tortures, particularly on Rabbis."[1]

The Lubavitchers in the United States became increasingly concerned and intensified their pleas to government officials. Lieberman was now unable to confirm whether the Rebbe was alive. Many felt that their "whole existence was at stake if the Rebbe was not saved"; he was the guiding force of the movement and the link between God and the community. His death would devastate the whole of Chabad.[2]

On behalf of many American Lubavitchers, State Senator Philip M. Kleinfeld of New York urged Robert F. Wagner, U.S. senator from New York, to ask Secretary of State Cordell Hull, whose wife had a Jewish father, to help ascertain the Rebbe's whereabouts.[3] Kleinfeld received most of his intelligence about the Rebbe from his dear friend and law partner Sam Kramer, Chabad's legal counselor; together, they wanted to facilitate the Rebbe's passage out of Poland. Wagner wrote Hull on 22 September 1939, enclosing several articles about the Rebbe and his movement, including reports of his 1929 visit to America, stressing his "high ecclesiastical position." Four days later Hull informed Wagner that communications with Poland had been suspended, and he offered to notify him when they were reestablished.[4]

Contrary to Hull's message and probably unknown to him, communications from Poland still existed. On 24 September, Mordechai Dubin succeeded in sending a cable from Riga assuring Jacobson that Schneersohn was in Warsaw at Zalman Shmotkin's house. Dubin probably received his information from one of the Lubavitch messengers who had traveled from Poland to Latvia. Exactly how

Cordell Hull and his wife, Frances, née Witz, in 1933, when President
Roosevelt appointed him secretary of state (United States National Archives)

these messengers made it in and out of the two countries remains
unknown, but their success is a testament to the Lubavitchers' resourcefulness. Most of them were either students or rabbis. The next
day, Dubin sent word that the situation was critical for the Rebbe
and that "every hour counts."[5]

Wagner wrote Hull again on 26 September to ask that the U.S.
minister in Riga gather "information as to the safety and whereabouts" of the Rebbe, emphasizing that many Jewish organizations
in New York had expressed concern. Wagner told Hull the Rebbe had
probably fled Poland for Latvia. In response to Hull's inquiry, the
American legation in Riga reported on 30 September that it believed
the Rebbe was ill in Warsaw, which turned out to be correct.[6]

The Rebbe's case attracted the attention of a number of high-
ranking officials, including Democratic congressmen Adolph J.
Sabath (Illinois), chairman of the House Rules Committee, and Sol

Bloom (New York), chairman of the Foreign Affairs Committee, as well as Justice Louis Brandeis. Brandeis, the first Jewish member of the Supreme Court, received a report on 29 September 1939 from Oscar Rabinovitz, a lawyer and one of U.S. Chabad's leaders, claiming that the Rebbe lay sick or wounded and trapped in Poland. Rabinovitz urged Brandeis to act quickly.[7]

Stories of Nazis atrocities had begun to trickle in. Rabinovitz, who had arranged the Rebbe's meeting with President Hoover in 1930, asked Brandeis for any assistance he could render. Rabinovitz reminded the justice that he had met the Rebbe nine years earlier and suggested he contact Attorney General Benjamin Cohen to help him. They should demand, he urged, permission from the German military authorities for the Rebbe's safe egress via Riga to Stockholm. Rabinovitz believed the "pressure which Cohen might bring to bear was highly urgent." Although Rabinovitz knew that thousands had bombarded the government with requests and that some had appealed directly to President Roosevelt, he felt justified in appealing to Brandeis because of the "extreme danger to Schneersohn's life and his great moral worth to Jewry."[8]

Brandeis took Rabinovitz's suggestion and consulted Cohen, one of Roosevelt's close advisers. The son of Polish immigrants, Cohen headed the National Power Policy Committee and belonged to several influential Jewish interest groups. Though initially he indicated that he could not intervene, on 2 October 1939 he wrote to Robert T. Pell, assistant chief of the State Department's European Affairs Division, who had contacts with influential German officials. "I don't know just who in the State Department could help in a matter of this kind," Cohen wrote, "and consequently I am turning to you for advice."[9]

Pell agreed that "it would be a very great tragedy indeed if any harm befell one of the leading Jewish scholars in the world."[10] He thought Cohen had contacted him mainly because he knew the chief administrator of Göring's Four Year Plan, Helmut Wohlthat, an ex-

Benjamin Cohen, who was instrumental in establishing the crucial contact with Robert Pell of the State Department's European Affairs Department (United States National Archives)

pert in international industry and economics and a Nazi Party member. Pell had met the ambitious and intelligent Wohlthat after the Evian conference of 1938, at which representatives from thirty-two nations had addressed the plight of Jewish refugees from Germany and Austria. Sadly, Romania and Poland had formally requested to be considered refugee producers, along with Austria and Germany, so that they could "dispose" of their Jews. Colonel Jozef Beck, Poland's foreign minister, had actually said in 1937 that out of the three and half million Polish Jews, "three million were superfluous and must emigrate."[11]

U.S. representatives at the conference refused to take any substantial number of Jews suffering under the Nazis or unwanted by Romania and Poland. Other nations followed suit. The Australian minister of commerce, Lieutenant Colonel T. W. White, cynically explained that "as we have no real racial problem, we are not desirous of importing one." White's statement reveals much about the xenophobic and antisemitic attitudes prevalent in many nations in 1938. A statement circulated among Jews described "the world [as] made of two types of countries: the kind where Jews could not live and the kind where Jews could not enter."[12]

The problems of the Evian conference were exacerbated by disunity among the twenty-one private Jewish delegations attending, which the weekly *Congress Bulletin* of the American Jewish Congress described as a "spectacle of Jewish discord and disruption."[13] Religious and political differences (Reform versus Orthodox, Zionist versus anti-Zionist) left many American Jewish groups conflicted as to how best to assist their persecuted brethren.[14]

Despite the failure of the Evian conference, Pell had succeeded in forging at least one decisive relationship. After the conference, the United States supported the Intergovernmental Committee on Refugees (ICG) and sent officials to Europe to discuss the refugee problem with the Germans. From late 1938 until the outbreak of war in September 1939, Pell, who eventually became vice-director of the ICG, met several times with Germany's representative to the ICG, Wohlthat, who privately assured Pell that if a specific case arose in which American Jewry expressed interest "he would do what he could to facilitate a solution." When Cohen contacted Pell about the Rebbe, Pell forwarded the request directly to Wohlthat.[15]

In the meantime, the Lubavitchers kept up their frantic efforts. Jacobson and Rabinovitz continued to remind Brandeis, Pell, and

Cohen of their leader's plight. Jacobson was a kind leader and a fine Torah scholar, but not a good lobbyist. Although he had succeeded in helping Jews emigrate to America in the interwar period, this case lay beyond his experience and abilities. In dealing with Washington officials and immigration protocol, he proved a poor organizer who failed to delegate enough tasks to those around him. Chaskel Besser, a prominent Hasidic rabbi and Agudah leader, said of him that "he was very inefficient in his dealings with people. He would let things often slide that needed to be paid attention to." Even his grandson, Rabbi Leib Altein, said he was very disorganized. On the other hand, he received no compensation for his duties and lived primarily from the small salary and the donations received from his Brooklyn congregation. He conducted his rescue efforts out of his intense love for the Rebbe and for the cause. What he lacked in organizational and lobbying skills, he tried to make up with enthusiasm and religious observance. He himself was lucky to be out of Europe. In August 1939 he had escorted to Otwock the six American students whom the Rebbe subsequently counseled to flee, and he had left Poland a few days before the war started.[16]

Jacobson was passionate to the point of extremity. On the ship from Europe in September, he and a few followers attempted to conduct Rosh HaShanah prayers. Ambassador Joseph Kennedy, the father of John F. Kennedy, was a fellow passenger and complained that Jacobson's service was disruptive. Furious, Jacobson cursed Kennedy and all his male heirs. That, at least, is the story that circulates in Lubavitch circles, where it originated.[17]

Pleas to save the Rebbe, including those of Justice Brandeis, Postmaster General James A. Farley (an adviser to Roosevelt), Cohen, and Pell, piled up on Secretary of State Hull's desk. Farley told Hull on September 27 that he had received many requests for help from Schneersohn's followers. The Lubavitch leadership had informed Farley that their community comprised more than 200 congregations, totaling 150,000 members in the United States and 10,000 in Canada. These numbers were exaggerated, but the Lubavitchers wanted to make their organization look more powerful.[18] The total worth of the Chabad organization, according to Jacobson's sworn affidavit, was $500,000. Perhaps Farley thought the Lubavitchers included sufficient numbers of potential voters to be worth listening to; Roosevelt had to think about the election coming up in 1940 and may have felt inclined to help for the good it would do him throughout the Orthodox communities.[19]

For months, Chabad and other Orthodox Jewish leaders had been demanding the rescue of some ten thousand Orthodox Jews, whom they considered the cream of Europe's Jewry. But, apparently, once the government indicated a commitment to rescue the Rebbe, Chabad refrained from pressing for the original list. The Rebbe was more important to the community than the thousands of others, and the group put all its efforts into rescuing him. On 2 October 1939, Hull informed Farley that the State Department would ask the American vice-consul in Riga to report on Schneersohn's situation at the expense of the interested American citizens.[20]

On 2 October, the Latvian embassy in Washington joined the chorus of voices and telegraphed the Latvian Foreign Office in Riga requesting assistance for the Rebbe. The Latvian embassy probably received information from Mordechai Dubin in Riga, who regularly heard from Mordechai Chefetz's messengers from Warsaw. By 24 September, Dubin had already informed Jacobson of the Rebbe's most recent address and had urged Jacobson to remove the Rebbe and his family from Warsaw immediately.[21]

On 3 October 1939, Pell, authorized by Hull, wrote Raymond Geist, the American consul general in Berlin:

> Rabbi Joseph Isaac Schneersohn known as Lubavitcher
> Rebbe, one of the leading Jewish scholars of the world

and a Latvian citizen, has been trapped in Warsaw. The most influential Jewish leaders and others in this country, including The Postmaster General, Justice Brandeis and Mr. Benjamin Cohen, have asked our assistance in obtaining permission from the German Military Government of Warsaw for the safe egress of the Rabbi to Riga via Stockholm. While the Department does not wish to intervene in the case of a citizen of a foreign country you might in the course of a conversation with Wohlthat inform him as from me and in view of our previous relationship of the interest in this country in this particular case. Wohlthat, who evidently wishes to maintain contact with the Intergovernmental Committee, might wish to intervene with the military authorities.[22]

Geist acted immediately. Since he did not expect any support from the German Foreign Ministry, he decided to contact Wohlthat directly. "I turn to you," Geist told Wohlthat, "because I know you, and you may be assured of the absolute discretion of the American State Department. I am aware of the considerable risk to any German persons intervening in this matter." Geist then telegraphed Hull and Pell that he had met Wohlthat, who had "promised to take the matter up with the competent military authorities."[23]

Wohlthat agreed that pressure from such influential sources warranted action. The United States had stunned the German authorities by recalling Ambassador Hugh Wilson after the Kristallnacht pogrom in 1938, when the Nazis arrested some thirty thousand Jews, burned hundreds of synagogues, and murdered more than a hundred people. U.S. relations with Germany had remained strained as a result of Hitler's persecution of Jews and his invasions of Czechoslovakia and Poland. Wohlthat therefore welcomed an opportunity to restore a modicum of goodwill between the two nations.[24]

TELEGRAM SENT

Department of State

Washington,

1939 OCT 3 AM October 3, 1939

AMERICAN EMBASSY

BERLIN

670

For Geist from Pell.

Rabbi Joseph Isaac Schneersohn, known as Lubavitcher Rebbe, one of the leading Jewish scholars of the world and a Latvian citizen, has been trapped in Warsaw. The most influential Jewish leaders and others in this country, including The Postmaster General, Justice Brandeis and Mr. Benjamin Cohen, have asked our assistance in obtaining permission from the German Military Government of Warsaw for the safe egress of the Rabbi to Riga via Stockholm. While the Department does not wish to intervene in the case of a citizen of a foreign country you might in the course of a conversation with Wohlthat inform him as from me and in view of our previous relationship of the interest in this country in this particular case. Wohlthat, who evidently wishes to maintain the contact with the Intergovernmental Committee, might wish to intervene with the military authorities.

Eu:RTP:AB

(Hull)

Enciphered by _____

Sent by operator _____ M., _____, 19___

Robert Pell, authorized by Cordell Hull, asks Raymond Geist, the American consul general in Berlin, for help in rescuing Rebbe Schneersohn (United States National Archives)

Hull made sure that the Lubavitchers, not the government, would shoulder the cost of the rescue. The success of the mission did not, however, hinge on finances. It depended on Wohlthat. In other words, a member of the Nazi Party had been charged to arrange the Rebbe's escape.

FIVE

The Nazi Connection

Helmut Wohlthat was an ambivalent Nazi, despite his high office. He had studied at Columbia University in New York from 1929 to 1933, and his time in America made him a logical choice to contact for help. Although it was dangerous to help Jews, there is evidence Wohlthat did so during the 1930s; in 1974, he claimed that he allowed thousands of Jews to take money and assets in excess of the legal limit out of Germany. He also had friends in the German resistance.[1]

Nevertheless, he also aggressively persecuted Jews. On 22 July 1938, on Göring's orders, he pushed through the Aryanization (the replacement of Jewish owners with "Aryans") of the German properties of a Polish businessman named Ignaz Petschek, valued at two hundred million reichsmarks. Why did Wohlthat agree to assist the Rebbe? Presumably he would not have acted without a direct request from the American government. It seems, too, that he had grown fond of Pell and felt obligated to act on his request to the extent possible.[2] Some Lubavitchers have claimed that Göring was involved in the Rebbe's escape. If so, Göring's support obviously would have profoundly influenced Wohlthat. But given Göring's position in the Nazi government, it is highly unlikely that he actively participated in the rescue of a Jewish leader. There is no evidence of his involvement in the episode, but he may have known something about it through his intelligence office, which tapped government phones and transcribed telephone conversations.[3]

Though Wohlthat believed the Rebbe's release would serve Germany's best interests, he knew Nazi authorities would object, so he had to carry out his mission in secrecy.[4] Wohlthat knew of one man he could trust, Admiral Wilhelm Canaris, the head of the Abwehr. Although a high-ranking official, Canaris often helped Jews. He was a man of many faces, most of which are difficult to unmask. Undistinguished in appearance, he stood only five feet four inches tall and had something of a Napoleon complex. His clear blue eyes and silver hair earned him the nickname "Old Whitehead," a term of endearment since most people who worked with him considered him a wise old man. He had a gift for languages, speaking fluent Spanish and possessing a working knowledge of English, French, Italian, and some Russian. He could memorize facts and foreign words with remarkable ease and he loved history.

In his youth, Canaris apparently believed that he was related to Constantine Kanaris (1790–1877), the naval hero of the Greek war of independence against Turkey and, later, prime minister of Greece. He and his family visited their "relations" in Greece, and most likely stories of Kanaris sparked his interest in pursuing a career as a naval officer. Early in his service, his superiors and comrades recognized his quick mind and admired his willingness to help others.[5]

During World War I, he served on the warship *Dresden* and was taken prisoner by the British after it was scuttled. Interned at Valparaiso, Chile, he soon escaped and made his way over the Andes to Buenos Aires, Argentina, using his language skills while posing as a young Chilean widower. In this disguise and with considerable acting skill, Canaris succeeded in making it back to Germany. He then

Admiral Wilhelm Canaris, head of the Abwehr, the German military secret service (Eliezer Zaklikovsky)

maintained his false identity to conduct undercover work in Spain. He also served as a U-boat commander, sinking three ships. After the war, when Germany was swept by revolution, he detested what the Socialists and Communists were doing to his country, developing a passionate hatred for the Soviet Union. During this tumultuous time, he continued in the navy in several different capacities.

When Hitler took power in 1933, Canaris supported him. A few years later, the admiral lectured his men about the "virtues of Nazism." Canaris explained at an Abwehr conference in 1938, for example, that "today, every German officer should unconditionally be a National Socialist" and feel bound by his oath to Hitler. Those who question Canaris's commitment to National Socialism cite his later involvement in the plot to remove Hitler from power. But no one knows with certainty what Canaris thought of Hitler and the Third Reich. In his initial actions, he seemed enthusiastic about Hitler's rebuilding of the Wehrmacht and his anti-Communist stance. He welcomed Hitler and his new movement as the best option for combating Communism and rebuilding Germany's prestige.[6]

After the establishment of the Abwehr in 1935, Canaris started working with Himmler, meeting frequently as well with Reinhard Heydrich, head of the SS Reich Main Security Office, whom he had known since the early 1920s. Heydrich and he lived near each other in Berlin, and his family often spent time and dined with Heydrich. The men also often took horseback rides together.[7] After witnessing the mistreatment of military officers and of the Jews, however, Canaris allegedly started to distance himself from Nazism and later avoided Hitler, even in the middle of the war, declining to dine with the Führer when invited. Yet he was able to hide most of his misgivings from those around him, especially from many Nazis and Hitler. Canaris had an amazing ability to adapt to his surroundings.[8] Given his skills, authority, and political outlook, he was an appropriate ally for Wohlthat to turn to in finding the Rebbe. There is a good chance Wohlthat knew that Canaris had already helped many Jews and people of Jewish descent escape Hitler's Reich.

In 1935, Canaris became head of the Abwehr, a small department of the War Ministry. His position often gave him the opportunity to brief Hitler on international affairs. In 1938, his power increased when the Abwehr grew to a group of departments attached to the OKW (Supreme Headquarters of the German Armed Forces). By 1939, he had developed the Abwehr into a highly respected intelligence-gathering agency.

The Abwehr functioned with unusual independence. Canaris made sure the SS did not have authority over his personnel or operations. The men Canaris employed had impeccable professional credentials, operating with a freedom unknown to most government officials and army officers. They were better educated and had broader experience than the average Wehrmacht officer.[9]

Wohlthat and Canaris were well acquainted through their dealings in government, and they were aware of one another's political misgivings. By 1939, Canaris, like Wohlthat, had demonstrated opposition to certain of Hitler's policies. Indeed, since 1935 he had been employing several men of Jewish background in his organization.[10] The way Hitler had acceded to Göring and Himmler's framing of Generals Blomberg and Fritsch in 1938 shook Canaris's faith in Hitler, who took advantage of their disgrace to remove many commanders from the military and place himself at the head of the Wehrmacht, allowing him to "decide over war and peace." Observing such moves, Canaris started to grasp "Hitler's perfidy and thirst for power." He also disapproved of the Nazi-Soviet Non-Aggression Pact signed in August 1939. After war erupted, he told Field Marshal Wilhelm Keitel that the Wehrmacht would assume blame for the SS's brutal executions in Poland, as they were carried out in the Wehrmacht's presence.[11] Keitel responded that Hitler had decided on this course of action, saying that if the army commander in chief did not wish to perform the executions, then he would have to tolerate the SS. Canaris felt unable to "officially" oppose this plan, although he told Vice Admiral Leopold Bürkner a few days later in Vienna that "a war conducted in contempt of all ethics cannot be won. There is a divine justice even on this earth."[12] The Abwehr chief gathered documents evidencing war crimes perpetrated by the SS and showed them to those he tried to convince to act against Hitler.[13]

After Wohlthat received the information about the Rebbe from Pell in early October, he met Canaris and told him about the case.

Perceiving the favorable consequences of granting the request of highly placed officials in Washington, Canaris agreed to the rescue and promised to send officers to Warsaw for that purpose.[14]

Another, more personal factor may have contributed to this remarkable decision. Canaris was demoralized. He apparently did not agree with Hitler's likely conduct of the war, and on hearing that German divisions had crossed Poland's borders, he said, with tears streaming down his face, "This means the end of Germany." He suspected that Hitler would lead Germany to defeat. Nevertheless, he was elated at the success of the Polish campaign. Canaris was a complex person. On the one hand, he hated the fact that Hitler had launched Germany into another major European war, but on the other hand, as a passionate officer and patriot, he worked tirelessly on counterintelligence and espionage activities against Germany's enemies even as he was helping plan Hitler's overthrow. He knew that Germany would be better without Hitler at the helm of the nation.[15] Perhaps he acted on behalf of the Rebbe to help a prominent person escape a hostile environment.

Canaris thereby not only put his career on the line but also risked the lives of those he ordered to perform the task. He knew about the SS's *Einsatzgruppen* (killing squads) that had been established by Heydrich, who took all his instructions directly from Hitler. They followed the army and killed undesirables, particularly Jews and the Polish elite.[16]

Understanding that the operation would be a delicate one, Canaris knew just the person to entrust with the job of escorting the Rebbe out of Poland: Major Ernst Bloch, a distinguished Wehrmacht officer who happened to be half Jewish. To prevent a paper trail, Canaris probably gave all his orders orally. He and Wohlthat had often dined with Bloch, who shared their animosity toward the Reich's antisemitic policies. Since the Abwehr was responsible for military information, it theoretically should not have engaged in such an operation, and Canaris knew he would need someone he could rely on. Perhaps he selected Bloch not only because he was an excellent soldier but also because of his Jewish background. It seemed logical to send a man of at least partial Jewish descent to save this Jew, despite the deeper irony of his serving with distinction in the Wehrmacht.[17]

SIX

Bloch's Secret Mission

Ernst Ferdinand Benjamin Bloch was born 1 May 1898 in Berlin, one of two sons of Dr. Oskar Bloch, a Jew, and his Gentile wife, Margarete née Schönberg. Margarete's first husband had died in 1897; he too was Jewish and she had two daughters by him. Mixed marriages were common in Germany; several thousand were taking place at the turn of the century.[1]

Bloch grew up in a wealthy home until his father died, in 1910, when the family fell on hard times. Besides doing odd jobs to help support his mother and siblings, he worked hard at school and excelled in his studies. At the outbreak of war in 1914, the sixteen-year-old Bloch left home without his mother's knowledge and tried to enlist in the army. Several regiments rejected him because he was too young, but eventually he convinced Infantry Regiment 132 in Strasbourg to take him.[2] Like many other young Germans, he felt thrilled at the prospect of serving his country and drawn by the adventure of war.

Bloch quickly saw action. During the battle of Ypres in Belgium in 1915, an enemy soldier bayoneted him through his lower jaw into

Ernst Bloch as a Wehrmacht officer in late 1935 or early 1936 (Author's collection)

his skull, destroying part of his chin and knocking out teeth. Placing a boot on Bloch's shoulder, the soldier then removed the blade from his head, leaving him for dead. He woke up in a field hospital. Remarkably, he suffered no brain damage and returned to the front a few months later to fight in the battles of Verdun and the Somme in 1916, Champagne in 1917, and Flanders in 1918, where he again sustained severe injuries, this time shrapnel splinters in both legs, an arm, and his head.[3] Bloch recovered again and returned to fight in the bloody trenches of the Western Front. By the end of the war, he had been honored with both Iron Crosses, Second and First Class (similar to the U.S. Bronze and Silver Stars), and the Wound Badge (akin to the Purple Heart). His brother, Waldemar, was less fortunate, dying in 1919 from wounds suffered during battle. After the war, Bloch remained in the army.[4]

Bloch's heroism did not protect him from antisemitism. In 1921,

Photograph taken for Bloch's military ID papers. The horrible wound on his face was quite pronounced in spite of several surgeries to repair it. (Author's collection)

he was rejected by a student fraternity for being Jewish.[5] His mother was shocked. So secular was the Bloch family that she did not consider her son Jewish. She could understand that the fraternity might not want to take religious Jews, but she never thought of her family in those terms. Her husband's being a Jew had not prevented him from becoming a successful medical doctor; even in his youth, he had been a member of a distinguished fraternity.

Enraged, Margarete wrote to her son: "I'm speechless and ashamed that even after the experiences since 1914 in the German Fatherland there are such narrow-minded people still around." She went on to express her fury that the fraternity had rejected him despite his bravery in battle. But she also blamed her son for the humiliation: "Did you have to tell them that your father was a Jew? Why then? You don't have to advertise that information on your nose, and besides, you have a Christian mother. . . . Your father didn't convert to Christianity because he didn't want people to think that he did so simply to better his status. There are also Jews who are at least as worthy as so-called Christians."[6] Bloch probably did say he was Christian, but his name most likely provoked questions that he answered truthfully.

Bloch continued his studies at Friedrich Wilhelm University in Berlin and in 1924 received a doctorate in economics cum laude. He remained on active duty as a Reichswehr officer throughout the Weimar Republic; his Jewish background was at that time not an issue. In 1930, he married Sabine von Bosse, a Gentile. His father-in-law, Hans von Bosse, welcomed him into the family, writing tenderly: "My dear Son, for the first time I'm sending you my best wishes on your birthday. . . . You will see that you now belong to us and that our hearts are bound to you. We especially thank your parents for this day, and now we have taken their role [Bloch's mother had died in 1922]. During this new year, you have committed yourself to Sabine, and thus God bless you and make you both happy! Happiness grows from the inside and cannot be hunted down but rather must grow like a healthy fruit nurtured by sunshine and rain. . . . In True Love, Your Father."[7] Having lost his father at an early age, Bloch must have been deeply touched by these kind words. Not surprisingly, his union with Sabine started out with a strong foundation. Throughout his married life, Bloch dedicated himself to her and never forgot his in-laws' generous welcome into the family. Society at large did not share the sentiments of his new family, especially after Hitler's assumption of power in 1933, but Bloch would not encounter antisemitism again until years after the fraternity episode.

In 1935, Admiral Canaris recruited Bloch to head the I/Wirtschaftsabteilung (Foreign Economic Intelligence Department), gathering data on the industrial capacity of foreign countries. Ca-

As head of the Abwehr's Foreign Economic Intelligence Department, Bloch often took foreign industrialists on tours of the Reich's factories, as on this occasion with Japanese businessmen in the spring of 1939 (Author's collection)

naris considered Bloch one of his most capable officers. Besides gathering intelligence on foreign industries, Bloch also led German and foreign businessmen on industrial tours of the Reich and, after Germany's occupation of the West in 1940, of Belgium, France, and the Netherlands. Canaris praised Bloch on one occasion, writing, "[Your department] has accurately discerned its objectives: to keep watch on the enemy [Belgium and France] munitions industry, discover its productive capacity, and ascertain the local situation."[8]

Bloch's Jewish paternity surfaced again in 1935, with the passage of the Nuremberg racial laws, which decreed the segregation of "Aryan" Germans from Germans of Jewish descent. On 14 November 1935, the Reich Interior Ministry issued a supplement to the legislation officially creating the "racial" categories of German, Jew, "half Jew (Jewish *Mischling* 1st Degree)," and "quarter Jew (Jewish *Mischling* 2nd Degree)," each with its own regulations. Hitler decided to treat half Jews for the time being as a separate group and not as full Jews. Full Jews had three or four Jewish grandparents. According to Hitler, when someone was more than "50% Jewish," he was evil (*übel*) and not worth saving. Half Jews had two Jewish grandparents, and quarter Jews had one Jewish grandparent.[9] Ironically, the Nazis had to apply religious criteria to define these racial categories, using birth, baptismal, marriage, and death certificates. Often stored in churches, temples, and courthouses, these records indicated what religion one adhered to or had left. If a Mischling practiced the Jewish religion or was married to a Jew, the Nazis counted that person as a full Jew (*Geltungsjude*).[10]

The 1935 Nuremberg racial laws provided the substructure for further anti-Jewish legislation aimed at maintaining the purity of the "Aryan" race. But article 7 of a supplementary decree of the Nuremberg laws authorized Hitler to Aryanize individuals labeled Jew or Mischling. Late in 1939, Canaris brought Bloch's case to the Führer, who signed documents declaring Bloch of "German blood" (*deutschblütig*), thus removing Bloch's "birth defect" with a stroke of his pen. Since there were many people who were valuable to Hitler who were of Jewish descent, he decided to give himself the option of keeping them.

The probable reason Canaris waited four years to get the exemption for Bloch is that his background had not been an issue until then. Many decorated veterans of World War I enjoyed several years of clemency after the promulgation of the racial laws. It was not until 1939 that they finally caught up with Bloch and the exemption that he had enjoyed earlier as a veteran became invalid.[11]

Bloch's application for Aryanization included his military records, his high school and college transcripts, recommendations from teachers and military superiors, as well as head-on and profile photographs. Hitler attached great importance to physical ap-

This photograph of Bloch, taken in late 1938, was probably sent to Hitler in 1939 with his application for Aryanization. On the basis of his good military history and his "Germanic looks," Hitler declared Bloch of "German blood," allowing him to stay in the Wehrmacht. (Author's collection)

pearances. Bloch's official Aryanization document probably read like most others, "I, Adolf Hitler, leader of the German nation, approve Ernst Bloch to be of German blood. His children may also claim this classification as long as Bloch does not marry anyone of foreign blood." Bloch and his family thus secured protection from racial discrimination.[12]

Liste von a k t i v e n Offizieren,
die selbst oder deren Ehefrauen jüdische Mischlinge sind
und vom Führer für deutschblütig erklärt wurden

N a m e u. Vorname	Dienstgrad u. R.D.A.	Dienststelle	Geburts- datum	Bluts- anteile
Adlhoch Franz	Gen.Major 1.11.42 (11)	Kdt. St.O.Kdtr. Rudnja	17. 6.93	Ehefrau 50%
Altmann Helmut	Oberst 1.2.42 (101)	Kdr. A.R.347	4. 1.97	selbst 25%
Andresen Hans	Major 1.1.42 (424)	b. Kw.Trsp.Abt.356 als Kdr.	6. 8.07	selbst 25%
A. .old Reinhard	Major 1.6.43 (6)	St. Gen.d.Pi. Abt. H.Gru.Nord	21. 5.12	selbst 25%
Aschenbrandt Heinrich	Gen.Major 1.12.41 (10)	Kdt. F.Kdtr.238	—	Sohn aus 1.Ehe, 25%
Behrens Wilhelm	Gen.Major 1.1.42 (5)	Kdr. Div. Nr.193	23. 8.88	selbst ?
Belli von Pino Anton	Oberst 1.4.58 (33)	F.Res.OKH, Dienst regelt Chef Kriegs- gesch.Abt.	13.12.81	selbst 25%
Bieringer Ludwig	Gen.Major 1.7.43 (1)	F.Res.OKH, kdt.zum Mil.Befh.i.Frkr.zur Einweis.i.d.G.eines Feldkdt.	12. 8.92	Ehefrau 50%
Bloch Dr. Ernst	Obstlt. 1.7.41 (45)	F.I.s.OKH, kdt.zur 213.I.D. z.Verw.als Btls.Kdr.	1. 5.98	selbst 50%
Bonin Swantus	Oberst 1.4.42 (544)	Vorstand Bekl.Amt Erfurt	—	Ehefrau 50%
Borchardt Robert	Major 1.6.43 (32d)	Pz.Aufkl.Abt.7 Wiedereinberufung als akt.Offz.genehmigt, aber noch nicht arisiert	9. 1.12	?
Borowietz Willibald	Gen.Lt. 1.7.43 (7)	Pz.Jäg.Tr.Schule, hat Ritterkreuz, ist in engl.Gefangenschaft	17. 9.93	3 Kinder (50%) arisiert, Ehe- frau(Jüd)verstb.
Braune Günther	Oberst z.V.	z.Zt. Gehilfe beim Mil.Attaché Madrid	18.10.88	selbst 50%
Bruhnke Dr. Johannes	Oberst-Vet. 1.8.41 (1)	Wehrkr.Vet.IX	—	Ehefrau 25%
Colli Robert	Oberst 1.7.43 (36a)	Kdr. Gren.Rgt.547	27. 6.98	selbst 50%
Emmenthal Karl	Oberst 1.10.42 (50)	Bev.Trsp.Offz.beim AOK 7	26. 6.01	Ehefrau 25%

A list from 1944 of "active officers who are either Jewish Mischlinge or married to Jewish Mischlinge and whom Hitler has declared of German blood." The "Blood Percentage" in the column on the far right shows Bloch as 50 percent Jewish. (Author's collection and Bundesarchiv)

Bloch's son Martin later wrote that "my father felt he was German, and as a German he served his country. . . . Moreover, he felt
protected by Canaris, in whose office he worked." Canaris described
Bloch in an evaluation on 14 March 1937 as a "reliable person, . . . a
diligent worker . . . [who] does his duty well." In June 1938, Bloch was
promoted to major. Later that year, Hitler sanctioned the awarding
of the Hungarian Knight's Cross Service Medal.[13] Obviously, Bloch's
Jewish ancestry did not matter to Canaris, but under Hitler's regime
Canaris had to be unusually careful to protect Bloch, whom he obviously valued.

Canaris chose other men of Jewish descent to help Bloch rescue
Rebbe Schneersohn. One was Private Johannes Hamburger, a quarter Jew who spoke French, Russian, and Polish and knew Warsaw.[14]
His grandfather had been a rabbi who converted to Christianity. Before the war, Hamburger had thought of becoming a priest. Instead,
he worked in the Abwehr, using his language skills and his uncanny
ability to persuade reluctant people to talk.[15]

His comrade Sergeant Klaus Schenk, a half Jew, was also useful
for the rescue mission.[16] He had a Jewish mother but, like most other
Mischlinge in the Wehrmacht, was reared as a Christian. He had distinguished himself in battle in Poland and received the Iron Cross
for defending against attacking Polish infantrymen and snipers. One
report claimed he killed more than twenty Polish soldiers and, when
he ran out of ammunition, threw grenades to hold the enemy back
until reinforcements arrived. He was the only survivor of his unit
of twenty. Like Bloch, he had a scarred face, but he had received his
mark from dueling with a fraternity brother.

Schenk was not only half Jewish but homosexual. He worried that
someone would find out about him. He had cause to worry since the
Nazis persecuted gays as sexual degenerates and would go on to kill
thousands of them. With two strikes against him, Schenk knew that
any transgression on his part would be viewed more harshly under
Hitler.[17]

Jm Namen
des
Deutſchen Volfes

erteile ich

dem Major (E)

Dr.Ernst B l o c h

die Genehmigung zur Annahme

des Ritterkreuzes

des Königlich Ungarischen Verdienstordens.

Berchtasgaden
Berlin, den   19. Oktober 1938

Der führer und Reichsfanzler

Hitler's decree awarding Bloch the Hungarian Knight's Cross Service Medal on 19 October 1938. (The signature was a stamped facsimile.) (Author's collection)

The fourth man on this unusual mission was Major Johannes Horatzek, head of the Abwehr office in Warsaw. His knowledge of Warsaw, the Poles, and the Polish language enabled him to play a key role in locating the Rebbe. After the successful conquest of Poland, Canaris traveled around Warsaw with Horatzek observing the destruction and confided in him that "our children's children will have to bear the blame for this." Canaris seems to have had a good working relationship with him.[18]

Bloch, Schenk, and Hamburger were not unusual figures in Canaris's Abwehr. Canaris employed a great many Mischlinge, including one of the principal men who collected information on Nazi war crimes: a quarter Jew named Hans von Dohnanyi, who, like Bloch, was Aryanized.[19] Karl Heinz Abshagen, a biographer of Canaris, writes that Abwehr personnel were often exempted from involved security checks on their family trees. As a result, although many were affected by the Nuremberg laws, they were allowed to remain. Thanks to Canaris, several Jews and half Jews were protected from the Gestapo by their service in the Abwehr.[20]

Unlike Bloch, a career officer, many Mischlinge in the Wehrmacht had been drafted. The Nazis made it mandatory for half Jews and quarter Jews to serve, and tens of thousands Mischlinge were in the Wehrmacht.[21] Most could not, however, become NCOs or officers without Hitler's personal consent. The German Jewish population had a strong tradition of serving in the armed forces; in World War I, a hundred thousand Jews served in the German military.[22] Coming as they did from military backgrounds, many Mischlinge hoped their service would protect them and their families from the rising tide of antisemitism. So the presence of Bloch, Schenk, and Hamburger in the Wehrmacht was not as bizarre as one might think.[23] Nor was it unusual that they should be selected—however odd the mission—to find and rescue Rebbe Schneersohn.

SEVEN

The Search Begins

From late September into early October, the Rebbe and his followers remained trapped in Warsaw and, despite the constant threat of arrest and persecution, continued rigorously to observe Orthodox tradition. On 25–26 September, at the height of the bombing, the Rebbe had a sukkah built for the coming holiday, inspiring his followers to believe that the Jewish spirit would not be defeated.[1] He told them, "For Hashem to do his part, we have to build a sukkah" and promised "a long life to whoever goes to gather the branches we need for the roof." Ironically, it was a secular Jew who scurried off to do the Rebbe's bidding.[2] From 28 September until 5 October, they celebrated Sukkot (Feast of Tabernacles), which traditionally marks the end of the harvest. During this holiday, Jews build a sukkah and live in it to commemorate the Israelites' flight from slavery in Egypt.

After Sukkot came Simchat Torah (Rejoicing of the Law) on 6 October, commemorating the annual reading of the Torah. During the course of each year, the entire Torah is read in synagogues, and Simchat Torah marks the completion of a full cycle of these readings from Genesis through Deuteronomy. The Rebbe said of Simchat

Torah that Jews seize the Torah and leap into dance. "[Men] dance with the Torah—they are making the Torah happy. In the midst of this joy, however, one needs to do some thinking. True, we are happy with the Torah. But is the Torah happy with us?"[3] As the Nazis set up their administration in Warsaw, many Jews had difficulty focusing on the holiday; the Rebbe may have felt the Torah was not happy with its people.

In many communities throughout Poland, the *Hakafot,* the ritual marching and dancing with the Torah scrolls at the end of the celebration, was probably omitted in 1939 to avoid attracting unnecessary attention from the German authorities. Chaim Kaplan wrote that "never before have we missed expressing our joy in the eternal Torah—even during the Middle Ages. After 7:00 P.M. there is a curfew in the city, and even in the hours before the curfew we live in dread of the Nazi conquerors' cruelty. The Nazi policy toward Jews is now in full swing. . . . Midian and Moab [ancient enemies of the Israelites] have joined forces in order to oppress Israel."[4]

At the beginning of October, rumors circulated in Warsaw that the French had invaded Germany and taken twelve cities. In reality, the French army remained idle. The news services had shut down, and no one really knew what was going on in the outside world. Most people, in any case, did not have time to think about politics and world events—they were too busy trying to find something to eat and drink. The Nazis rounded up Jews for forced labor, and, puzzled by the persecution, Kaplan exclaimed on 18 October: "Great God! Are you making an end to Polish Jewry? 'Your people' cannot understand: Why is the world silent?" Many in the Rebbe's group feared for their lives, and the Germans must have forced several of the younger men to go on work details. Many Jews resigned themselves to a fate they felt would soon end in death.[5]

Back in America, Chabad's legal counsel Sam Kramer suggested the Lubavitchers ask his friend Max Rhoade, also a lawyer, to start the paperwork for getting the Rebbe and others out of Europe—

namely, his sons-in-law, Rabbi Menachem Mendel Schneerson and Rabbi Samarius Gourary; their wives, Chaya Moussin and Chana; and the Gourarys' son, Barry.[6] But the process was complicated by the absence of birth certificates. Many of the relevant documents were in the Soviet Union and therefore impossible to obtain.[7] Senator Borah had tried to help Gourary and his family leave Europe since early 1939, but obviously without success.[8] Yet the fact that Borah wanted to help Gourary shows how connected the Lubavitchers were in Washington, as well as how difficult it was even during prewar days to get entry visas to the United States.

Since Hitler had taken power in 1933, the number of rabbis seeking refuge in America had increased dramatically. Section 4(d) of the Immigration Act of 1924 allowed "ministers" of religion to enter America on nonquota status.[9] Many, though, had to prove they were employable, something Visa Division officials doubted. The division was headed by Avra M. Warren, a man not inclined to help Jewish refugees. And in January 1940 Roosevelt would pick Assistant Secretary of State Breckinridge Long to oversee European refugee policy. Long's fundamentally ungenerous spirit and self-avowed antisemitism would prove deadly for refugees. When he took over from Warren, he found there was already a tradition of unwillingness to help those in need.

Given the State Department's indifference and hostility to Jewish immigrants, it is hardly surprising that those under Warren's, and later Long's, aegis made the process of applying for visas as difficult as possible. Visa Division agents working under Warren and his second in command, Eliot B. Coulter, regularly questioned the sincerity of the rabbis they investigated. They thought most would become public charges and, interpreting the immigration laws in the most restrictive way, rejected their applications. Needless to say, Max Rhoade faced incredible odds in his effort to help the Rebbe reach the safety of the United States.[10]

The Lubavitchers in America had become increasingly worried

Avra M. Warren, head of the U.S. Visa Division until January 1940
(United States National Archives)

about the Rebbe—a month had passed without good news since the
initial flurry of appeals to politicians. Nothing seemed to be happening. On 26 October 1939, Jacobson telegraphed Chaim Lieberman,
the Rebbe's secretary in Riga, saying, "We received word through
State Department Washington that German military authorities in
Warsaw desirous of cooperating have dispatched officers to locate
Rabbi and then accompany him to Riga."[11]

Soon Oscar Rabinovitz, the lawyer who was responsible for several of Lubavitch's political contacts, informed Justice Brandeis of
the Rebbe's address. Brandeis relayed this information to Benjamin
Cohen, who told Robert Pell. On 28 October, Pell wrote the U.S.
chargé d'affaires in Germany that Schneersohn "may possibly be located at the Gourari home, Bonifraterska Street 29." Wohlthat received this information and notified Washington on 4 November
1939 that an officer (Bloch) had been charged with finding the Rebbe
and helping him escape.[12]

By November, Nazi persecution of Polish Jewry was becoming codified. The Germans required Jews to wear an armband with the Star of David, and many walked in fear of being harassed and arrested by the Germans.[13] Both Jewish converts to Christianity and religious Jews were compelled to wear the armband. Sadly, some Jews took a perverse pleasure in observing the persecution of converts. Kaplan wrote: "I shall, however, have revenge on our 'converts.' I will laugh aloud at the sight of their tragedy. These poor creatures, whose number has radically increased in recent times, should have known that the 'racial' laws do not differentiate between Jews who become Christians and those who retain their faith. Conversion brought them but small deliverance. . . . This is the first time in my life that a feeling of vengeance has given me pleasure."[14]

Many Jews believed that those Jews renouncing the Hebrew faith weakened the body of Israel and betrayed their people. And all too often, Jewish converts demonstrated cruelty to Jews. The truth was that while some Jews converted out of religious conviction, others did so to improve their social status. The Rebbe looked down on such converts, calling them "apostates" and *nebbich* Jews (Jews to be pitied); he was even more aggressive about those "light-minded ignoramuses" who followed disbelievers and atheists. For observant Jews like the Lubavitchers, abandoning Judaism, regardless of the reason, was a sin against God.[15]

Day after day, in the midst of all the confusion, Bloch combed the sections of Warsaw where Orthodox Jews lived, inquiring after the Rebbe. As might be expected, most Lubavitchers feared the army major and revealed nothing. One time he confronted a Lubavitcher rabbi on the street, asking him to pass the news to the community that he had come to Warsaw to save Schneersohn. The Lubavitcher rubbed his eyes in disbelief, stood frozen, and finally moved away, stumbling. Another time when Bloch approached a religious Jew and inquired after the Rebbe's whereabouts, the man's eyes widened, his mouth opened, and his shoulders slouched. He slowly raised

An Orthodox Jew carrying a suitcase runs through the wreckage of Warsaw
in a photograph taken by the German military on 4 October 1939
(United States National Archives)

his hand, stroked his beard, then turned and disappeared down an
alley.[16] That German soldiers were seeking to help the Rebbe must
have struck him as absurd.

Frustrated by his fruitless search, Bloch asked Hamburger what
to say to religious Jews when he met them. The major realized that
the proper military greeting—name, rank, and mission—did not encourage the divulging of information. Smiling, Hamburger said, "To
start with, say Shalom. Shalom is a good word."[17] Bloch grinned and
repeated the word a few times.

Bloch and his men sometimes proceeded through Warsaw in
civilian clothes. Protocol probably prevented them from discarding
their uniforms entirely; nor, most likely, did they want to come un-

der the scrutiny of the Gestapo. Their gray tunics provided ano-
nymity among the thousands of Wehrmacht soldiers stationed in
Warsaw. Since there had been long-standing friction between the SS
and the Abwehr, especially in foreign intelligence activities, any help
in disguising their activities was welcome. Canaris had all his men
pay close attention to the SS in Poland.

On the basis of documents available in Washington, it seems that
Bloch and the others, probably including Major Horatzek, discussed
a strategy for convincing the Rebbe of their good intentions, since
they were persuaded he was refusing, for obvious reasons, to reveal himself. Bloch and Hamburger agreed that instead of confront-
ing men on the street they should try going door-to-door. They did
not know if the Rebbe was alive or dead, and they had made little
progress since their arrival. The direct approach was the only way,
Bloch said.[18]

By that time, news of the soldiers' search must have reached the
Rebbe, who probably sent Samarius Gourary out to ascertain the
Germans' intentions. This proved difficult since most Polish Jews
did not trust the Germans. If the Lubavitchers were suspicious of the
German soldiers who claimed to want to come to their aid, Bloch and
his men, for their part, probably felt little kinship with the Orthodox
Jews of Warsaw.

The Lubavitchers felt justifiably skeptical of them, even if they
were Mischlinge. Many German Mischling soldiers, people just like
Bloch, who served in Poland reacted negatively to Ostjuden or issues
of Jewishness. In this respect and others, many Mischlinge felt the
same antisemitic feelings as non-Jews and were often disgusted by
the Hasidic Jews' appearance, habits, and living conditions. Many
today believe that racism was felt only by non-Jewish Germans, but
antisemitism had spread to Mischlinge through years of propaganda
and assimilation. Two totally different cultures were colliding.[19]

Many veterans report seeing other soldiers cut off Jews' beards,
force Jews in traditional garb to push military wagons, or prod Jews

with guns.[20] Many Mischling soldiers mistakenly believed the anti-semitism directed at Ostjuden would never affect them or their families.[21] Because most Mischlinge did not "look," act, or feel Jewish, they misjudged Hitler's true intentions. By the same token, the Lubavitchers would not have accepted as religious brethren these children of converts whom the Rebbe called apostates. So, even if the Lubavitchers had known that Bloch and some of his team were Mischlinge, it is unlikely that they would have placed their trust in any soldier of the German Reich.

EIGHT

A Lawyer's Work

On 18 October 1939, American Lubavitchers held a fund-raiser at the New York City Jewish Center for the Rebbe's rescue. A letter from America's Chabad headquarters had gone out to several Jewish organizations at the beginning of October saying that "every Jew, having a spark of Judaism within his breast, must conscientiously work to help save the Rabbi from the lurking peril." Sam Kramer and several others attended the fund-raiser, but, although many turned out in moral support, only two thousand dollars was collected. The organizers had hoped to raise at least ten thousand.[1]

Kramer, Chabad's legal counsel, was a close friend of the Rebbe's. A veteran of the American navy, he had helped found the YMHA (Young Men's Hebrew Association), the Sons of Israel synagogue, and Israel Zion Hospital in Brooklyn, organize the first eastern board of directors for the Anti-Defamation League, save a Swedish Protestant church from bankruptcy, and, finally, support and run Chabad in America.[2]

Although a Lubavitcher, Kramer was clean-shaven and wore modern clothes. He lived according to Torah values, but he wanted to

Samuel Kramer, legal counsel for Chabad in the United States. He was responsible for contacting Max Rhoade, who helped organize the rescue. Kramer also provided much of the funding. (Debby Kramer Neumark)

bridge the ways of old Jewish Orthodoxy with modern society. He felt that as a religious Jew he must not separate himself from the world but rather should live within it and try to make it better, using the religious foundation he respected and loved. Since he knew how to translate the Lubavitchers' wishes into effective political action, he proved indispensable to the rescue effort.

Realizing that the Lubavitcher rabbis had little knowledge or experience in dealing with governmental authorities, he wrote to his close friend Max Rhoade for assistance. According to Rabbi Israel Jacobson, he and Kramer hired Rhoade "with instruction not to rest till the Rebbe had been saved." Jacobson told Rhoade: "I need not emphasize the importance of the work we are doing because I understand that you are fully aware of the great and outstanding role the celebrated Rabbi Schneersohn has in the life of the Jewish people, and thus I am sure that you will please continue your excellent work and help us to bring about the speedy rescue of the Lubavitcher Rabbi." Rhoade decided to take the case because of his "deep" friendship with Kramer, whom he could not turn down.[3]

In October, Rhoade took charge of the legal aspects of the rescue. He was the kind of competent and rigorous attorney who believed everything should be done according to regulations. He was also well connected, acquainted with the likes of Justice Brandeis. The fact that he spoke Yiddish, the main language of most Lubavitcher rabbis, made him an excellent liaison between the Lubavitcher community and the government.[4]

Rhoade expressed to Kramer his concerns about the Rebbe's escape route, indicating that he thought it best to approach the Swedish authorities as there was fear of war in the Baltic States. He discussed how Washington should support the immigration of this group of Jews and how information should be channeled to the Germans working on the case. And last, he discussed money.

Apparently, Rhoade had done legal work for the Lubavitchers in the past on a pro bono basis, but this time he felt compelled to re-

Max Rhoade, the Washington lawyer who helped organize the rescue. He was also successful in mobilizing political support for the Rebbe's cause. (Eliezer Zaklikovsky)

quest payment. He knew he would spend an unusual number of hours on the case. On 28 October, in a letter to Kramer and Jacobson, Rhoade requested that his fees and expenses be paid on time to preserve his "peace of mind and ability to concentrate on the matter as you wish." In another letter a few days later, he wrote Kramer that he had talked to Jacobson and made "entirely clear my non-mercenary or rather non-profit motives in connection therewith."[5]

Jacobson made a special trip to Washington to discuss the situation with Rhoade and to deliver important documents. He encouraged Rhoade, telling him that rescuing the Rebbe would not "be solved in a day or so, with a call or letter here and there, all on a charitable basis. You have done many favors for us till now, let us make an arrangement so you can work for us on a permanent basis and expedite the whole affair and bring it to a quick and successful conclusion."[6] Although this sounded as if Jacobson intended to pay, Rhoade remained skeptical. On 25 October, he wrote to Jacobson to tell him he had enjoyed meeting him, but emphasizing that, regardless of the honor involved in working on such a case, he needed to be paid: "It is only too obvious that the situation demands enormous concentration and time, with resulting serious impairment of my current income. . . . I therefore hope, to enable me to continue tackling this job with some sort of mental comfort and freedom from undue distraction, that you will carry out your own plan promptly regarding myself. I wish I could afford otherwise."[7] Both the tone and the substance of Rhoade's letter suggests that he worried about the sincerity of the Lubavitchers' intention to pay. He often reminded Kramer and Jacobson of their commitment to him. Despite his concerns about money, he began to prepare the applications for U.S. residency visas for the Rebbe and his group.

According to some Lubavitcher rabbis, Jacobson probably knew his organization could not pay Rhoade's fees and was less than candid in discussing them. Jacobson and his followers were desperate and likely believed that, once they hired Rhoade to rescue the Rebbe, God would provide the means to pay him. Jacobson knew the case stood little chance of success without a high-powered lawyer like Rhoade. He may also have felt that Rhoade would come to realize the Rebbe's importance and change his mind about payment. Not all share these opinions, however: Rabbi Avraham Laber believes Jacobson had the money and was just late with his payments.[8]

To obtain visas, Rhoade needed to prove to the U.S. Immigration Service and the State Department that the Rebbe and his group were rabbis and thus "professors" of Jewish theology who could find employment as teachers. Providing sufficient proof would be difficult as there was strong anti-immigration bias in the "visa decision machinery," and the State Department's attitude toward Jews suffering under Hitler was callous.[9] Rhoade would have to work exceptionally hard to open America's gates for the Rebbe and his associates.

The plan was contingent, however, on the Germans' finding Schneersohn and avoiding the clutches of the SS. With each passing day, hope dwindled that the Rebbe had survived. The whole of Lubavitch prayed for his survival. Without word from Europe, several Lubavitchers started to express their frustration with Rhoade even though he had been working on the case for only a few weeks. Jacobson wrote Kramer on 30 October 1939 that "I have not seen anything tangible about the Rabbi's affairs as yet." While understanding their distress, Rhoade found the Lubavitchers' constant inquiries and complaints annoying. On 4 November, Rhoade wrote to Kramer, who also doubted Rhoade's diligence, assuring him that he would "work at top speed to close this case."[10] Rhoade's tone indicated slight irritation not only at Kramer's inquiries but also at the Lubavitchers' behavior.

On 4 November, Rhoade wrote Benjamin Cohen that those interested in the Rebbe's welfare were in a state of "the greatest anxiety" for news about the Rebbe and felt "perturbed over the lack of word from the German authorities." Rhoade encouraged Cohen to ask the State Department to have the American consulate in Warsaw "urge Rabbi Schneersohn to cooperate with the German military officer [Bloch] assigned to facilitate his safe egress to Riga, and to notify them of the Rebbe's condition and needs." Rhoade realized that Bloch was probably experiencing difficulty winning the Rebbe's confidence because no independent authority had assured the Rebbe of Bloch's intentions. Rhoade believed that if the American consulate could communicate with the Rebbe, he would follow Bloch. By now, Lubavitchers in Riga and Vilna knew about the German plan (probably from the U.S. telegraphs) and had sent secret messengers to Warsaw to convince the Rebbe of the German's sincerity.[11]

Rhoade still had to figure out how to convince the U.S. immigration authorities that the Rebbe was worthy of their help. Believing the case warranted the involvement of the State Department, Rhoade bombarded it with letters, confident that, as he explained to Cohen, "the Department will gladly make an exception in the case of Rabbi Schneersohn, consistent with the extraordinary action already taken upon Secretary Hull's instructions at your request. . . . It seems logical, that if the State Department went out of its way in one phase of this matter, it might just as well complete the job."[12] Rhoade's tactic of presenting State Department action on behalf of the Rebbe as a fait accompli was surprisingly effective in getting the department to do what he felt should be done.

The scope of the rescue expanded to include additional members of the Rebbe's family and close associates numbering well over a dozen. Rhoade hoped that Jacobson had arranged employment with various synagogues for the rabbis in the Rebbe's entourage, because he needed proof as soon as possible for the American government. The fact that most of the Rebbe's group were born in Russia eased Rhoade's job since that country's quota remained open. He nevertheless needed detailed information about Chabad "to give a clear picture to the American Consulate of the past and present earning capacity of the Rebbe and the other heads of the families who wish to come to America, as indicating a source of future income."[13] Despite the goodwill of many in the government, the fact remained that if the Rebbe could not support himself he would not be welcome. If someone was likely "to become a public charge," the officials handling the case would deny a visa. Therefore, a person required "an American sponsor to have $5,000 or more in a bank account" to prove that he or she would not be a drain on society.[14]

Rhoade asked Jacobson to provide him with the number of Chabad members throughout the world, the number of Lubavitch synagogues, the estimated total income of the Chabad organization for the last five years, the source of Chabad's income, the organization of Chabad, the name and address of its chief financial officer, the estimated total and nature of the Rebbe's personal annual income

for the past several years, and similar information for the rabbis accompanying the Rebbe.[15] Obviously, Rhoade had no knowledge of
Chabad's infrastructure. Jacobson, although an energetic leader, did
not have a real office and did not speak English well (his primary
language was Yiddish); his young daughter often had to help him
understand the letters he received.[16] He had no financial staff. Since
his office was not organized or operated as a corporation, it could
not provide the detailed information Rhoade needed. By its nature,
charismatic religious leadership like the Rebbe's makes no distinction between personal assets and institutional property even though
such distinctions are important in secular law. All this greatly ham-
pered Rhoade's efforts to prove Chabad could support the Rebbe.

Frustrated with Jacobson, Rhoade wrote him on 4 November: "I
hope you will not mind my impressing upon you the necessity of
reading my letters carefully and answering me on every point, because I cannot constantly keep track of these things and necessarily
depend upon you to carry out anything I suggest and unless all of
this is done very promptly we shall find ourselves delayed at various
junctures." Jacobson constantly disappointed Rhoade in these matters, even though as far back as February 1939 the Rebbe, fearing
that war might break out, had requested him to obtain visas for him,
his family, and his inner circle.[17]

The Rebbe's escape route also troubled Rhoade. He feared that
the Soviet Union might invade the Baltic States, and that the Rebbe's
host countries might prevent him and his group from leaving without proper papers. He also feared that the Gestapo would intervene
if the Rebbe and his family received emergency visas in Berlin.

Since the acting chief of the Visa Division in Washington, Eliot B.
Coulter, advised Rhoade that "it was impossible for either emergency visitors' visas or immigration visas to be prearranged," it
seemed best for the Rebbe to travel to Riga and wait there until
the United States could complete the necessary paperwork. Helmut
Wohlthat had informed Robert Pell that he planned to evacuate the

Lubavitchers to Sweden but needed more time. Wohlthat reserved the right to send Schneersohn to Riga via Vilna, if necessary, a route to which Rhoade objected because of the looming Soviet threat.[18]

Rhoade continued to worry about his fees—an issue no one wanted to discuss. He wrote Kramer on 6 November, saying, "I had already indicated that because of the monkey wrench which this matter has thrown into current income for weeks past, I prefer remittance now, rather than at the conclusion of the matter." Perhaps the reluctance to pay Rhoade stemmed from the fact that Kramer was personally bearing the brunt of the financial responsibility and was struggling with the expense. Rhoade knew this and suggested that Jacobson, together with the Lubavitcher community, should relieve Kramer of this burden. Rhoade said that he hoped "Jacobson and his colleagues will be able to effectuate a 'catch up' plan this week, for any further allusion to the subject is quite embarrassing."[19]

On 8 November, Rhoade protested to Jacobson that he had "not yet forwarded the check payable to the Swedish Legation for the amount of $4.82" and that his fee of $48.27 from October was still outstanding. Jacobson's reluctance to pay is difficult to understand. He had access to discretionary funds to cover such expenses, especially when $2,000 had been raised specifically for the Rebbe's rescue. If Chabad in America did possess assets of $500,000, it could have taken out a loan or mortgaged real estate to pay legal fees.[20]

The same day, Rhoade received a letter from Jacobson in which he failed to answer Rhoade's questions about Chabad's resources or to explain why bills remained unpaid. The lawyer replied angrily, "As I understand your letter, you do not have, and apparently do not care to secure from [Chaim] Lieberman any concrete, factual information on the past of Rabbi Schneersohn and the other prospective immigrants." Rhoade informed Jacobson that the absence of this required information would prove "a definite handicap in obtaining even quota visas for these people." Jacobson's inability to comply perplexed Rhoade. "Despite the greatest good will and prear-

ranged friendliness," he emphasized to Jacobson, even "ordinary rabbis" accompanying the Rebbe had to demonstrate the ability to earn
enough income to support themselves; "mere generalities" about
Schneersohn's "importance as a spiritual figure and the spiritual importance of Chabad" would not suffice. Although that type of argument might convince Lubavitchers, U.S. immigration officials would
hardly be impressed. No one disputed the Rebbe's spiritual authority
in the eyes of many Jews, but it was irrelevant to his ability to earn
an income. Furthermore, the rest of the Rebbe's entourage had no
such claim to greatness. Rhoade needed data from Jacobson that
would prove the "*bona fide* nature of the synagogue contract-affidavit
material." He would not take responsibility for failing to bring the
Rebbe safely to the United States if Jacobson did not provide it. "I
just want to record for future reference," he said, "that I asked for
this information and could not get it." He would not have done his
job, he continued, "if I failed to warn you about this problem, which
is very apt to arise."[21]

Jacobson notwithstanding, Rhoade made progress with the State
Department. Benjamin Cohen thought Rhoade should discuss the
information he had with Robert T. Pell, who was handling the case
under Cordell Hull's oversight.[22] After meeting with Rhoade on
8 November, Pell described the Rebbe as "a sort of modern St. Fran-
cis of Assisi" deserving aid and succor. The following day, Rhoade
asked Pell to ask Wohlthat whether the Germans had discovered
Schneersohn's whereabouts. Rhoade also requested that Pell cable
the Warsaw consulate to locate the Rebbe and inform him of Bloch's
mission.[23]

Rhoade felt the need to pass on the information about the officer's
intentions again since it appeared that neither the Rebbe nor his followers wanted to reveal themselves to the Abwehr man.[24] Rhoade requested on 9 November that Pell send Bloch the Rebbe's old address
"since we suspect that the Rabbi is in hiding and fears to entrust

himself to the German officer."[25] Surely the Rebbe knew about the search by now, but he had probably experienced difficulty verifying Bloch's credibility.

Rhoade felt this confidential information might convince the Rebbe to trust Bloch. With stories of German atrocities becoming widely known in Warsaw, it was critical to persuade the Rebbe that Bloch indeed aimed to help him. Hull authorized Pell to send the information to the U.S. embassy in Berlin.[26]

With the help of Congressman Sol Bloom of New York, Rhoade talked to Latvian diplomats. He also wrote to Alfred Bilmanis, Latvia's diplomat in Washington, on 8 November, reminding him that a German officer had been assigned to facilitate the Rebbe's escape and asking him to tell his people in Latvia to reassure the Rebbe of the officer's trustworthiness. Rhoade needed Bilmanis's cooperation to ensure that the Rebbe would not be detained at the Lithuanian or Latvian border. This was important in that these countries had been reluctant to allow Jewish refugees to immigrate.[27]

The Rebbe would probably have to travel through Lithuania without his passport and other necessary documents, which had been lost. The route through Lithuania might prove better than through Königsberg, Germany, where the "danger of molestation by anti-Jewish elements" was greater. Rhoade hoped that Bilmanis would intervene since the Rebbe was one of Latvia's "distinguished citizens." Rhoade had to persuade the Latvian diplomat to help not only the Rebbe but also his entourage of seventeen people. Although Bloch had not yet located Schneersohn, Rhoade insisted that Bilmanis have visas prepared for the speedy departure of these Lubavitchers. Rhoade's fear that the Soviet Union would invade the Baltic States grew each day, and he worried that if the Russians caught the Rebbe, he would be as good as dead. The Russian threat combined with Latvia's apparent inaction would seem to justify the curt tone in which he all but demanded that Bilmanis fulfill his requests.

He hoped that Dubin and others of Chabad's friends in the Latvian government would pressure their officials to issue the appropriate documents.[28]

Meanwhile, Bloch and his group were scouring Warsaw for the Rebbe. They soon found the destroyed building Schneersohn had registered with the police as his address. Bloch's team reported to Canaris that since the building the Rebbe had claimed as his address had been "completely demolished during the bombardment at the end of September," it would be impossible to determine whether the Rebbe had perished. Indeed, Bloch assumed that the Rebbe might already have died, but he continued his search.[29]

Walking from house to house, Bloch's team asked scared and hungry Lubavitchers about the Rebbe, but no one dared to talk. On one occasion, a little girl opened the door and asked what the soldiers wanted. Suddenly, a mother's arm pulled the child away from the entryway and slammed the door. Another time, a young man opened his door and, on seeing the officers, lost control of his bladder. Bloch and his men nonetheless continued to go door-to-door, explaining they wanted to help the Rebbe, not to harm him.

Perhaps they had so much trouble finding the Rebbe because the Lubavitchers "all felt that if the Nazis ever captured the Rebbe that would have been a great prize for them." Many were convinced, understandably, that "the Nazis were after him."[30] The Lubavitchers were terrified and the atmosphere in the city had become horrific. As one Jew wrote, "Darkness rules the streets of Warsaw [and] dominates our minds."[31] Time was running out for the Rebbe. Soon the borders would be closed and no Jews would be able to leave Poland.

Back in Washington, Rhoade feared that Schneersohn would not entrust himself and his followers to a German officer. On 9 November, Rhoade cabled Lieberman and wrote Kramer, emphasizing the need to convince the Rebbe to trust Bloch. Rhoade looked to Lieberman to accomplish this task since he had lost hope that the rather apathetic representatives of the Latvian government would locate the Rebbe. Indeed, the Latvians were worried as the Soviets looked menacingly at their country; the rescue of the Rebbe must have yielded to other, more important priorities. Rhoade and Kramer nonetheless were perturbed by the Latvian government's inaction. Rhoade found it strange that the Latvian Foreign Office had failed to act on information from Bilmanis or in response to the presumed efforts of Latvian Senator Dubin. He suspected that "Latvia is displeased with the Rebbe—only a naturalized Latvian citizen—for having overstayed in Poland with something akin to a presumption of expatriation." Rhoade and some of the Lubavitchers in the United States agreed that unfortunately Dubin and Lieberman were "evidently weak with the Riga Foreign Office." Rhoade worried that the State Department might lose interest if it discovered that the Lubavitchers lacked strong Latvian support.[32]

"Perhaps the Latvian Foreign Office has done its best," Rhoade speculated, "but failed for reasons of its own (unless we are to assume gross negligence), to apprise Bilmanis of the nature of its action." While voicing concern for the Rebbe, Bilmanis told Rhoade that he could not go further without embarrassing himself and his government and suggested that Senator Dubin deal with the Latvian officials on the Rebbe's behalf. Rhoade did not tell Bilmanis that Dubin had only minimal influence with the Latvian government, because he feared the information might discourage Bilmanis from exerting continued effort. Bilmanis might have done more, Rhoade felt, but the many competing demands from others in dire straits probably discouraged him. To impress and influence him, Rhoade arranged for the two of them to meet Justice Brandeis. Rhoade told Kramer that the meeting "gratified [Bilmanis] a great deal."[33]

The lawyer urgently needed an ally with some political clout in Riga, but he did not know where to turn. His remaining tactic was to pressure American Jews to change the "lukewarm" attitudes of the Latvian Foreign Office. Rhoade feared, however, that Dubin and other friends of the Rebbe assumed that, now that the United States had become involved, they could fold "their hands in total inaction." He did not wish to "believe that they were such saps." Because of the confusion, Rhoade insisted that Kramer help him gain approval from the authorities to call Dubin or Lieberman personally in Riga to determine what was going on. Rhoade also sought to talk with the American ambassador to Latvia, who was to prepare the visas for the Rebbe and his group. Rhoade commented that the Latvian government should be contacting the United States government and not vice versa. He continued to worry that Latvia might be upset with the Rebbe, who, although a Latvian citizen, had chosen to live in Poland for years. If the Latvians felt the Rebbe did not really care about their country, which on the face of it seemed the case, they might not help.[34]

Rhoade soon received news that the German authorities had obtained the Rebbe's new address. He immediately requested Pell to ask Wohlthat to confirm that this address was not the "demolished building."[35] The next few days were filled with arrangements for the Rebbe's escape. Despite his financial concerns, Rhoade worked diligently on the case, primarily because of his friendship with Kramer. He attempted to open channels of communication with Latvia, though Pell advised him that the American embassy in Berlin could not, for diplomatic reasons, establish contact with the Latvian legation there. Rhoade suggested to Kramer that they inform Lieberman of this fact. Something had to change quickly with Latvia, Rhoade felt, or they would never get the Rebbe out. He also suggested that they contact the American embassy in Riga to solicit its help with the Latvians.

On 15 November, Pell reassured Rhoade that he was greatly interested in the case and promised that he would leave no "stone unturned" to discover the Rebbe's whereabouts. Pell further assured Rhoade that the American embassy was impressed with the international interest attached to the case and was communicating information about the Rebbe's situation to the Warsaw consulate. Although

Latvian support had diminished, Rhoade found increasing support in the United States, primarily from Pell, under the direct authority of Hull.[36]

Concerned about the Abwehr team, Rhoade wrote Kramer on 16 November, saying he had "misgivings about reposing too much confidence in the German [soldiers]." The lawyer believed that "no one can depend on the German attitude, particularly under the present regime, and in war time."[37] However, he had no choice but to trust the Germans, who seemed to be acting in good faith.

Lieberman echoed Rhoade's concern that Lubavitchers in Latvia were experiencing trouble securing that country's support for the escape. With the help of the Red Cross, Rhoade hoped to put the Latvian Foreign Office "on the spot" to take action to help rescue the Rebbe.[38]

On 20 November, Rhoade and his wife, Helen, joined Bilmanis at the Latvian embassy for a reception, at which Latvian officials gave the impression that they would cooperate.[39] Despite the efforts of the United States, the Abwehr, Latvia, and the International Red Cross, no one had yet located the Rebbe.

The Lubavitchers continued to stall in paying their bills. Rhoade protested to Kramer yet again on 21 November, saying he had tried to keep costs to a minimum, "but in a matter like this," cables, telephone calls, and large expenditures of time were inevitable. Rhoade reported that he had received neither his fee for the previous week nor payment of his last expense statement. He would have also been deeply offended by Kramer's complaints, he explained, "except for my knowledge of the sacrifices you are making yourself." Then he made it absolutely clear that working on the Rebbe's rescue had resulted in a "heavy personal loss."[40]

Apparently, Sam Kramer paid most of Chabad's expenses personally. One wonders why Jacobson and the American Chabad leaders, who had by now raised five thousand dollars for the Rebbe, allowed their bills to remain outstanding. Rhoade was aware of this fund, and it is strange that he did not mention it. Perhaps he thought it was to remain untouched to convince government officials that the Rebbe could support himself once he was in the United States.[41] His letters to Kramer indicate that he believed the Lubavitchers were more than capable of paying their bills.

On 25 November, Rhoade again wrote Kramer to request payment for fees and expenses. In response, Kramer seemed to be preparing Rhoade for the inevitable reality that the Lubavitchers would not pay him. Consequently, he should take solace in the good deeds he was performing and the appreciation he would receive. The Lubavitchers probably felt that since Rhoade was Jewish he should feel an obligation to work to save the Rebbe whether or not they paid him in full; they likely viewed it as an honor to have been chosen to rescue the Rebbe. Kramer had already written to Rhoade that he would reap not only financial but spiritual rewards: "As I have already indicated, compensation for your services will have to come from heaven, with the hope that the blessings from the Lubavitcher [Rebbe] and the numerous other rabbis interested in his welfare will be reflected in the happiness and prosperity of yourself and your dear Helen. I am confident that what you have done and will continue to do in this matter will be 'spreading bread upon the water' which, in due time, will bring its own compensation to you."[42] Rhoade did not appreciate such arguments. Blessings from ungrateful rabbis playing the guilt card did not pay his rent.

Rhoade also felt frustrated because the time he was spending on the case was significantly more than he had anticipated. As a perfectionist, he was intent on leaving nothing unexplored that could help with the rescue, but in so doing he neglected other cases that would have netted more cash. As a result, he became resentful of this case he felt bound to complete out of friendship and a sense of duty. Although Chabad did not pay nearly enough for his services, and although he doubted it would pay him in full, he could not, without losing face, just drop a case that had brought him in touch with some of the highest government personalities.

On the one hand, at a time when the Rebbe's life stood in peril and when the Nazis were persecuting thousands, one is taken aback by Rhoade's obsession with his fees. On the other hand, one would suppose that a dedicated follower like Jacobson would have been more than willing to pay any amount necessary to save the Rebbe.

NINE

The Angel

Acting on promising new information from Wohlthat on 25 November, Bloch and his team inspected an apartment house where they thought the Rebbe lived. When an old man answered, staring at them with hostility and fear, Bloch explained that, though soldiers, they had orders to help the Rebbe escape occupied Poland. The old man denied knowledge of the Rebbe's whereabouts and closed the door. After Bloch left, however, Schneersohn instructed his staff and family that, if the officer returned, they should give him "truthful information."[1] Perhaps the Rebbe had finally been informed that Bloch had been assigned to help him and could be trusted. Messengers were going back and forth between Riga and Warsaw, and since Riga received several telegrams from the United States, where information was being obtained from Wohlthat, their task was definitely to pass this information on to the Rebbe.

Probably at this time, the Rebbe dispatched Samarius Gourary, his son-in-law and de facto foreign secretary, to inform the soldiers that he would accept their help. The tall, stocky Gourary was a learned Hasid of the old Lubavitch world, a Torah scholar who often handled political situations for the Rebbe. After telling a group of Germans, probably Bloch's men, about the Rebbe, he started to return home. On the way, several soldiers, obviously non-Abwehr personnel, cut off half his beard, vertically dividing his face. When he returned, others explained he should feel lucky since some Jews lost not only their beards but their ears as well.[2]

It remains unknown whether the information Gourary passed on actually reached Bloch. Convinced, however, that the old man who answered the door had been hiding something, Bloch decided to return. He was sure the Rebbe was there. Some believe the soldiers must have been instructed as to how to convince the Rebbe they meant no harm, for "the Rebbe would never have left with Nazi soldiers unless they had some way of proving their intentions."[3]

Bloch went into action, ordering several of his men to dress in full battle gear and to prepare for all contingencies. He needed to get to the building quickly, secure the perimeter, and then assess the situation. He knew he had to get there before the SS, who would lay claim to the Rebbe if they reached him first. The SS and the Abwehr had been competing with each other in Warsaw, and Bloch wanted to avoid complications. When he and his soldiers returned to Herschel Gurari's house, where the Rebbe lived, they broke down the door.

They found themselves in a dark hallway smelling of sewage. The bombing had destroyed the plumbing and the household used buckets for toilets. A small child's cries echoed down the corridor, and a woman's soft voice could be heard comforting the baby. In the chaos that ensued, the Rebbe did his best to maintain his composure. Loud German voices yelled orders. The dozen or so Lubavitchers turned white and remained silent.[4]

Four German soldiers ordered all to stand and face the walls. The Jews obeyed, putting their hands in the air. Many shook as they turned their backs to the Germans. The Rebbe's grandson Barry Gourary knew he would feel the cold steel of a barrel against his neck. Many started to pray and breathe heavily. The clatter of metal cleats on the wooden floor and the jingle of holster straps swinging on rifles reverberated through the room. A few people started to cry.

Some thought of their families and others thought of God and death. They heard one German counting, *"Eins, zwei, drei, vier . . ."* Another started calling out names. Each person called was asked to turn and face the Germans. One by one, they turned, all eyes gravitating to the swastikas on the men's uniforms. When the German finished calling out all the names, another handed the Jews travel papers, explaining that the documents were necessary for their escape. The Lubavitchers stared blankly at the men and at the papers. After taking some time to get over the initial shock of this encounter, apparently the Lubavitchers were distressed that so few had been chosen to leave.

Soon thereafter, Wohlthat reported to Washington that Bloch had found the Rebbe and that, allowing time for the Rebbe to recover his health, he would probably be able to leave Warsaw by 1 December under the protection of a "German staff officer."[5] The Rebbe was exhausted. His cheeks were sunken, his eyes were hollow, and his complexion was yellow. He needed to recover his strength.

Bloch's mission was not yet complete. He now faced the daunting challenge of spiriting the Rebbe past the SS and the Gestapo.

TEN

The Escape Route

On 27 November, Pell reported to Rhoade with good news. Wohlthat had informed him that the German soldiers had found the Rebbe alive and that he was now under the protection of a staff officer. Pell also told Rhoade that, in response to the Rebbe's plea for funds, which the Abwehr had passed on, he had sent $250 through the State Department.[1] The burden of uncertainty must have left Rhoade's shoulders—the Rebbe had finally been found.

The Rebbe, remarkably, seemed concerned most about his library. On 27 November, he sent Lieberman a telegram explaining that he lived in horrible conditions and had "no dwelling now, and find myself in the home of friends with the whole family in one room, and therefore have no place for the books." The Chabad library seemed as sacred to the Rebbe as his own life. In his telegram to Lieberman, he specifically asked that the authorities not only rescue his staff and family but also help move his "valuable library." The Lubavitchers valued these books, some 40,000 volumes, at "about $30,000" and wanted the United States to obtain permission from the German consul in America for their removal.[2]

Two things remained crucial for the escape: visas to enter the United States and a safe route from Warsaw. Rhoade renewed his efforts to prepare immigration affidavits. He still lacked proof, however, that the Lubavitchers could support themselves. Julius Stulman, a wealthy Lubavitcher in New York, agreed to support Schneersohn and some family members and applied for visas for Schneersohn, his wife, and his mother. A few weeks later, Jacobson wrote Stulman asking for more help, saying, "I am sure that you will kindly comply with my request and the merit of this great Mitzvah will sustain you and your family, and you will be blessed by G-d."[3] Stulman's support might have helped Schneersohn and some of his immediate family, but Rhoade still had to convince the authorities that the additional seventeen people with the Rebbe would not become public charges.

Pell and Rhoade were well aware that they were still dependent on Wohlthat for the Rebbe's safe passage out of Poland. They had previously decided that the best route would be from Warsaw to Berlin and from there on to Riga, but Rhoade now favored an escape route through Italy. Pell pointed out that Wohlthat had accomplished an extraordinary feat by arranging a military escort for foreign Jewish citizens into Germany, sidestepping the Gestapo. Although the Gestapo, he observed, usually respected military authorities, of which Wohlthat, as a member of Göring's staff, was a part, they might "butt in" if a situation looked unusual. Pell therefore advised staying with the original plan since changing the route to go through Italy or Switzerland would attract the attention of the Gestapo. The Rebbe would be in grave danger if they ever caught him.[4] Ultimately, Pell and Rhoade decided to leave the decision in Wohlthat's hands.

In the same meeting, Rhoade learned that, although Pell exerted no direct authority on the granting of visas, he would do his best to influence the Visa Division chief, Avra M. Warren, and Warren's assistant Eliot Coulter, who often acted in his place when Warren was absent. Even though Coulter had told Pell that the division's "hands are tied respecting procedure," Pell believed that it would make the necessary exceptions for the Rebbe and his group. It appears that Coulter did help where he could.[5]

Harry T. Troutman of the Visa Division also attempted to help, working diligently to get the rabbis in the entourage nonquota visas, probably after receiving information proving they were "ministers." Troutman argued that these "ministers" were unique because they represented the heads of a religious body, and he carefully prepared the paperwork for the legation in Riga required for their emigration.[6] The Rebbe was fortunate that men like Troutman and Coulter did what they could for him and his followers, because a few months later their boss, Warren, made a special trip to Europe to instruct consular officials to curtail the entry of refugees.[7]

Those advocating on behalf of the Rebbe kept his multiple sclerosis a secret. Disease and sickness seemed to block others from receiving visas, lest they become public charges. The Visa Division rejected one person because he had favus of the scalp, a contagious skin disease, and flat feet, which kept him from earning a living. Even though he could serve as a rabbi, the division stood firm.[8]

Up to that time, most official discussions had focused on Rebbe Schneersohn, with only brief mention of his group of intimate followers and family members. The Rebbe's group at this stage included his wife, Nehamah Dinah; his mother, Sarah; his son-in-law Samarius Gourary; his daughter Chana Gourary; his grandson Barry Gourary; his son-in-law Mendel Horenstein; his daughter Sheina Horenstein; his secretary, Haskell Feigin; and Feigin's wife, two sons, and three daughters. Soon more would be added. Rhoade appealed to Pell on 28 November to ask Wohlthat to guarantee safe passage to Riga for all of them. Rhoade also asked permission to warn Warren of the problems that would arise when the members of the Rebbe's group could not produce proper identification. Then, in a letter to Warren, Rhoade stressed that he should deal "liberally with the situation" when in doubt. Rhoade felt "the Rabbi's world prominence" justified a generous attitude.[9]

On 30 November, Rhoade further asked Pell to request the U.S. consulate in Warsaw to issue visitors' visas to the Rebbe's group. To prove that Stulman would support Schneersohn, his wife, and his mother, Rhoade enclosed copies of financial documents. Rhoade also promised to provide affidavits for the other people in the group as soon as possible. Stulman sent these additional affidavits shortly thereafter.[10]

Although it looked as if the Rebbe and his entourage could lawfully enter the United States, they still had to escape the watchful eyes of the SS, which had begun to move Jews into ghettos throughout Poland. Extracting the Rebbe and his group from a secured ghetto would be difficult. Bloch had to take them out of Warsaw before the ghetto walls closed.[11]

Anxious about the Rebbe's prospects for safe passage out of Germany, Rhoade became intensely involved in the details of the plan. He still felt that passing through the Baltic States, which Stalin seemed on the verge of conquering, was dangerous. He preferred that the group wait for their ship to the United States in Sweden. If Wohlthat knew the United States had provided "pre-arranged transit visas," he might approve travel through Königsberg, Berlin, and the port of Sassnitz, where the group could leave by ferry for Sweden. Rhoade had arranged Swedish transit visas to be picked up in Berlin; he nevertheless feared for the group should it have to wait there long for visas. He requested that Pell ask Wohlthat to arrange for the visas to be stamped on board the Sassnitz–Tralleborg ferry. Rhoade now regarded this course as more advantageous than the route through Lithuania. Should Wohlthat opt for the route through Vilna to Riga, he said, someone at the American embassy in Berlin would have to officially approve the plan, with a caution to avoid Soviet-occupied territories at all cost.[12]

When Jacobson learned that Rhoade was again proposing differ-ent escape plans to Pell and others, he became irritated. He wrote Kramer, saying that "approaching influential people every day with new plans" left them "exasperated." Jacobson thought it had been agreed that if no alternative plan was quickly carried out, the Rebbe would proceed to Riga.[13] Jacobson obviously wanted Kramer to reel Rhoade in. Tempers were rising, and the Lubavitchers were im-patient. They also expressed resentment of Rhoade's fees. When Kramer asked him about his charges, Rhoade answered, "While I don't blame you for being sensitive to the expenses, it is very difficult to exercise normal conservatism. Whenever I am in doubt, I resolve it in favor of the Rabbi, as time is of the essence."[14]

Although he had received no official response, Rhoade hoped the Germans had agreed to guarantee safe passage to the seventeen indi-viduals accompanying the Rebbe. He wrote, "The silence of Berlin on the request for enlargement of the escort to include the entire group consisting of the Rabbi's relatives . . . indicates that no ob-jection has been made. . . . All the adult males are Rabbis, thereby entitling the entire group to non-quota status."[15]

On 30 November, the world was shocked to learn that the Soviet Union had invaded Finland after it refused to concede territory north of Leningrad that Stalin claimed was necessary to ensure the Soviet Union's security. Many Lubavitchers feared that, once the Soviets had forcefully seized the Finnish territory they wanted, Stalin would turn his military might against the Baltic States and the Rebbe would fall into Russian hands in Riga.

Meanwhile, in the Visa Division, Coulter urged Rhoade and Pell to send to the American consulate in Berlin the evidence proving adequate financial provision for the Rebbe and his followers once they were in the United States. Rhoade protested that sending such information to Berlin was not only impractical but also dangerous because of the Gestapo. Nonsecret cables regarding the financial ar-rangements might easily precipitate a Gestapo extortion plan and take the matter out of Wohlthat's hands.[16] He asked Pell if he could obtain assurance that the Berlin consulate would provide the Rebbe and his followers with emergency visitors' visas "without going into the details." Rhoade had little faith in the possibility of convincing the consulate of the appropriateness of the nonimmigrant clause, because the group's "entire condition contradicts the 'tourist' idea." In other words, they had to get visas to enter the country on a permanent basis.[17] Rhoade officially labeled all the members of the Rebbe's group as the Rebbe's "dependents" to avoid extensive investigation into their financial resources and those of the Chabad organization and to thereby expedite the granting of visas for the entire group. In a further attempt to move the Visa Division to action, Rhoade compared the Rebbe's situation "to what might happen if war conditions in Italy compelled the Pope and his associates at the Vatican to seek temporary refuge in the United States for the purpose of carrying on the world affairs of the Catholic Church."[18]

In the meantime, Wohlthat and the Abwehr had decided on an escape route from Warsaw via Berlin and Riga to Stockholm, and then on to the United States. Now Rhoade needed Pell to help "secure American visitors' visas for the Rebbe and his group upon their arrival in Berlin." Rhoade hoped that Pell could convince Wohlthat to instruct the military escorts to take the Rebbe and his group first to the American embassy to receive their travel documents. To get their visas, the group would need to answer American officials properly "regarding their intentions" upon arrival in Berlin.[19]

As a backup plan, Rhoade had contacted a well-connected Cuban lawyer about prearranged Cuban visitors' visas for the group. Cuba demanded five thousand dollars per person, meaning it would have cost around one hundred thousand dollars to send the entire group there. Rhoade wrote Kramer that Cuba might prove their only option to secure safe passage to North America even though the Cuban authorities were more than willing "to financially exploit the opportunity presented by refugees in distress." Rhoade advised that they "should avoid these *'gaslonim'* [thieves] if possible." Nevertheless, Cuba was like a "'Schwester im Dorf' [a sister in the village] though . . . a mightily punk 'Schwester.'"[20] For now, everything hinged on the Germans; they still had to help the Rebbe and his entire group leave German-occupied Europe.

Rhoade reasoned to Pell in a letter of 29 November that the German officials who seemed willing to help "would not wish to do things half way and certainly would not wish to deprive the Rabbi, who is a sort of Pope, of his immediate disciples."[21] He insisted that Pell at least request that the group be escorted to safety. Pell thought their entry into the United States would not pose a problem, since the Rebbe and most of his followers were Russian-born and the quota for Russia remained open. Those who could not qualify for the Russian quota could possibly receive nonquota visas because they were rabbis, though such an approach would be difficult. Rhoade expressed the hope that, since the German authorities had done so much already for the Rebbe and his group, they might also arrange for their transportation to Lithuania. Annoyed by the long list of new demands, Pell advised Rhoade that the Germans would be unlikely to consider so many options.

Rhoade now foresaw another danger. The heavy use of international cables, albeit in diplomatic code, to transmit sensitive information troubled him. He again feared the Gestapo might intercept the cables, "develop an extortion plan, and take the matter out of Wohlthat's hands."[22] Although Pell had far more experience in dealing with such matters, the lawyer urged the utmost secrecy regarding financial support for the Rebbe.

ELEVEN

Flight

Having gone to such extraordinary lengths to locate and rescue the Rebbe, Bloch was shocked to learn that the Lubavitchers expected him to arrange for the escape of more than a dozen additional Orthodox Jews, not the few family members he had been ordered to help. Although the Rebbe was a "great leader," Bloch told Schenk, in his own community he lived a life "totally divorced from reality." The Rebbe failed to see that he was not in command of the situation. He simply could not understand the hazards he would bring on himself, as well as on the soldiers sent to protect him, if Bloch was forced to escort a large group of Orthodox Jews back through Nazi-occupied Poland, much less through Germany. Bloch was also surprised by what he considered the irrational complaints of the Lubavitchers. For instance, when he returned after his first meeting with the Rebbe with cheese, bread, and sausages for them, they refused the food because it was not kosher. Bloch was dumbfounded. "These crazy people," he grumbled, "they are hungry and sick. Indeed, a strange people—they don't even know when somebody is trying to help them." Schenk regretted not having told Bloch to tell them the meat was beef. (Of course, they wouldn't have accepted nonkosher beef either.)[1]

There had been confusion as to the size of the group in the United States as well. For example, in late November, in a conversation with Rhoade, Pell expressed surprise that Rhoade assumed the Germans would save all of the Rebbe's entourage. Pell explained that "up to the present there had been only the question of the Rabbi. My request to Herr Wohlthat was made in behalf of the Rabbi and in his reply he had extended that to include the Rabbi's wife and child. . . . A request to extend Wohlthat's action to include a large number of people might prejudice the whole affair." Rhoade pleaded with Pell to at least ask Wohlthat if he would do so. Pell refused, fearing he might "react unfavorably against the Rabbi."[2] Soon after the conversation with Rhoade, Pell started to push for the entire group. Probably Rhoade's aggressive tactics convinced him to ask Wohlthat to include them, which Wohlthat in fact did.

Bloch procured a truck and wagon to transport the Lubavitchers to a railroad station outside Warsaw. Here they would board a train for Berlin, and from there one for Riga.[3] Wohlthat's office had already received funds for Schneersohn's travel and by 13 December had arranged for him and all his dependents, except for Mendel and Sheina Horenstein, to travel directly to Riga.[4] (Since the Horensteins were Polish citizens, they could not leave Europe owing to U.S. restrictions.) The operation required the coordinated effort of a number of people; Bloch needed a truck, fuel coupons, and train tickets. He also had to arrange clearances to pass through military and SS checkpoints and special approval for "foreigners" to enter Berlin.

Only two months after the rescue requests to Wohlthat, the U.S. embassy in Berlin reported on 22 December 1939 that Rebbe Schneersohn as well as his family and some of his followers had left Warsaw for Berlin and Riga.[5] The report failed to describe the difficulties Bloch and his team faced in transit. Before leaving, Bloch advised the Rebbe's group that they would have to follow his exact instructions, warning that many times he might have to handle them roughly to prevent SS members or other Germans from becoming suspicious. In a dire emergency, he might have to touch some of the women, he explained, although he would do his best to avoid that insult to their beliefs.[6]

As they left the building, the Lubavitchers must have felt nervous excitement at finally escaping Warsaw. As they entered the street, passersby must have wondered why a German was leading off this group of Hasidic Jews. Were they to be killed? Although Warsaw had returned to a semblance of normality, with people again at work, it was an occupied capital dominated by the Nazis. As the Jews stepped onto the waiting wagon and truck, Polish children watched them and ran their index fingers along their necks to signify execution. Schenk brushed the children away and reassured his charges that they had nothing to fear. They carried their suitcases and religious books and cast their gaze downwards. A few of them held hands and whispered to one another quietly.

Only yards away, the hard clanging sound of marching troops echoed through the streets. It was an SS unit, armed with rifles and side arms. The skull-and-crossbones insignia sparkled on their black uniforms. As the group approached, Bloch considered the possibilities. If the SS was after the Rebbe, he and his men could not defend the people under their protection. Suddenly, Bloch yelled, "OK, you pigs. Get in the truck and wagon. I said *now*." Schenk started herding the Jews roughly onto the truck and the horse-drawn wagon, yelling, "Faster."[7] The SS unit marched by without paying much attention.

Bloch rode in the truck with the Rebbe. Along the road, they observed the charred remains of Polish armored trucks and troop carriers, carcasses of horses, and the fresh graves of civilians caught in the maelstrom of war. Schenk later recalled that the Rebbe looked out at this horror, shook his head, put his old, wrinkled hand to his face, and rocked back and forth mumbling to himself.

When they reached the first checkpoint outside the city, the SS asked Bloch to step out. Bloch presented his papers and then carefully viewed his surroundings. He scolded one SS soldier for not saluting properly. Schenk heard the man apologize halfheartedly. Picking up on this, Bloch took out his notebook and asked for the names of the man and his superior. The man knew he was in trouble.

As two soldiers busied themselves with Bloch, another two walked up to the group in the wagon. One looked at what must have been for him a group of strange people. In the young man's blue eyes, Schenk saw not hate exactly but a fierce curiosity. He asked Schenk who these people were. Schenk told the man that all questions should be directed to Bloch, his superior. "What unit are you with?" the SS man demanded. Schenk replied, "We are members of the Abwehr." The young man's eyes opened wider, then he turned his gaze to the ground and returned to his post.

Bloch walked back to the truck, breathing heavily. He looked at Schenk and said, "We made it through this one. I told them these Jews were prisoners sent for by special authority in Berlin. They seemed to want no further explanation. Anyway, the Wehrmacht should be at these checkpoints, not the SS."[8] Bloch looked back at the guards as the truck started up and moved slowly through the opened field gate. Instinctively, he placed his hand on his pistol.

At some point, the Rebbe again asked Bloch why he was rescuing them. When Bloch told him he was half Jewish, he asked if Bloch felt Jewish. It must have seemed odd to talk to this man who looked like a character out of the Bible and try to understand why he had asked such a question. Surely taken aback, Bloch probably hesitated. Then he told the Rebbe that he did not but that he had always been intrigued by his Jewish past. "You have a strong Jewish spirit," the Rebbe responded. The fact that Bloch was rescuing him seemed to verify Bloch's Jewish loyalty for the Rebbe, who saw him returning to his roots in performing this brave act. Bloch most likely did not reciprocate the Rebbe's feelings of kinship; he simply performed his duty to the best of his abilities. The Rebbe felt, however, that God was conducting the whole event, and what better instrument to use than a fellow Jew. Also, as one Lubavitcher rabbi explains, the Rebbe believed that praising someone could help that person rise to future challenges; creating a bond with Bloch might make Bloch more effective in taking the next steps in the rescue.

The motley group passed columns of soldiers and military trucks, some with the large white SS runes painted on their sides. Despite the horrors and dangers surrounding them, the Lubavitchers remained focused in their faith. Some tried to convince Schenk that their way of worshiping was the best way to observe God's laws. As Schenk understood their argument, a harmonious world would arise only when all Jews recognized their Rebbe and his doctrine. Once this unity was achieved, the Messiah would come. The Lubavitchers thanked Schenk and the other Germans for ensuring that the world would not lose its greatest living leader, who held "mankind's destiny in his hands."[9]

One checkpoint right outside Warsaw proved particularly difficult. As the truck started to go through the inspection process, an SS soldier shouted at Bloch, pointing his finger at the Rebbe. The SS were confused. They looked at Bloch, an officer, then they gazed at the Orthodox Jews whom they had just forced to step out of the truck, surrounding them with rifles lowered. Although the sky was a light gray, the shadows of the soldiers danced around the Jews, who kept their eyes to the ground. Several SS men pointed their rifles directly at the Rebbe's face. Schneersohn's hands shook.

Bloch told the SS commanding officer, a tall, ordinary-looking man in a jet-black uniform, that he had special orders to take these Jews to Berlin. The SS officer sniffed, blinked, and shook his head, saying he was shocked he had not been informed about this cargo. He threatened to detain the Jews and hold Bloch and his men at his headquarters until he received authorization from Berlin; the whole thing "smelled rotten" to him. "Why does the Abwehr care about

Orthodox Jews?" he asked, gesturing toward the group. "They are ignorant scum who should be shot." Then he turned back to Bloch and asked, "What are you really doing?"

For a moment, Bloch feared the SS had been informed about the mission. He felt that he was about to lose the group and possibly his own clemency. A sweat broke out across his shoulders and his breathing became more rapid. He later told Schenk that if the Berlin SS had known that he, a half Jew, was helping over a dozen Orthodox Jews escape Warsaw, they would have had his head delivered on a platter.[10]

"I don't understand why these Jews are being taken to our capital," the SS officer insisted, his face reddening with frustration. "Secondly," he continued, "I don't like taking orders from an army officer who is incapable of telling me why these creatures are being escorted to Berlin or who has ordered him to take them." The SS man ended his diatribe with a malevolent grin. Bloch's fists clenched and the blood rushed to his cheeks as he shouted harshly that Canaris had issued his orders. He had contact with several regiments in the area, he said, naming them and their commanding officers. If the SS man did not let the group through, he would personally see to it that he was arrested and "properly dealt with." The officer starred at Bloch, summing up the gravity of his threat. After some uneasy hesitation, he ordered the roadblock opened and let Bloch's group through. The bluff had worked.

A few miles past the roadblock, Bloch told the Rebbe everything would be all right, adding, "The SS is not Germany." The Rebbe did not look persuaded. Schenk registered the deep irony of their situation. Here were SS personnel who wanted to kill the Jews, and Wehrmacht soldiers who wanted to help them—and both groups were German. In fact, many of the Lubavitchers believed Bloch was not a real German officer but a Jew playing soldier to save the group.

The Rebbe probably recounted this horrible scene to his secretary, Chaim Lieberman, who later wrote: "As soon as they saw us, the German soldiers were as bloodthirsty as wild animals to hurt our group of Jewish men with beards and side locks. . . . A German Jew who had served in World War I and wore a uniform covered with medals helped the Rebbe and his family escape this danger."[11] Bloch, the World War I veteran, obviously told the Lubavitchers about his Jewish father to calm their fears and perhaps even because he felt, in a strange way, akin to them. The fact remains that they believed a fellow Jew was rescuing them. Some saw Bloch as a guardian angel sent by God. Perhaps this idea struck them as more plausible than that of a "friendly Nazi," and more in keeping with the stuff of their faith. Viewing these rather unusual Germans as acting under God's command would not have been unusual for the Lubavitchers.[12]

At the train station, Bloch's group again attracted the attention of the authorities. An army officer questioned him as to why Jews had been issued first-class tickets. Bloch or one of his men may have told him that the Jews were traveling under diplomatic protection and then said a few other things that caused him to leave without further questioning.[13] Sitting in a train full of Nazi officials and military personnel made the Jews uncomfortable. One can only wonder what they felt as they crossed the border into the Greater German Reich and passed through towns bedecked with swastika flags. This was not their world. As one Lubavitcher described it, they were now in the "very heart of the evil Nazi kingdom."[14]

On 15 December, Bloch brought the Rebbe and his group to Berlin, where they stayed one night at the Jewish Federation. They probably picked up the visas there that would ensure their escape. The next day, they boarded another train, again in a first-class cabin, for Riga, accompanied by their German escorts and delegates from the Latvian embassy.[15]

When asked why Jews were traveling in the first-class section of the train, a "German officer," most likely Bloch, was reported to give the same response as earlier, that they were traveling on diplomatic orders and should be left alone. At the Latvian border, the Germans bade the Jews farewell. It was probably the last time Bloch saw the Rebbe. As they left German soil, the Rebbe and his group rejoiced. "We felt so good once we reached the Latvian border," Barry Gourary says. On its way to Riga, the train stopped at Kovno (Kaunas), where several of the Rebbe's followers met the train and danced with joy as he arrived.[16] He had returned to his world.

TWELVE

Waiting in Riga

When news reached Jacobson that Schneersohn, his family, and his staff had reached Riga safely, Jacobson arose from a meeting and ran out into the street. There, he jumped up and down, did "hand-springs on the sidewalks," and shouted ecstatically. "I could not contain my joy." He then returned to his office to continue planning the Rebbe's journey. That day, he also received a phone call from the Rebbe thanking him and the American Lubavitchers for all their efforts on his behalf.[1]

On 20 December, Rhoade telephoned Pell and immediately afterward wrote him a letter to express appreciation for his "wonderful efforts." But the case was not yet closed. The Rebbe's group still lacked visas for entry into America.

Foreseeing a bureaucratic roadblock—"insufficient proof" of guaranteed employment in the United States—Rhoade asked Pell to help him obtain exemptions for them. He emphasized once again that the status of the group created "a novel and perhaps even a non-precedented situation and, therefore, requires unusual handling. The situation, in principle, is analogous to the problem that would result if forced evacuation of the Vatican occurred as a result of war and the Catholics in America desired to bring all the ordained ministers of religion (priests) of the Vatican to the United States for the purpose of transferring the seat of the Catholic hierarchy to this country. In such a situation, the status of the Pope and other high prelates of the Catholic hierarchy as ministers of a religious denomination, even though not officially affiliated as priests of any particular congregation, could not be properly questioned. That is likewise true of Chabad hierarchy." Rhoade explained that section 4(d) of the Immigration Act of 1924 sufficiently defined the Rebbe and his rabbis as "clergymen" worthy of nonquota status. To drive home his point, Rhoade quoted the Department of Labor on the subject of section 4(d): "The intent of the law is to enable religious bodies . . . to bring needed ministers . . . from foreign countries." Rhoade carefully insisted that although the members of Schneersohn's group did not have congregations to take care of them, they still would find sufficient support from U.S. Chabad. He concluded that American Lubavitchers should not be deprived of the "spiritual welfare" provided by the hierarchy.[2]

In case his argument did not persuade Pell and the Visa Division, Rhoade also worked on securing quota visas. Here the burden of proof lay on the U.S. Chabad headquarters. For all of Rhoade's eloquent pleading, and for all the time Pell gave the case, the simple fact remained that Jacobson was going to hamper their efforts if he did not obtain the necessary information. Besides proving that the men could support themselves, he had to prove that they could "qualify as Rabbis within the meaning of the law." Without such documentation, the whole case would be jeopardized.[3]

Rhoade continued to experience problems with Jacobson, the person from whom he needed the most help. He wrote Jacobson on 21 December about the lack of "sufficient concrete details and financial information" and his fear that the present affidavits were inadequate for the issuance of visas. He also complained that the

Chabad rabbis were pestering him about his work. The case, he said, was "without precedent" in view of the "legal technicalities involved in connection with the Immigration Act, which I cannot possibly take the time to explain by letter or expect you gentlemen to understand. Therefore, you will please restrain your impatience and assume that I am moving heaven and earth to accomplish the desired result. Don't expect the impossible just because such unusual things have already been accomplished."[4]

Besides dealing with Jacobson, Rhoade continued to struggle with the State Department. On 22 December, he wrote Kramer that "our Rabbis are not the conventional type so even if we regard them as superior we [have] to anticipate difficulties with a goyish mentality by carefully formulating the facts."[5] They had to persuade the Visa Division that these men were not only invaluable to Chabad but also beneficial to American society.

Rabbi Judah Gourary, under Jacobson's guidance, had developed the strategy of focusing solely on the hierarchy angle to create a fast regulatory bypass of the quota system.[6] In the documents, it was argued that under section 4(d) of the Immigration Act of 1924, the Rebbe could be classified as a "minister" since he had practiced his religion for at least two years and wished to enter the United States "solely for the purpose of . . . carrying on the vocation of minister" of his religious denomination. Naming the members of the Rebbe's group the hierarchy helped to classify them as ministers of an entire movement and thus to secure nonquota visas without proving they had separate congregations to support them. This enabled Rhoade to sidestep the laborious process of obtaining affidavits from several congregations for every rabbi.[7] Starting in mid-December, Rhoade discussed this idea with the State Department, which seemed remarkably open to it. The tactic also relieved Rhoade of having to depend on Jacobson for affidavits from various congregations, affidavits he had still failed to procure after three months, along with documentary proof that the Rebbe and his group were indeed rabbis.

Rhoade wrote Hull on 23 December that, "inasmuch as these Rabbis, as a hierarchy, are even superior to ordinary Rabbis, their nonquota status both with respect to their past vocation as ministers of a religious denomination and their purpose to continue their vocation of discharging their high religious functions after admission to the USA is obvious." The lawyer had done all he could with the information he had. He told Kramer, "Pell is our man 100% and has done everything possible with the Visa Division. I don't think anyone can do more." He reminded Kramer not to "minimize the technical difficulties at this end. As an old, and may I add rather successful, hand at immigration matters, I am not a bit ashamed of the progress so far and it is almost impossible (and a terrible waste of time) to justify and explain everything that is being or not being done."[8] Rhoade was so confident he could count on Pell that he took the Lubavitchers' request about their library to him. On 23 December, he wrote Pell: "As the Nazis have quite a record for destroying literature, and in view of the plans now in progress to transfer the seat of the world hierarchy to the United States, I have been asked by . . . *Chabad* to request you to please [help]. . . . I understand that some of the manuscripts are priceless. The value of the collection alone is sufficient to render immediate action imperative."[9]

Pell explained to Rhoade that he would have to prove the library was American property. This task would prove daunting. And even though the Rebbe argued that the books were essential to the movement, he could not make the same case for his jewelry and what turned out to be his pots, pans, silverware, and other household items—things he also wanted to get out.[10]

Back in Riga, the Rebbe remained agitated about the status of his precious library. He wrote Jacobson on 26 December 1939, saying, "Surely I will receive within a few days a detailed letter about all that has been done for the saving of my library and about taking it out from there. . . . There are about a hundred and twenty boxes of books and three boxes of manuscripts of our revered and holy parents, the saintly Rabbis . . . and you will surely do all you can to bring them to your country. There are also the remainder of our other valuables that was left over after the great conflagration . . . the jewelry, etc. . . . I have already advised several times by telegram, and also my son-in-law [Gourary] has spoken with you several times over the telephone about the books and the manuscripts and you have as yet not answered anything. I repeat and say again and request most earnestly that you kindly hasten this matter as soon as possible."[11]

Since some of the manuscripts documented Lubavitch history, the Rebbe considered them essential to the preservation of the traditions of his people.[12] He may have thought of the famous rabbi and leader of the Pharisees during Roman times, Rabban Yohanan ben Zakkai, who is credited with saving Judaism after the Jewish revolt of 66–70 C.E. After sneaking out of Jerusalem to meet with Roman authorities, Yohanan requested only to go to the town of Yavneh, outside Jerusalem, to establish a center of Torah study and worship, which he believed were the primary reasons God had created mankind. So instead of pleading with the Roman authorities to spare Jewish lives, Yohanan did all he could to save several scholars and carry on the religious traditions of study and worship he felt so essential to Jewish survival. And survival, he believed, depended on setting up a center for scholars to study Torah and the ancient Jewish texts. The Rebbe shared Yohanan's convictions about Jewish survival. His library was essential for saving his Jewish community's way of life, a life of observing God's laws. Some of the books were sacred remnants, having, like the Rebbe, survived the Soviets and, if the escape was successful, the Nazis.[13]

Even so, thousands of the Rebbe's manuscripts were not religious, and Chabad could have easily replaced hundreds of the books since they were still in print. Others were actually antireligious books published by the Yevsektzia, the Jewish section of the Communist Party, or secular ("heretical") ones like Dante's *Inferno*. The Rebbe had collected books avidly for years. "He collected anything having to do with Judaism or if the book was written in Hebrew," writes historian Arthur Green. "He was fanatic in collecting any- thing he could put his hands on and frequently petitioned publish- ing houses and authors for books." Throughout the 1920s and 1930s, the Rebbe "publicly appealed for book donations."[14] Though the fu- ture of the movement did not depend on the preservation of most of these books, the Rebbe hated to part with any of them.

Why in the midst of the chaos and horror of war was the Rebbe worried not only about his books but also about his gems and house- hold goods? One must not forget that the Rebbe had undergone horrible persecution under the czars and Stalin and that he prob- ably viewed the treatment under the Nazis as another stage of suf- fering he had to endure as a Jewish leader. The Rebbe had not ex- perienced ghettos or concentration camps and thus may not have recognized the need to focus exclusively on saving lives that seems so clear today. He simply wanted to be free of Nazi persecution. Only in hindsight do the Rebbe's efforts to save his personal posses- sions seem perplexing. His actions should not be construed merely as shortsighted or selfish: he believed them necessary for the con- tinuation of his work. He probably did not think that the money and effort expended for his books and possessions would interfere with his ability to help people in need. He paid three hundred dollars for a lawyer in Poland and probably several hundred more for packing, storage, and shipping. It is unlikely that he viewed saving his library and saving Jews as mutually exclusive efforts. Yet even the famous Jewish sage Rabbi Akiva noted Yohanan's mistake in not asking the Romans to save Jerusalem in addition to his students and library.[15]

The Rebbe's obsessive quest on behalf of his library has unsettled many. Historian Ephraim Zuroff, an Orthodox Jew, asks, "How can one justify expending even a small amount of resources and ener- gies to try and save the rebbe's library at a time when the rescue of lives should have taken precedence?" One wonders why no one talked about using the funds and political contacts necessary for retrieving the books to save more Jews, but the Lubavitchers never discussed this matter. As Zuroff writes, Lubavitchers "do not consider such a set of priorities controversial or in any way problematic."[16] In other words, if the Rebbe wanted it to be done, then such an order was not questioned. According to Rabbi Shalom Dovber Levine, head of Chabad's library and archives, "There was something very secret and holy in building the Library from the start. . . . In the worst times of depression in Russia and Europe, he gave his life for it. He viewed it as part of the rebuilding of the Lubavitch movement."[17]

This talk about saving books was premature, however, as the visas had not been issued. To convince those in Riga of the Rebbe's status, Rhoade asked people like Senator David Walsh of Massachusetts and Secretary of State Hull to forward requests to the American consulate in Riga: "Shall appreciate favorable consideration of applications of Renowned Chief Rabbi Joseph Isaac Schneersohn and Associate Rabbis World Chabad hierarchy for non-quota visas. American Branch Chabad denomination desires removal of hierarchy to America due to war situation and evacuation from Poland. In view of information given me have every reason to believe that representation by Rabbi may be relied upon."[18] Upon receiving a request for help, Postmaster General James A. Farley responded on 28 December that obtaining a temporary visa for the Rebbe would not "be an easy thing to arrange. However, I will do whatever I can."

Rhoade continued to urge his contacts to apply pressure on the Visa Division. He probably asked Senator Wagner to contact the chief of the division, Avra Warren, directly. On 29 December, Wagner wrote Warren for an update. Those involved with the rescue obviously felt Warren needed prodding. Coulter, rather than Warren, replied to Wagner a few days later, telling him that the Riga legation had already received information about the visa applications of the "aliens." Coulter mentioned that while several issues still needed clarification Wagner should feel "assured that the applications of the aliens in question will be given every consideration consistent with the immigration laws."[19]

On 29 December, Rhoade asked Cohen to appeal to Hull again to "prod the Visa Division into more rapid and definite cooperation." Recognizing that "ordinary cases" did not merit such extraordinary action, Rhoade argued that it was a "matter of life and death" for the Rebbe, the "recognized world spiritual head of a whole orthodox Jewish denomination, numbering hundreds of thousands of adherents." Rhoade reasoned that since Cohen was partly responsible for the Rebbe's successful escape to Riga, he would have a vested interest in "seeing the job completed. . . . Otherwise, all the weeks of immense effort may prove in vain." Cohen advised Rhoade to be patient with the overworked Visa Division, where things had slowed down because of the Christmas and New Year celebrations. On 2 January 1940, Rhoade countered Cohen, saying that although they had "to reckon with certain limitations, this is the sort of case where it is proper to cut the red tape. There is unquestionably enough evidence in the hands of the American Consulate in Riga to warrant immediate issuance of the non-quota visas to the rabbis comprising the hierarchy of this religious denomination." On 3 January, answering the lawyer's plea, Coulter stated that making an exception for the Rebbe "would, of course, be inconsistent with the Immigration Laws and established practice."[20]

Concerned about the delay and the increasing hostilities in Europe, Rhoade wrote Congressman Adolph J. Sabath that Riga was unsafe "because of the possible spread of the present Baltic conflict and the danger of Russian domination of Latvia." Rhoade continued to pressure every high-ranking official he knew. State Senator Philip M. Kleinfeld of New York promptly responded to Rhoade's request. Postmaster General Farley, Senator Wagner, and Senator Walsh, among others, also sent cables to Riga similar to the following: "Will deeply appreciate favorable action on application World Chief Rabbi Joseph Isaac Schneersohn and associate Rabbis of World

Chabad Hierarchy for non-quota visas in compliance with desire American Branch Chabad denomination for removal of this hierarchy to America due to coming war peril and evacuation from Poland. My request is prompted by assurance from distinguished American friends of Rabbi and his associates that representations can be relied upon."[21]

On 4 January, Coulter assured Rhoade in bureaucratic style that he could not ask the consular officer in Riga to go outside the immigration laws. He explained that Rhoade should send proof about the Rebbe to Riga because "the burden of proof is placed by law upon an alien applying for a visa to establish his eligibility." Coulter ended his letter by saying that "the cases of the aliens concerned will receive every consideration consistent with the immigration laws." Rhoade responded on 6 January that "Pell had referred to your Division the visa phase in the hope that an acceleration plan could be devised in view of the urgency and importance of the hierarchy aspect." Rhoade reminded Coulter that the Rebbe was the celebrated world rabbi of Chabad and that his followers were "not merely ordinary Rabbis of individual congregations." He challenged the need for identification, which the Rebbe and his group could not possibly provide. Since "the reputation of applicants is such as to render their claims entirely trustworthy, there is no need of extremely exacting and time consuming requirements, especially in time of war danger." He also warned that if the Soviet Union conquered Latvia, the Russians might execute the Rebbe and his group as counterrevolutionaries.[22]

This fear was warranted, for in June 1940, the Red Army would occupy the Baltic States and many Jewish leaders would disappear.[23] Unbeknownst to those involved with the rescue, they had a few months to make sure the Rebbe left Riga, but they felt they had only days. The mounting tension strained the friendship between Rhoade and Kramer. Kramer criticized Rhoade for making suggestions to politicians before consulting the Lubavitchers; Rhoade felt the pressure of time acutely and preferred to try too hard rather than not hard enough.[24]

In a particularly bold effort, Rhoade attempted to gain the ear of Pell's boss, Myron C. Taylor, a former U.S. Steel executive who was chief of refugee work for President Roosevelt and his personal representative to the Vatican. Rhoade argued in a letter to Kramer that Taylor's dedicating "himself to the humanitarian refugee work" of rescuing the Rebbe would be "a concrete illustration of Christianity's efforts on behalf of stricken Jewry."[25] If Rhoade believed that Taylor might obtain help from the Vatican, he was to be sorely disappointed. Although the Catholic Church protected Jewish converts, it did not protest Nazi antisemitic policy. Sadly, the Catholic leadership was even passive "regarding the murder of its own adherents, Poles, Gypsies, and even its priests." More realistically, Rhoade hoped that Taylor would call the embassy in Latvia and persuade the office to issue immediate visas to the Rebbe and his group. Rhoade also suggested prevailing on Judge Samuel I. Rosenman, who often advised Roosevelt on Jewish matters, to appeal directly to the president.[26]

Rhoade discussed with Kramer other matters weighing heavily on him, namely, his fees. He complained that hundreds of dollars in bills remained outstanding and he needed his friend's support to rectify the situation. "Because frankly," Rhoade wrote, "this thing has reached a point where it is absolutely pulverizing me, though for your sake and the sake of the cause, I am still grimly carrying on."[27]

The government needed to conduct a special investigation of Chabad to verify the information it had received to date. The U.S. embassy in Riga had actually sent a request to Hull, who apparently sent it on to Troutman or Warren in the Visa Division.[28] Rhoade knew the investigation was important and eagerly awaited the findings. Visa Division special agents were assigned to meet with the American Chabad leaders at the beginning of January. What appeared to be glacial progress made Rhoade nervous. In the absence of news, he wrote Troutman asking him to do his best to "accelerate" the investigation: "Owing . . . to the impracticability of establishing the new seat of the hierarchy at Riga or in any country other than the U.S.A., each day lost results in great damage to the denomination. I refer particularly, of course, to the American branch of that denomination. . . . You know from the file, of the great efforts expended by the State Department through diplomatic channels in bringing about the evacuation, with the consent of the military authorities. Under these exceptional circumstances, I am sure you will not regard our constant insistence upon exceptionally speedy handling as unreasonable." Rhoade noted that any interviews would have to begin by 3:00 P.M. on 5 January: "This particular denomination is extremely religious. The Jewish Sabbath commences at sundown Friday and at this time of the year it is necessary for the offices to close at 3:00 P.M. Friday (through Saturday) in order to permit preparations for the Sabbath. It will be appreciated if you will kindly call this to the attention of the investigator."[29] Apparently, agents scheduled a meeting for 5 January.

But on 5 January, when Special Agent Tubbs showed up for the appointment in the late afternoon, no one met him at the office. The Sabbath was more important than completing the paperwork necessary for Schneersohn's rescue. There was also some confusion caused by Chabad's using several addresses and giving the agents the wrong one. A new appointment was scheduled for the ninth, and this time Tubbs successfully met with a delegation of Chabad, including Jacobson and Sam and Hyman Kramer, and verified much of the information. The delegation assured him that fifty thousand dollars would stay in the United States as salary for the hierarchy.[30] Sam Kramer, according to Jacobson, "launched into a brilliant exposition of what the Chabad movement is" and "the important work they accomplish for the Jewish community." Chabad also probably provided proof that the Rebbe had a contract to act as the rabbi of congregation Anshe Lebovitz of Chicago, with an annual salary of four thousand dollars for at least five years. After several hours, the agent left with the information for his report.[31]

In his report, Tubbs expressed skepticism about the Lubavitchers' investing their assets in the United States in light of the importance they placed on outreach and maintaining communities overseas. Since most Jews lived overseas and "will permanently continue to remain in Europe and . . . the greater portion of the influence and efforts of this organization will certainly continue to be in that direction," Tubbs remained doubtful about their intentions to invest only in the United States. Seemingly baffled that almost all the money raised for Chabad went to the Rebbe for him to use as he saw fit, Tubbs concluded that, since the Rebbe would focus on his followers, most of the money would go abroad. He believed that the hierarchy sought sanctuary in the United States not out of desire to become Americans but because of their precarious situation in Europe. From the document, it is clear that Tubbs doubted the contributions the hierarchy would make to America as a whole.[32] It seems, however, that his damning report was ultimately disregarded, presumably because of the large number of high-ranking officials already involved in the case.

On 9 January, Rhoade received confirmation that visas would be issued to the Rebbe and most of his entourage as soon as officials completed their investigation.[33] He set to making arrangements for the Lubavitchers to travel from Sweden to France and Italy, where they could board an Italian-American ocean liner. They could also travel through Germany if Wohlthat helped them, but many were fearful about that route. After much debate, and Wohlthat's probably having the final say, it was decided that the Rebbe's group would fly from Riga to Stockholm and take a train from there to the port of Göteborg for the transatlantic voyage.

On 13 January 1940, the State Department finally approved the visas. Only the Polish Horensteins were not granted visas, as they were citizens of a country conquered by the Germans. They would have to remain in Europe. A few weeks later, the embassy in Riga told Hull that the evidence of the hierarchy's ability to support themselves had been submitted and that visas would be forthcoming.[34] The Rebbe and his entourage were fortunate. Throughout 1940, tens of thousands of Jews would wait to leave Europe for the United States. Under the four-year administration of Breckinridge Long, who would shortly take control of immigration matters, hundreds of thousands of Jews would be denied permission to enter the country.[35]

The United States allowed 105,000 refugees from Nazism into the country between 1933 and 1940, but these numbers reflected only a minority of those who had tried to enter. U.S. leaders condemned Nazi atrocities but took no corresponding action. The tragic story of the *St. Louis*, which set out from Germany for North America in 1939 with 930 Jewish refugees, is a case in point. When the American government refused its passengers refuge, it was forced to return to Europe, where most of its passengers went to their deaths. Similar fates befell refugees on the *Ordina, Quanza,* and *Flanders.*[36]

Supply ships returned empty from Europe that could have helped rescue refugees. Many requests to use these ships were sent to the government, and apparently Roosevelt passed them off to the Visa Division. Under Warren's leadership, the failure to use the ships to save those in danger mirrored the State Department's reluctance to pursue a policy of active rescue.[37] Warren's successor, Long, viewed the impassioned response of many Americans to the plight of the refugees as "'an enormous psychosis' which he attributed to 're-pressed emotions about the war.'" In summer 1942, when the opportunity arose to rescue five thousand orphaned Jewish children stuck in Vichy France, Long actively prevented it. Even though Eleanor Roosevelt pushed hard for their rescue, Long's efforts delayed the action so long that, before any of the children could leave, the Germans sent most of them to their death in the East.[38]

Breckinridge Long (left) with Representative Sol Bloom of New York. As director of immigration matters from 1940 until 1944, Long was responsible for keeping hundreds of thousands of refugees out of the country. (United States National Archives)

Since American Jews admired Roosevelt and were greatly impressed with his New Deal, the average Jewish citizen could not fathom that the president refused help to people in need. Roosevelt did not generally act unless he was pushed on an issue, and he was not pushed to rescue Jews under Hitler. In fairness, Roosevelt was heavily engaged in providing jobs for millions who had just emerged from the Great Depression and in preparing for a war to defeat Nazi Germany and imperial Japan. As Roosevelt's attorney general and close adviser, Benjamin Cohen, said after the war, "Things ought to have been different, but war is different, and we live in an imperfect world."[39]

With antisemitism prevalent in the State Department, especially under Avra Warren and Breckinridge Long, it is remarkable that the

Rebbe and his group received visas at all. Refugee aid organizations protested Long's obstructionism to Roosevelt, but the president did not remove him. By mid-1940, Long had cut immigration by 50 percent.[40] Had Roosevelt wanted things to change, he could have made Long alter his tactics, but he seems not to have cared about the situation.

The U.S. government may have finally issued visas for the Rebbe's group not only because of political pressure but also because it finally received enough documentation about Chabad's financial resources. Chabad reported that its U.S. operation received $35,000 annually, and it projected that it would obtain $50,000 if the leaders of the movement were granted admittance to the country. They enclosed bank statements showing that the Rebbe had $5,000 in personal accounts.[41] This information seemed to convince the State Department. On hearing the news, Philip Kleinfeld wrote Cordell Hull on 17 January to thank him and Robert Pell on behalf of Chabad. He also acknowledged Coulter's important role in the Rebbe's escape.[42]

But the Lubavitchers were not satisfied merely to save the lives of the Rebbe and his staff and family. At a time when few Jews in Nazi-occupied lands were being saved, they still wanted to rescue the Rebbe's books. On 22 January 1940, Rhoade told Kramer that unless Chabad could prove that it held "title to the library," he could not approach the authorities for it.[43] The documents showing title never materialized, and even had Rhoade received them, he would have had somehow to get the books out from under the Nazis.

The Rebbe refused to give up the fight. On 7 February, while waiting in Riga, he was informed that Jacobson had been unable to effect the rescue of the library. He hired a lawyer in Warsaw to arrange the shipment of 135 to 145 cases of his books and 11 cases of household goods from Poland to New York via Italy.[44] The Nazis would not allow all his possessions to be returned to him. The SS commander in Warsaw would later notify the commissioner for the ghetto that

"Rabbi Schneersohn's cases, which included his crystal, china, and silver, were considered unregistered Jewish property" and therefore subject to forfeiture.[45]

His work largely done, Rhoade resigned as the Rebbe's lawyer in February and turned the assignment over to Henry F. Butler, who worked for a lower fee. Butler took over the few remaining legal matters. Jacobson made sure he also looked into saving the Rebbe's books and personal items.[46] Rhoade probably left for financial reasons. Throughout December and January, he continually reminded Jacobson and Kramer about his bills and reiterated how tired he was of working without compensation.[47] It is unknown whether Rhoade was ever paid in full for his services.

Despite the resolution of the visa issue, the Rebbe did not leave Riga immediately. Health issues had become a problem. On 20 February 1940, he notified Jacobson that they would have to delay their departure to allow his mother to recuperate from a stomach operation. The Rebbe himself had fallen and broken his arm, so he would spend the time healing as well. He was also reluctant to leave Riga for America without his daughter and son-in-law Sheina and Mendel Horenstein. The Rebbe was supported by charity and loans from friends in Riga. Fortunately, his daughter Chana Gourary, the mother of Barry and wife of Samarius, had hidden a large sum of money in her clothes and underwear, and they had lived off that for several weeks. But their funds were drying up.[48]

In the meantime, things had become worse in Warsaw. Twice in February 1940, after receiving reports about the brutal deportations of Jews, Assistant Secretary of State Adolf A. Berle tried to get Hull to take some action. He encouraged the American government to object directly to the German government: "We should register a protest. We did so during the far less significant, though more dramatic, riots of a year ago November [Kristallnacht]; and I see no reason why we should not make our feelings known regarding a policy of seemingly calculated cruelty which is beginning to be apparent now." But Hull did not follow Berle's recommendation, and the fate of the Jews in Warsaw continued to drift into the abyss of the Holocaust.[49] Riga was no longer safe either. If the Rebbe did not leave soon, he faced danger from either the Soviets or the Nazis— whichever moved first to take over Latvia.

THIRTEEN

Crossing a Perilous Ocean

On 6 March 1940, Finland sued for peace and surrendered its territory to the Soviet Union. Although the Soviet victory had come at a high price, with the loss of two hundred thousand men to Finland's twenty-five thousand, Stalin's desire for expansion was not deterred.[1] He took over the Baltics in June. Had the Rebbe and his group still been in Latvia, they would probably have died.

The day Finland surrendered, the Rebbe's group left Riga by plane for Stockholm, catching one of the last flights from Latvia to Sweden. Those escaping with the Rebbe were his wife, his mother, his son-in-law Samarius Gourary, his daughter Chana, his grandson Barry, his secretary Chaim Lieberman, his nurse, Seina Locs, and three other Lubavitchers. His secretary Haskell Feigin, Feigin's wife, their five children, and a few other Lubavitchers scheduled to leave Sweden a bit later did not make it out.[2]

Several members of the hierarchy and their families remained under the Nazi jackboot. Only Rabbi Mendel Schneerson and his wife were relatively safe, living in France. During his time in Riga, Schneersohn had tried to rescue twenty-one other people in that city,

The Swedish liner *Drottningholm* (Eliezer Zaklikovsky)

thirty-five in Warsaw, and thirty-three in France, most of whom had to remain in Europe. The Rebbe was pained to leave his brethren, and during the journey he muttered remorsefully, "Now we are orphaned!" He had obtained visas for eleven families of Chabad leaders, but they had to wait until later to travel, and many would not escape.[3]

From Stockholm, Schneersohn's party traveled by train to Göteborg, where they boarded a Swedish liner full of refugees, the *Drottningholm*, for New York.[4] It was a dangerous passage. German submarines operated in the North Sea and the North Atlantic, the exact route the Rebbe's ship had to take. Nazi torpedoes had already sent hundreds of vessels to the ocean's bottom. Quite often, the German U-boats struck with such surprise and in such a devastating fashion that most of those onboard perished.

Passenger liners were in no way immune to war. On 3 September 1939, Germans had torpedoed the liner *Athenia*, killing 120 people, 28 of them Americans. Between 5 and 6 September, German submarines also sank the merchant ships *Bosnia, Royal Sceptre,* and *Rio Claro* off the coast of Spain. Only the crew of the *Rio Claro* survived. A few days later, the British aircraft carrier *Courageous* went down with 500 men. In September 1939 alone, Germany sank approximately fifty ships. A month later, it sank another prestigious English vessel, the battleship HMS *Royal Oak,* taking 833 officers and men with it.[5] By the time the *Drottningholm* set sail, the Germans had spent six months honing their U-boats' hunting skills.

No ships were safe from German attack—not even those of neutral countries. The Germans had already sunk ships of several neutral countries, including Norway, Holland, Spain, and Sweden (often, probably, because the ships were difficult to identify). And as the war progressed, neutral countries' losses from German U-boats increased. Indeed, the distinct possibility presented itself that the Germans would mistake the *Drottningholm* for an Allied ship or— although it was painted white with a large circle on its funnel and *Sverige* (Sweden) prominently written on its side—would refuse to believe it was a mercy ship and would sink it. At 538 feet long and 60 feet wide, it presented a fine target.[6]

In addition, several German pocket battleships and other warships roamed the seas ready to sink or capture Allied vessels. Many on the *Drottningholm* may have wondered what would happen to the Jewish passengers if the Germans boarded the ship, since most were refugees. The ship on which Rabbis Altein and Greenberg had traveled in September had been stopped by a U-boat and searched, but fortunately it was released.[7] There was a chance the Rebbe would not share their luck.

Mines were another problem. The Germans' indiscriminate laying of them had caused enormous damage to Allied and neutral shipping. Many mines were magnetic and could explode without contact with the vessel. The Luftwaffe and navy had dropped thousands of these magnetic mines over hundreds of square miles of the Baltic Sea, North Sea, and Atlantic Ocean.[8]

The Rebbe's ship sailed first along the coast of Norway, docking at Bergen after two days at sea. It had encountered mechanical problems and needed to be repaired.[9] Although the group was not aware of it at the time, even small delays could have proven disastrous. Only one month later, Germany would invade Denmark and Norway. The German navy had already sent thirty-two submarines to Norway's coast at the beginning of March in preparation for the invasion.[10] Four were positioned near Bergen. Repairmen worked on the *Drottningholm* all night, and, to the relief of all aboard, the ship resumed its journey on 9 March. Soon, however, the captain announced that he had to stop because of heavy fog, as they were in a rocky pass. With the engines shut down, the ship bobbed lazily up and down in the ocean—a sitting target. Although it was late at night, many passengers got out of bed and nervously walked into the hallways to find out what was wrong. The fog lifted the next day, and the ship continued on.

Before the Lubavitchers made it to the open ocean, German submarines stopped them twice. One can only wonder what they felt as the submarines surfaced and unfurled their red flags with the black swastikas. Both times, the Germans boarded the ship, searched it, questioned the captain, but allowed it to go on its way. They were looking for assurances of the ship's neutrality by checking to see that it did not carry any military cargo.

On 13 March, after four days at sea, a warship stopped them. It turned out to be British, and, after some intense moments of uncertainty, it let them continue. According to the Lubavitchers, they were stopped two more times by British warships, but they were again released and allowed to go on. In April, having conquered Norway and Denmark, the Germans would block the Baltic Sea from the Atlantic.[11]

It is remarkable that a Jewish leader like Rebbe Schneersohn made it out with American help, because many other rabbis did not get the support they needed to escape Europe. In October 1940,

Chairman James G. McDonald and Executive Secretary George L. Warren of the President's Advisory Committee on Political Refugees would write in a memorandum that several rabbis living in the Baltic countries had been put on lists by the immigration office but were not rescued since "action on their behalf was never from the start more than a gesture of sympathy."[12] Most of the Hasidic leaders in Eastern Europe did not escape, and they died in the Holocaust.

FOURTEEN

The Rebbe in America

On hearing that the Rebbe was on his way, Chabad sent out a notice to several rabbis saying, "If our mouths had the sea's capacity for song, it would not suffice to praise and thank G-d for the miracles and wonders He has performed for us and for the entire House of Israel by salvaging for us this teacher of his people, this leader of *his* nation, the Rebbe." Their prayers for God to save the Rebbe were indeed answered. The Rebbe's ship arrived in New York harbor late in the evening on 18 March, but passengers had to wait until the next day to disembark since the authorities had already closed the port.[1] In February and March, the Germans and their allies sank seventy-six ships; the Rebbe was lucky his ship had not been one of them.[2]

On 19 March, a boat with immigration officials and a committee of the Rebbe's supporters, including Hyman and Sam Kramer, Kleinfeld, and Jacobson, met the *Drottningholm* before it entered port. Even a representative from Mayor Fiorello La Guardia's office was on hand to greet the Rebbe. The Swedish sea captain asked the Rebbe whether he would like to leave the ship first. No, the Rebbe replied, he wished to leave last. Through those who disembarked

Rebbe Joseph Isaac Schneersohn on 19 March 1940, waiting in his stateroom on the *Drottningholm* to step onto the shores of America (Eliezer Zaklikovsky)

before him, he requested that his followers waiting on the pier be instructed to recite the benediction "Blessed is He Who gives life to the dead" when they first caught sight of him.[3] Although he deeply regretted having left so many "brethren in devastated Europe," he felt relieved to be alive and in the United States, where he believed he could do the most to help his yeshiva students and other Chabad leaders still in Poland, Russia, and the Baltic States.

Schneersohn told Jacobson before being rolled onto American soil in his wheelchair, "The sufferings I endured in prison in Russia do not compare to the torments of the 12 weeks I spent under *their* rule."[4] The day was cold and rainy, but that did not stop a crowd of supporters from coming to welcome the Rebbe. Before the Rebbe appeared, his eighty-year-old mother was carried off the ship on a stretcher, sending a hush through the crowd. Next, eager eyes watched for the Rebbe to emerge. When he was wheeled off the ship dressed in his traditional Hasidic garb, including his shtreiml, a large round fur hat, several hundred people, mostly Lubavitchers, erupted with cheers, prayers of thanksgiving, songs of "Heveinu Shalom Aleichem" (Peace unto You), and joyful dances. His escape was viewed by his followers as an act of "mystical significance, leadership and heroics."[5] The Rebbe's face was pale, "tormented and terrified," that "of a man rescued from a fire." Zalman Posner, one of the onlookers, later described seeing the "legendary" Rebbe step foot on U.S. soil as "a tremendous event in my life."[6]

A few hours later, at a special reception at the train station, the Rebbe asked those present to pray for Jews trapped in Poland. In a slow, slurred, but passionate voice, he said, "We should begin with a *brachah* [prayer of thanksgiving], thanking God for saving us from a very troubling situation and bringing us out of distress to abundance. To my great sorrow, I will have to interrupt the joy which we are all feeling right now. The great pain which our brothers and sisters are enduring without mercy at this moment does not let me rest. The cries of our brothers and sisters in Poland, and of the many *yeshivah* students in particular, haunt me wherever I go, and I cannot rest until *Hashem* has helped and saved them." He went on to say, "Jews are being mercilessly massacred, there exists in Europe a holocaust which defies description. America's conscience must be awakened, and above all, American Jewry must alert itself to the life saving mission now on its hands as never before in the history of mankind." He hoped that American Jews would intensify their efforts to help their brethren, whom the Nazis were "annihilating" in Europe. Rabbis and communal leaders were in the most danger of extermination, he said, naming several of his students who should be first on the list of those saved. If American Jewry did its part, then the U.S. government would follow suit. As he spoke, the tears of those standing around him dripped down on his shoulders and hat. Although he did not grant any interviews, the Rebbe later issued a statement through Rabbi Gourary appealing for the rescue of "3,500,000 Jews in Poland who are 'on the verge of annihilation.' . . . You of our brethren in America, who cannot imagine what modern warfare is like, . . . should create a vast fund to alleviate the lot of your Polish brethren, who have been made to suffer for all Israel," a "'communal sin offering' for the Jewish people."[7]

Equally painful to him on his arrival was his followers' caution not to expect too much from American Jews, who did not live observant lives. The Rebbe set as his goal to "salvage" the American children of the "lost generation" and give them back their Jewish identity. He retired to bed saddened by how far he felt American Jewry had become assimilated and fallen from Jewish observance. "The endless tears that accompanied my first [bedtime prayers] on American soil," he said, "shall remain undescribed."[8] As the Rebbe did not have his library, he soon borrowed or bought several religious books. He then spent long hours reading at his desk amid huge stacks of them. Some have argued that he was trying to find an explanation for the explosion of violence in Europe.[9]

A few days after his arrival, the Rebbe again publicly asked everyone to do their best to help those in Europe. On 24 March 1940, he gave a talk at the Greystone Hotel in New York City, where he said, "I cannot recover from my experiences in Warsaw, the fearful, life-threatening twenty-seven days of war . . . as well as the pain-filled, cruel eighty-one post-war days, . . . days lived in dread of death. The horrible life conditions of our brothers and sisters, the oppressive fright, the pitiless deeds of (today's) Haman [the Persian king's minister in the Book of Esther who tries to kill the Jews]—thoughts of these give me no rest. I must cry out—American Jews—of every kind, every description: Save Your Brethren Now!"[10] Unfortunately, his pleas seemed to reach no farther than the Lubavitchers and some other Orthodox communities.

Although the Rebbe never mentioned Bloch or the team that

helped him escape, he thanked Cordell Hull on 25 March for his support: "You can imagine how delighted and happy we are to set foot again on the friendly soil of the United States . . . after the dreadful experience we had in Poland of the war and Nazi regime."[11] He also sent a letter overflowing with appreciation thanking Justice Brandeis for his assistance. In April, the Rebbe asked to meet with Roosevelt to extend his gratitude, but the president's busy schedule, it was said, made a meeting impossible. In August, the Rebbe repeated his request through Congressman John W. McCormack of Massachusetts, who helped many Jews. The Lubavitcher who wrote for the Rebbe informed McCormack that the Rebbe was the "head of the Protestant Jews," who numbered "3,000,000 in this country and 8,000,000 in the world. This man got out of Poland through the kindness of the President and he wants to thank [him]." These figures were grossly exaggerated. One of Roosevelt's secretaries answered McCormack, telling him that the president did not have time at the moment, "but I do hope that things will ease up so Rabbi Schneersohn may see the President at some not too future date."[12] A meeting with the president would have been a good opportunity to plead for the rescue of more Jews.

In public, the Rebbe praised Roosevelt and later, on 12 September 1941, he wrote to him, "I wish to convey to your Excellency our profound gratitude for all you have done and are doing in the cause of Justice and righteousness in this land and other lands, and for the protection of all that is sacred and dear to all right thinking human beings . . . [and] to ensure lasting benefit, both spiritually and materially, to the people of Israel in all lands." The Rebbe had composed a prayer for the president to be recited in synagogues throughout America; it read in part: "We beseech Thee, O Merciful God! Inscribe our gracious President [and his ministers who] are fighting in the cause of justice and righteousness, unto a happy, blessed and successful New Year."[13] In December 1942, the Rebbe and Rabbi Gourary wrote to Roosevelt in the name of Chabad, again

RABBI I. SCHNEERSOHN
OF LUBAWITZ

סף יצחק שניאורסאהן
ליובאוויטש

1940 MAR 29 PM 3 40

DIVISION OF
COMMUNICATIONS
AND RECORDS

RECEIVED
DEPARTMENT OF STATE

Hotel Greystone,
Broadway,
At 91st Street,
New York.

March 25th 1940.

Hon. Cordell Hull
The Secretary of State
WASHINGTON D.C.

Dear Sir,

        I have pleasure in informing you that I
have arrived safely in New York together with my
son-in-law Rabbi S. Gourary and other members of
my family.

        You can imagine how delighted and happy
we are to set foot again on the friendly soil of
the United States and to find a haven of peace in
this free and blessed country, after the dreadful
experience we had in Poland of the war and Nazi
regime.

        We feel deeply grateful to you for your
kind help in the issuance of our emigration visas
to the United States, and our heartfelt thanks to
you for your kindness.

        Blessed is this country with its famous
and beloved leader President Roosevelt, the greatest and most outstanding figure of our age, famed
for his humane feelings and love of peace, and its
equally famous and great Secretary of State.

        May the Almighty bless you and grant you
long life, good health and every success in your
work for this country and humanity as a whole.

                Truly and respectfully you

                Rabbi Joseph Schneersohn

RIS/NM.

The Rebbe thanks Secretary of State Cordell Hull for rescuing him
(United States National Archives)

praising him and asking God to grant him and the armed forces
strength against the "enemies of mankind."[14] The Rebbe's letters and
his prayer acknowledged the great responsibility the president and
the government carried, even though the Lubavitcher community
in its newspaper made it known that they felt government leaders
were ignoring their tragedy.

RABBI I. SCHNEERSOHN
OF LUBAWITZ
770 EASTERN PARKWAY
BROOKLYN, N. Y.
SLocum 6-2919

TRANSLATION

By the Grace of G-d,
Elul 20, 5701.

(Sept. 12, 1941.)

His Excellency,
The President of the United States of America,
Honorable Franklin Delano Roosevelt,
The White House,
Washington, D.C.

Peace and Greetings !

        In the name of the Chabad-Lubavitz adherents throughout
the wide world, whose teacher and spiritual leader I have been
destined to be, following in the path of my forefathers, the Heads
of Chabad for six generations, and

        In in behalf of the Agudas Chasidei Chabad of the United
States and Canada, with several hundreds of Congregations in the
United States, comprising some 150,000 members, Chabad adherents,
citizens and legal residents of this country,

        I wish to convey to your Excellency our profound gratitude
for all you have done and are doing in the cause of Justice and
righteousness in this land and other lands, and for the protection
of all that is sacred and dear to all right thinking human beings.

        Millions of Jews throughout the world, in addition to all
Jewish subjects of this land, feel certain that your Excellency who
has been invested by the grace of Almighty G-d with the leadership
of the United States under the banner of freedom, justice and equal-
ity, recognize with the purity and wisdom of your heart, the worthy
traits of the People of Israel, and have given thought, which with
the help of G-d you will also materialize, to ensure lasting benefit,
both spiritually and materially, to the people of Israel in all lands.

        I have the honor of enclosing herewith the text of the
special Prayer which I have composed for Rosh Hashana (New Year) and
Yom Hakipurim (Day of Atonement), the Days of Judgment when the
Lord of the Universe takes to account all human beings; this Prayer
to be recited in all the Synagogues throughout the land where our
people shall congregate during these coming Solemn Days, a prayer
for the success and welfare of this land, for the triumph of justice
and truth in all lands and that the Almighty bless your Excellency
with long life and many happy years, that you may lead your subjects
in the path of justice, equity and peace.

        With heartfelt blessings,

            Respectfully yours, Rabbi JSS

On 12 September 1941, the Rebbe wrote to Roosevelt to express Chabad's
support for all that he was doing for humanity (Franklin Delano Roosevelt
Library)

Throughout 1940 and 1941, the Rebbe successfully sent food packages to Torah scholars and their families in Poland and Russia. He relied on Rabbi Mordechai Chefetz in Riga to funnel food packages to Poland via Latvia, often breaking the British blockade to do so. The Lubavitchers in America received reports that several families received this aid. But after the German invasion of Russia in the summer of 1941, the sending of food to most of Western and Central Europe stopped.[15]

On his arrival in 1940, the Rebbe immediately began efforts to rescue his students who had remained in Poland. He applied to the Joint Distribution Committee for money, asked his American students to write letters to the authorities, and worked tirelessly to secure visas and safe passage.[16] His students, he said, were "the very kernel of the existence and establishment of the [movement] in America." He obtained visas for thirty students, having raised the money for their travel arrangements with the Russian company Intourist and for visas, which allowed them to journey from Vilna to the east coast of Russia, China, or Japan, where they waited for money to board ships for America. On 13 January 1941, the Rebbe expressed his disappointment that not more money was being raised. His rescue fund had raised $5,040 for thirty students (probably for their travel), but he needed another few hundred dollars for two additional students. He had taken so many loans that he did not know where to turn anymore. The thirty who had already received documents and money traveled to Kobe, Japan, where they patiently waited for further instructions. The Rebbe pleaded for funds through his newsletter in March 1941. He appealed for assistance in saving "Jewish treasures that the greatest amount of gold" could not replace, and he urged rabbis to impress on their congregations "that every hour is dear not only in this life but also in the life to come. We must save Torah scholars and in doing so save ourselves."[17]

It appears that in 1941 the Rebbe's Pidyon Shvuim (Redeeming Those Imprisoned) fund obtained five hundred to six hundred visas for rabbis and students stranded in Poland, Lithuania, Latvia, Estonia, Finland, Sweden, Bulgaria, and France, but it is unclear whether these students had enough money to leave. Probably most of them had travel arrangements but did not escape before the United States canceled their visas out of fear that saboteurs would exploit an open immigration policy (an absurd theory promulgated by Breckinridge Long and others in the State Department). By the time a visa was granted, it was often too late to save the person. A report on the department's shameful record submitted to Secretary of the Treasury Henry Morgenthau stated, "It takes months and months to grant the visas and then it usually applies to a corpse."[18]

The Rebbe seemed to focus only on other Lubavitchers. With the situation in Europe getting more desperate by the minute, Schneersohn applied his efforts to Jews he felt most able to save—specific individuals whom he could identify and to whom the authorities might respond. One Chabad rabbi explained that, according to Jewish law, one is always supposed to save one's family first in any crisis, and all Lubavitchers were the Rebbe's children. Other Orthodox Jewish organizations in America also focused exclusively on rescuing rabbis and yeshiva students they deemed worthy instead of on rescuing anyone in need—a controversial policy bitterly debated among American Jews.[19]

Unfortunately, in June 1941 the United States also canceled the visas of those students stuck in Japan. The "close relatives edict" prevented refugees who had relatives under Nazi occupation from entering the United States. "For Jews, of course, no exception was made if the relative was starving to death in a concentration camp," observes historian Henry L. Feingold.[20] On 11 December 1941, soon after the United States entered the war, Schneersohn wrote Roosevelt, "In this grave hour, when the security of America has been challenged by a wicked treacherous enemy, we desire to express our unqualified solidarity with our president, government and the people of the United States, and our solemn determination to selflessly do our duty and privilege in the defense of our land." The next day, the president's secretary replied, "Permit me, in the President's name, to thank you for your telegram. . . . For the splendid assurance conveyed in your message he is more appreciative than he can say."[21] One wonders how Roosevelt would have responded if the Rebbe had asked him to ease the restrictive immigration policies. Perhaps the Rebbe did not because he felt that he should not offend those responsible for saving his life. Perhaps he felt that Jews relied too much on governments for salvation or that asking the president to save European Jews would not accomplish anything, although Roosevelt had played a small role in his own rescue.

Soon after his arrival, the Rebbe had told his followers that although "democratic countries" did not pay attention to the Jews' horrible situation, he could not blame them, "because self-preservation is the first rule of nature." He felt powerless in the face of a government he thought did not care about the "cruel treatment meted out to us everywhere." An article in his newspaper explained in February 1942: "We haven't anyone to champion our cause and intervene on our behalf with our torturers, though it would not do any good if such a champion were available. . . . We were warned against awaiting any salvation from our surrounding world other than that from our G-d, blessed be He."

Once the Rebbe recognized that diplomacy would not work with the Nazis, and that the U.S. government was not willing to do more, he focused on the spiritual survival of the Jews. Jewish history and Torah philosophy, he said, always saw war on two fronts: first, people must do everything possible in natural ways to save their lives and the lives of all innocent people; at the same time they must pray to God for salvation. Ultimately, a combination of both the natural effort and the power of faith were key to survival. Even after natural efforts had been exhausted, the Rebbe declared, Jews must never forget that their survival was guaranteed by the Jewish people's commitment to God and to spiritual integrity, which he felt they were failing at during this critical time in history. Awareness and commitment to the values and practices of Torah were the passport to Jewish survival and endurance. The difficulties they faced, Schneersohn argued, citing classical Torah texts, meant that Jews should examine their own lives to find what they could do better or repair. The Rebbe's organization believed the Jewish world was being afflicted because it had been "flooded with all sorts of idol worship known as Reform, Assimilation, World Culture, Socialism, and various other isms." The Jews were at the forty-ninth stage of impurity (if they reached the fiftieth, they would disappear); the tenth plague had afflicted the world and the end was in sight. The organization warned that those Jews who "stubbornly persist in their proclamation of and their adherence to the . . . truly earthen idols, civilization and democracy, risk the loss of their lives." The Rebbe announced in August 1941 that if every Jewish home did not cleanse itself of the forty-nine stages of impurity, the Jews would be stricken by the "destroying angel."[22]

Discouraged by the U.S. government, the Rebbe explored other options for the thirty students, who now had to leave Japan for Shanghai, China, owing to the outbreak of the Pacific war.[23] He needed the students, feeling that without a strong Lubavitch Torah center the world would suffer even more. Eventually, he secured visas for nine of the thirty to go to Canada. The other twenty-one students had to remain in China for the rest of the war.[24]

In addition to his students, the Rebbe especially tried to get his daughters Sheina Horenstein and Chaya Moussia Schneerson out of Europe. Sheina and her husband held Polish citizenship, which disqualified them for U.S. visas. Sheina, her husband, Mendel, and the entire rest of the Horenstein family died in Treblinka in 1942. The Rebbe appointed Samarius Gourary to arrange the escape of Chaya Moussia and her husband, Menachem Mendel Schneerson, even though the two brothers-in-law had an awkward relationship.[25] With emergency visitors' visas Samarius helped them obtain, Chaya

The sixth Lubavitcher Rebbe, Joseph Isaac Schneersohn (left), with the future seventh Lubavitcher Rebbe, Menachem Mendel Schneerson, in Austria in February 1935 (Eliezer Zaklikovsky)

Moussia and Menachem fled Vichy France for the United States in 1941; many of the Jews who remained in France soon boarded trains for the death camps.[26] It seems that the only reason Rabbi Menachem made it out was that Rebbe Schneersohn convinced the U.S. consulate officials that he was invaluable to the Chabad hierarchy as a "great Torah scholar" who would contribute to America.[27] Besides the fact that Menachem was married to the Rebbe's daughter and was himself a great rabbi, perhaps the Rebbe also pushed hard for Menachem's escape to ensure that the Lubavitcher movement would have proper leadership after his death. When Menachem arrived in the United States in the summer of 1941, the Rebbe appointed him head of the educational department as well as of "the movement's social-service organization and its publishing house." The Rebbe was clearly grooming Menachem to be the next Rebbe.[28]

It has been argued that Schneersohn should have urged Brandeis, Pell, or even Hull to work for the rescue of all Jews under Hitler. Conceivably, he could have met with them to discuss rescue efforts, but the record shows he did not. Some Lubavitchers familiar with the history counter that the ailing Rebbe was doing everything he could to rescue his followers, and that meeting or petitioning government officials would not have accomplished anything.[29] Yet other Orthodox leaders who met with officials in Washington pleaded for their brethren in Europe and accomplished a great deal. They focused on saving lives in Europe whereas, historian David Kranzler says, the Rebbe felt he could do little for those in Europe and thus focused on saving Jewish souls in the United States.[30]

Historian Ephraim Zuroff writes that, compared with what they had done for the Rebbe, even Lubavitch "activists invested proportionally . . . little effort in saving the rebbe's students, who were also stranded in the Warsaw area." But much as when a military general and several of his men are captured in war, the most effort goes into rescuing the leader. Certainly the Lubavitch activists were not unique in the Orthodox world. Other Hasidic groups in the United States gave top priority to saving their rebbes.[31]

In an act of great solidarity, the Rebbe made a few public pleas for the Gerer Rebbe, who, remarkably, was also rescued by German soldiers (he, too, made it out with several family members). Bloom, Brandeis, Hull, and Wagner were also involved in the rescue, but it is not clear if those connections were established by Chabad, although one can assume they were. Schneersohn also worked for the rescue of Rabbi Aaron Rokeach, the well-known Rebbe of Belz, and Rabbi Ben Zion Halberstam, the Rebbe of Bobov. In April 1941 he wrote to the Belzer Hasidim asking for information about the Belzer Rebbe's location and names of his family members, promising that "I will do whatever I can" for him. Ultimately, Rabbi Rokeach of Belz made it out of the Bochnia ghetto in 1943 with the help of a Hungarian officer. The efforts for the Bobover Rebbe, however, were unsuccessful, and he perished in the Holocaust.[32]

Schneersohn also wrote to the Joint Distribution Committee in February 1940 begging for money for Polish Jews to obtain visas and pay transportation expenses. Later in 1940, after he arrived in the United States, he pleaded for funds for many Jews stranded in the Baltics for their travel and food expenses. Beginning in April 1941 he turned to the Quakers in Philadelphia, who had extensive contacts with humanitarian services throughout Europe, asking them to help save as many Jews as possible. With the Nazis tightening their grip on millions, and the doors of the United States closing shut almost completely, the Rebbe was exerting his strongest efforts to rescue those he might be able to actually save. There was only so much he felt he could do. Sadly, the feeling of impotence was common among Jewish leaders in the United States. Historian David Wyman has written, "American Jews lacked the unquenchable sense of urgency the crisis demanded." Granted, in 1940 death camps, gas chambers, and genocide were still unimaginable.[33]

Even though he did not employ the political contacts that helped him escape Europe, the Rebbe did use the Pidyon Shvium fund to help rescue people, asking readers to donate to it in special ads in his newsletter. But the fund was also used to build schools and support study. Some of the money raised was used to rescue a few Lubavitchers and, according to Rabbi Shalom Dovber Levine a large portion of it supported those suffering under the Soviets throughout the war.[34] Since most of the Rebbe's followers were located in western Russia, this latter focus was understandable.

One of the key players in organizing the Rebbe's escape, Latvian senator and fellow Lubavitcher Mordechai Dubin, endured horrible hardship. After the Soviets occupied the Baltics in June 1940, they deported Dubin and other Lubavitchers from Riga to the Soviet Union, where many of them disappeared. Dubin later returned to Riga, but in poor health. The Soviets sent many Lubavitchers to Siberian concentration camps; most perished.[35]

With Dubin and others in mind, the Rebbe sent a delegation to the White House in March 1941 to obtain emergency visitors' visas. It appeared that the Soviet authorities had deported most of the people named to concentration camps. Since they had opposed the Communist regime and were Russian citizens, their rescue would prove difficult even though the Soviets maintained close diplomatic contact with the United States. With the help of Clarence E. Pickett of the American Friends Service Committee in Philadelphia, the Lubavitchers arranged a meeting with Eleanor Roosevelt.

Pickett wrote Mrs. Roosevelt on 5 March, saying, "Three distinguished rabbis of the bearded sort pled with me to ask you to see them." She agreed to meet with the delegation, and on 18 March 1941, Philip Kleinfeld, Rabbi Samarius Gourary, and a few others visited her at the White House. Although they mentioned many people, they focused primarily on rescuing Mordechai Dubin, a man who had done so much to help the Rebbe throughout the years.

The Lubavitchers presented her with a two-page memorandum. The first page was about Dubin. They appealed to the "First Lady of the Land, famous for her kindness and great humanitarian work, to kindly intervene in behalf of a distinguished public worker and humanitarian, Senator Mordechai Dubin, through the above mentioned channels, with a view to securing the early release of . . . Dubin, and his deportation together with his family to this country, where asylum and refuge are awaiting him." They listed others, mainly yeshiva students, on the second page and concluded their memorandum by saying, "Intercession is earnestly appealed for in behalf of the above mentioned victims of intolerance with the view of procuring their release and deportation from the Soviet Union to this country, where hospitality and refuge has been offered to them." Although the Rebbe had made a public statement in 1940 on behalf of all Jews in Poland, his organization now did not request help for Jews under Nazi oppression or ask that Hitler's atrocities be made more public. As historian David Kranzler says, "Chabad focused on its mission to rescue American Jews from assimilation and rebuild its community, working against incredible odds. It focused on its own mission."[36]

It is not clear what the Lubavitchers' meeting accomplished. Mrs. Roosevelt reportedly tried to be helpful.[37] She presented the matter to Undersecretary of State Sumner Welles, asking him to approach the Russian ambassador. Welles wrote her on 31 March that he had brought the matter to the ambassador's attention but that they could not intervene for non-American citizens "since the Soviet Government consistently refuses to entertain representations from this Government on their behalf." Despite the First Lady's good intentions, her requests were often brushed aside. After receiving a copy of Welles's letter, Pickett thanked her on 22 April for her effort and noted, "It looks as if nothing further can be done. I have sent copies of this letter on to the persons who visited you in Washington." Mrs. Roosevelt often had difficulty convincing those in power, especially Warren and Long, to help people in need, but that did not prevent her from trying; unfortunately, she did not have the power to change the situation for many desperate Jews.[38] Her relationship with her husband was not good, and many of those surrounding the president did not take her seriously. If she had had a large group supporting her, maybe she could have done more. As historian Holger Herwig says, "Roosevelt allowed Eleanor to bring information, but he usually ignored her requests."[39] Pressure from a source Roosevelt respected was what was needed.

When the Rebbe failed in 1940 and 1941 to rescue many of the Lubavitcher students, Chabad leaders, and family members he had hoped to save, he began to concentrate on his spiritual mission, wanting more than anything to make American Jewry observant. He might not have eased up on rescuing those stranded in Europe had he thought there was a chance of success, but having encountered so many obstacles, he felt it unproductive to continue working with a government uninterested in the plight of the Jews. He turned his energies to what he believed to be an obtainable goal of rebuilding Jewish life in America.

The Rebbe's rescue efforts might have been more successful had he joined the Vaad—the Orthodox rescue agency—or other groups working to save Jews. Unfortunately, Chabad's relationship with the Vaad was less than friendly. In the fall of 1940, Chabad presented a request to the Vaad to help 156 rabbis emigrate from Lithuania to the United States, a request the Vaad apparently ignored. Furthermore, in a letter to Rabbi David Rabinovitz at this time, the Rebbe discussed the Vaad's raising money for all yeshivahs, including those of Chabad. Yet he had not received any funds and requested Rabinovitz to obtain "the $1,000 they owe me," saying that he felt deeply hurt by the Vaad's ill treatment of him. He claimed that throughout his life in all his fund-raising he never made a distinction between Chabad and non-Chabad institutions and had given hundreds of thousands of dollars to non-Lubavitch schools. "If I were to demand from them to pay me back for the money I spent in order to support and save their yeshivahs over the years," the Rebbe continued, "they would have to give up even their girdles." According to Chabad, the Vaad refused to give the Rebbe the $1,000. Rabbi Alex Weisfogel, who worked in the Vaad with one of its greatest leaders, Avraham Kalmanowitz, says, "The reason the Vaad probably did not act on their requests as they would have liked is that the Vaad focused on all Jews, not just on Lubavitchers. The problem with Chabad then was that it focused just on what it needed." David Kranzler has a different perspective: he believes it was difficult to help anyone at this stage, requiring a lot of money and influence. The Vaad wanted to help, he says, but used its meager resources first to save its members. (It was able to rescue only a handful of yeshiva students initially.) According to Kranzler, in other words, the conflict had to do less with ideology than with finances. Regardless of the reasons, the lack of help disappointed the Rebbe greatly. Many in the Lubavitcher com-

Rabbi Avraham Kalmanowitz, one of the most prominent leaders of the Orthodox Jewish rescue organization Vaad. His efforts, and those of Rabbi Aron Kotler, helped save thousands of lives. (Agudath Israel of America)

munity still feel the Vaad was anti-Hasidim and therefore ignored Chabad's needs.

According to Moshe Kolodny, director of Orthodox Jewish (Agudath) Archives of America, the problems between the Vaad and Chabad arose from differences in ideology. Many in the Vaad, according to Kolodny, viewed the Lubavitchers as absorbed in their claim to have found the only way to live a Jewish life. The Vaad also disagreed with Chabad's focus on the Messiah and their Rebbe. Since Chabad apparently did not offer the Vaad reciprocal support for its endeavors, Kolodny notes, one can argue that it was unreasonable for Chabad to expect it to have helped Lubavitchers. In any event, the Rebbe felt he could not work with it.[40]

Schneersohn condemned Jewish spiritual leaders whom he felt compromised their religious duties unnecessarily to work with non-Orthodox, or even Christian, organizations. Orthodox Rabbi Aron Kotler of the Vaad worked with both non-Orthodox and secular leaders. Many Orthodox rabbis criticized him for his willingness to work with such people. To such criticism, Kotler replied that he was ready to "work with the Pope" and even prostrate himself before the Catholic leader "if it would save . . . one Jewish child."[41] Kotler's colleague Avraham Kalmanowitz agreed with him and worked with Reform Jews and even atheists. These courageous Orthodox rabbis helped rescue thousands.[42] The Rebbe did not agree with methods like theirs and said in 1943, "These false prophets and iniquitous rabbis have brought our people to the ludicrous state in which rabbis have themselves photographed with clergymen; rabbis are invited to officiate at a *Seder* in a church and Christian clergymen are invited to synagogues to listen to the Sounding of the *Shofar* and to [hymns sung at the table during Sabbath], to [prayers for Yom Kippur]. Genuine rabbis, Torah scholars, stand abashed. They cannot lift their eyes out of shame—for the Destruction that is being brought upon the Jewish street."[43] The Rebbe most certainly did not oppose working with Christians to save innocent lives. He had done so himself with the Quakers. He felt, however, that to ensure the survival of Judaism, clear religious and ideological borders had to be erected between Jews and Christians. This was similar to the notion of rabbis in the early days of Christianity who believed that if Jews did not segregate themselves religiously from the Christian community, Judaism could disappear over the course of time. Combining Judaism and Christianity compromised much of what Judaism and Torah stood for, and if this happened, according to the Rebbe, it would only help undermine the spiritual power needed in difficult times like the Holocaust.

As a result, the Rebbe preached during the war that it was a mitzvah to denounce those who transgressed by "desecrating the practical *mitzvot*, such as *tefillin* and the prayers, by irresponsibly spurning the restrictions of kosher dietary laws and the family purity laws; by giving their children an irreligious education in *treifah* Talmud Torah schools whose men and women teachers are godless, and in *yeshivos* that match; and by attending temples with their faithless rabbis." The Rebbe's organization claimed in September 1941 that, had the Jews been better educated and had they "lived according to the precepts of the Torah," the present "catastrophic situation would not have developed." In other words, instead of working with secular Jewish leaders or with rabbis who were joining with Christian leaders or violating Jewish law, the Rebbe was encouraging his followers to denounce such men and other "perfidious rabbis" and their "unkosher" ways. He believed the Holocaust was God's punishment on the Jews for abandoning their faith. Only renewed obedience to God and belief in the Prophets would end the punishment—continued disobedience and disbelief were "perverse Jewish Nazism." Political action to end the Holocaust or save lives was futile as long as Jews failed to follow the commandments. With this ideology, the Rebbe could not aggressively seek the help of those he felt were violating God's laws. One sees, too, that the Rebbe would have been quite difficult to work with since he obviously would have cooperated only with those willing to accept his dictates and support his policies.[44]

In a speech in 1943, the Rebbe attacked secular, Reform, and Orthodox Jewish leaders who conducted events and protested the government's lack of action on Holy Days and the Sabbath: "These leaders brazenly defy God and scoff at Him. Even their mournful demonstrations—which the godless leaders of certain Jewish parties believe are going to save Jews in peril, and for which they have cooperation of unprincipled rabbis—are called for Friday evening. This planned desecration of *Shabbos* is a rebellious response to the commandment from the G-d of our fathers to keep this day holy, and a senseless and shameful affront to their fellow Jews. This they do while our brothers and sisters are being slaughtered, murdered, buried alive, with a cruelty that the world has never witnessed; while the blood of Jewish old and young, fathers, mothers and tiny toddlers, is flowing in rivers throughout all the occupied countries." The Rebbe viewed their tactics as damaging to the plight of Jews rather than helpful in increasing public awareness.[45] Those few who demonstrated in fact accomplished much, and the Orthodox who conducted activities on the Sabbath and Holy Days did so in the spirit of saving lives. In their minds, they were fulfilling a mitzvah to save life at any cost and thereby obeying God's law. The Rebbe agreed that one must break the commandments, if to do so will save a life, and in a 1942 letter he advocated the use of "natural"—that is, political—means to that end.[46] He did not agree, however, with the way many Jewish leaders were breaking the commandments.

The Rebbe wanted to save European Jews, but he had a higher priority: preparing himself, the Jews, and the world for the imminent arrival of the Messiah. He felt that the Holocaust challenged all humanity to root out evil, not just its symptoms, at its source. In a sense, his strategy (bring the Messiah, who will end all evil, including the Holocaust) was very similar to the U.S. government's policy (win the war, and Hitler and his Holocaust will end automatically). The Rebbe believed absolutely that his religious efforts were just as important as, if not more important than, America's all-out war effort. Both would bring victory to the just, and in the Rebbe's world, God could achieve more than any military or political strategy.[47]

The Rebbe and his followers felt that American Jewish leaders who believed that the only hope for Jews was to defeat Hitler were "wrong" and "leading their followers astray by uttering false prophecies." This seems to have been his predominant message after his failed rescue efforts in 1940 and 1941. Such leaders, he explained, had "traded our proven method of pleading for [God's] intervention for politics and diplomacy." They had forgotten the great hope and

"joyous news" of God's promise of Messiah, a Messiah the Rebbe
thought was "about to arrive—he is already standing within reach
of us!" Only with the proper focus on living righteously and preparing for the "final deliverance" would life improve. In a time when
the "Jewish people [were] drowning in [their] own blood," the Rebbe
regarded as irresponsible Jewish leaders who focused on a "diet of
worldly prospects, ignorant of the real cause of the world catastro-
phe," which was the lack of penitence and prayer. These spiritual
leaders, like the world press, were "abysmally ignorant" of the "truth
in the developments of the war." Without an announcement from
these leaders that the Jews were on the "eve of the era of redemption"
and that "the present Jewish sufferings are pre-messianic travail,"
all efforts with the government were fruitless. The Rebbe felt abandoned by Jewish organizations that ignored his call for redemption.
He was saddened that they had given up on the Messiah and were
working solely in the secular world to get things done. Only his own
call and warning about the situation were "true and timely." Physical conquest of Hitler (rescue through victory) was fruitless without
making spiritual activity a priority and acknowledging that God was
the "only controlling power in the world."[48] The Rebbe once said his
movement's politics were strictly "Torah and *mitzvot.*"[49]

Thus, it is not surprising that in several of his letters the Rebbe
discouraged mass demonstrations when others saw the need for
them.[50] In 1941, for example, the mere threat that 50,000 to 100,000
African Americans were going to march on Washington prompted
President Roosevelt to issue an executive order to help increase employment opportunities for "Blacks."[51] A march on Washington by
over 400 members of the Union of Orthodox Rabbis of the United
States and Canada on 6 October 1943 helped create the War Refugee Board, which saved thousands of lives in 1944 and 1945.[52] Even
though the Rebbe supposedly had control over 160,000 followers,
he viewed demonstrations, especially if they violated Jewish law, as
offensive and counterproductive.

On 6 October 1943, more than four hundred Orthodox rabbis marched on Washington to protest America's inaction in helping Jewish victims of Hitler. President Roosevelt refused to meet them when they arrived at the White House. (Agudath Israel of America)

Many did not agree with the Rebbe's tactics. Philosopher Jacob Klatzkin wrote the Rebbe on 8 March 1943 to say that his heart ached not to see Jewish leaders going into the streets of America dressed in mourning to protest the lack of government effort and to awaken Americans to the "murder of tens of thousands of our brothers." Asking "Why are our Orthodox leaders silent?" he begged the Rebbe to lead Orthodox Judaism in the cause.[53]

The Rebbe responded in a twelve-page letter on 31 March 1943, expressing sadness at Klatzkin's sentiments. Never, in all his years of communal service, he said, had there been a time like this, when righteous Gentiles willing to protect Jews were nowhere to be found. There were groups to protect "cats, dogs, maybe even mice, but no groups to protect Jews." The countries and governments that benefited from "our wisdom and wealth are now turning their backs and eyes away. These people a few years ago treated us nicely, but now their eyes are shut and ears closed to the spilling of the blood of Israel in the conquered areas under evil Nazism." To "our embarrassment and shame," Schneersohn explained, "and to the shame and embarrassment of all humanity" the government just tells them "to calm down and rest assured that when the war is over, then they 'will see what we can do for you.' Until then, we are, God forbid, disowned crumbs [i.e., remnants of leavened bread that must be swept away] on the eve of *Pesach*."[54]

Demonstrations aimed at inspiring the Jewish people were no use: Jews already knew what was going on. If they sought to mobilize the "gentile Press," then "we see so clearly that they are sitting behind a diplomatic curtain. We do not know if they are laughing or gloating on the evil deeds, but what we do know is that they are pretending all is in order. If demonstration is for the government's benefit, the world sees that their ears are closed to the screams of our 'corpses' and their eyes are closed to the river and streams of blood. . . . The one thing that we can do, should do, must do is to awaken the compassion of our Father, our King in Heaven. In order to awaken the compassion of Heaven, why do we have to make a demonstration?" The Rebbe's strategy in this titanic struggle against evil was to seek God's help, since humans appeared unable or unwilling to save the Jews. He believed God had sent the Germans to "collect on His debts" since the Jews had not been following his commandments.

The "chutzpah" of secular and nonobservant Jewish leaders was "leading Jews to sin." At a moment when "our brothers and sisters are being murdered with the greatest cruelty in fire and water and burned alive" and when hundreds of thousands of Jewish men were serving in the armed forces, Jews the world over should humble themselves before God and return to Judaism. "Precisely in the time when the dark clouds of antisemitism are covering this country and the haters of Israel are sharpening and shining their weapons to kill Jews (may their swords go into their own hearts and may their bodies fall into their own pits)" and when false information was being spread throughout the world, Jews needed to pray to God for forgiveness and study Torah.

The Rebbe claimed that nonobservant Jews, or *kofrim* (apostates), were the ones who needed to do the most to stop Hitler's genocide. Instead of bothering him with letters, Klatzkin should go to his kofrim brothers and protest that they were not keeping the Sabbath holy, not wearing tefillin, not eating kosher food, and not obeying God. They should return to the way of life they knew was right and then things would get better. God, the Rebbe explained, had brought him to America to build his yeshiva and keep the "Holy Torah alive." Having witnessed how far the Jews had strayed from God, he had immediately published a newspaper about their coming destruction. His warnings, he felt, foresaw the terrible things to come and "the birthpangs of the Messiah," all "very serious topics and secrets of our sages."[55]

The Rebbe had little experience with democratic government, and the governments he had known in Europe, primarily under the Soviets, had often proved brutally intolerant toward Jews. He did what he had been taught and what he had always done, pray and study, which among the Lubavitchers made him a saint. They would often watch him pray so as to observe ultimate holiness, especially during times of hardship. They admired that he prayed on behalf of all Jews and lived a life of self-sacrifice in order to help them live according to God's commandments.

Most religious leaders would agree about the power of prayer, but very few would suggest that prayer and study should dominate one's action in the face of danger. It was political action that had saved the Rebbe's life, and yet he condemned that very tactic. Perhaps the most puzzling feature of the Rebbe's inertia is the fact that he, unlike most other Jewish leaders, had experienced Nazi atrocities firsthand (albeit for a short time). But his theological vision guided all his actions. Even before departing the ship that brought him to America, he had told Jacobson that "our work is Torah, and the strengthening of *Yiddishkeit* here, and Torah and *Yiddishkeit* overseas." As soon as he turned Jews to strict Torah observance and fortified their "fear of Heaven," God would drive their tormentors "to the gallows." The Rebbe himself would plead with God to send his angels to welcome "thy people Israel" and end the persecution and war.[56]

Historian Avrum Ehrlich argues that the Rebbe's move to the United States can be viewed as tantamount to a commander's leaving his troops in a losing battle while he retires to safety. Yet, most of his followers saw his escape "as part of a larger mystical-military mission." The spreading of Chabad in America, a land viewed by most ultra-Orthodox Jews as heretical (the impure country—the *treife medina*), was the beginning of the "final struggle" that would usher in the redemption of the nation of Israel. Despite the fact that the United States was the only place left open to the Rebbe, his move was seen as a brave effort to fight assimilation in the Western world.[57]

The Rebbe saw the war, the inability and unwillingness of the democracies to rescue Jews, the infighting among Jewish groups, and Hitler's persecution as the fulfillment of the prophecies about the end times. The Jews were now entering the stage of redemption from exile they had experienced after the destruction of the Second Temple in 70 c.e.; the time of the Messiah was near at hand. He wished to awaken Jews to this reality and to teach them how to make the coming of the Messiah as painless as possible.[58]

Since the Rebbe looked at the situation largely in spiritual terms, he took drastic spiritual action. Wanting even children to understand that something was dreadfully wrong in the world, he directed that, as long as Hitler slaughtered the Jews, Lubavitcher children should not have candy. He called for a worldwide fast in 1941 so that "our brothers and sisters" who by the "hundreds and thousands . . . are being tormented by deadly terrors" would return to God "in wholehearted repentance," enabling the Messiah to come. He concentrated on rebuilding his community in the United States and on carrying his spiritual message to the masses, sending emissaries all over America to strengthen Jewish communities.[59]

Given the Rebbe's chronic health problems, many of his followers found it remarkable that he was functioning at all. His multiple sclerosis and strokes prevented him from walking on his own, and he had a difficult time even picking up a pencil. He needed help eating, washing, and dressing. He mostly remained in his room and relied on newspapers, radio broadcasts, and his followers to keep him informed of outside events and of how his plans for Lubavitch were being implemented, especially since he did not speak English. Even in his fragile state, his mind was sharp. He retained authority over the movement, and his ideas served as the guiding light for his followers. Sickness makes most people more introspective, which may partly account for his turn away from the political. Combine his personal experience with the Soviets and the Nazis and one can perhaps understand why the Rebbe felt that God's wrath was ushering in the last days.

In his talks, attended by twenty-five to fifty of his trusted followers, as well as in his newspaper, the Rebbe repeatedly explained his numerous beliefs about the Holocaust—why God was allowing it and what could be learned from it. His newspaper even boldly claimed to be the "only publication that interprets our times from the genuinely Jewish standpoint. . . . Learn the truth, and be prepared to guide yourself according to your own best interests."[60]

In March 1941, the Rebbe said at his headquarters in Brooklyn that Jews who "refuse to return to living Judaism are forced to return to the Jewish cemetery!" An article in his newspaper in April called on Jews to stop changing their names, language, garb, and appearance to appease their Gentile neighbors; "weakling" Jews were doing so out of feelings of inferiority. Deuteronomy warns of the dangers of assimilation: "Your sons and daughters will be given over to another people" and "you shall beget sons and daughters, but they will not belong to you" (28:32, 41). To please God, Jews were to keep the

Sabbath and a kosher home. Since they had not remained faithful to God's commandments, their "sins have kindled a fire under our feet. We forgot to be Jews; now we are being reminded by the powers above that we must return. . . . Only penitence can save us from the consequences." If they did not repent, Satan and his human agents ("professional atheists") would win by deceiving them into relying on secular means rather than God.

"Our brothers and sisters overseas now find themselves in a most perilous and frightful situation," the Rebbe explained in October 1941.

> Hundreds and thousands of congregations and entire communities of our brothers and sisters are being persecuted and tortured to extermination. Those remaining alive are exposed to famine, imprisonment and exile. And one is not certain that these tribulations will not spread to other countries. Maimonides tells us, apropos of the laws on Fast days, that on the occasion when a great calamity befalls our people, it is incumbent upon us to offer prayers to the Almighty and acknowledge that the trouble is in punishment for inobservance of the Torah, and thereby bring about G-d's mercy upon us. . . . We behold in all these trials and tribulations the approach of Messiah. . . . Brothers and sisters, HAVE COMPASSION UPON YOURSELVES, UPON YOUR SONS AND DAUGHTERS, SO that you be not destroyed in the birth pangs of the coming Messiah. Forsake your evil ways of desecration of the Mitzvot. Entreat our FATHER IN HEAVEN for forgiveness for the past misdeeds.

Since Hitler's Holocaust had been ordained from above, the Rebbe claimed, the Jews should take hope in the fact that, if they followed God's commands, things would get better. In an article in his newspaper in April 1941, Jews were encouraged to realize that "now that all nations are arming to the teeth, we Jews must think of our own unique defenses. Our armament—Torah, prayer, penitence, good deeds, and observance of the 613 commandments—will protect us against all the blitzkriegs of our enemies. . . . Without Torah and penitence we would be helpless and doomed."

The Torah gave Jews proof that God would not abandon them, his chosen people. He would never let the Jews be totally annihilated if they focused on Torah. But to hasten God's rescue and new reign, Jews needed to become observant and trust his promise that he would rescue them in times of trouble. These were the last sufferings before redemption and the Messiah, and once he came, the horrors facing the Jews would be replaced by "deliverance and triumph." Although the Rebbe knew that the "Jewish star will rise" again and that the "world-destroyer" would be annihilated, he still felt great pain and was often seen crying because of all the hardships and misery the Jews were undergoing. Knowing how emotional he was, his followers did their best to prevent his seeing articles about Hitler's slaughter.[61]

In 1943, the Rebbe said, "For the wise man at this time—in this era on the eve of the Redemption, in this era of the birthpangs of *Mashiach,* when the Almighty is cleansing the sinful world and sinful men, in this era when harsh edicts . . . have been decreed on the saintliest individuals within the House of Israel—this is a time to *remain silent.* One's head is dulled, one's heart is bruised, one's spirit is battered: it is natural to fall silent." He continued in 1944, "About the plight of Jews in the Nazi-occupied countries there is nothing to say," and "the principles underlying the current rescue plans are no more than political talk."[62]

The ancient Talmudic sage Rabbi Nachman said that when the Messiah comes it will be a terrible time for humanity. What worse event could one possibly imagine than Hitler's Holocaust? An article in the Rebbe's newspaper explained, "Our Sages have said: 'When disaster comes upon the world—look forward to salvation!'"[63] The prophets Ezekiel and Isaiah describe the destruction of the world that will take place in the end days before the Messiah comes, and from his writings, it is clear the Rebbe felt humanity was approaching the Jewish Armageddon.[64] Just as Moses came to lead the Jews out of bondage in Egypt under Pharaoh, so now the Messiah would deliver the Jews from the Holocaust.[65] The Rebbe wrote in June 1941 that Chabad had "been rousing American Jewry to become aware that we are living in the last days before the Redemption." God ruled the world and caused all events, and the slaughter of Jews under Hitler was "pre-messianic travail" that would give them their "final deliverance." It was a mistake to believe that Jewish deliverance was dependent solely on the defeat of Hitler.[66]

Just as God had punished his chosen people with exile, slavery and bloody tyrants in biblical times, the Nazis were instruments of God's displeasure because many had violated God's commandments, especially American Jews, who had brought this misfortune on the House of Israel with their "golden calf and the broken tablets." Writing in July 1941, the Rebbe pleaded for Jews to stop their idolatry and turn away from their sins so that the punishment would stop.[67] In August 1941, he said that American Jews' "coldness and indifference . . . towards Torah and religion" were just as destructive as the fire in Europe that threatened "to annihilate more than two-thirds of the Jewish people."[68]

Of course, it was the more Orthodox, Torah-observant Eastern European Jews who were bearing the brunt of God's retribution. Because he loved the Jews so much, the Rebbe said, it pained him to point out that it was the pious who suffered for the others and that suffering was "being paid up in lives."[69] This "bloodbath" should inspire all Jews to return to the Torah and thus clear the path for the "Righteous *Mashiach*." The Rebbe viewed the destruction of European Jewry as "the birthpang that precedes" the Messiah's coming. The "suffering of world Jewry today is a voice from heaven calling" all

Jews to "*teshuvah* [repentance] of unfaithful ways," and if they heed the call, a "beautiful and luminous world will arise." God "sends hardships to cleanse us of our sins. They should be received with true affection, because their purpose is our benefit. . . . Whom G-d loves He afflicts." The Rebbe believed that the murder of Jews was not "accidental . . . but the result of an edict from heaven"; his followers needed to accept the destruction of their "brothers and sisters overseas" as a sign from God to be more observant. "Do not be deluded into thinking that we Jews can be helped only by mortals and politics," he said in 1941. "The 'wise and understanding people' must not be influenced by such foolishness." In 1944, he reiterated that "the Jewish people will be saved not by statesmen nor by presidents nor by kings, but by G-d's Will, which will act only when we return in *teshuvah*."[70]

Perhaps the reason he himself had been saved, according to his theology, was that he had been exceptionally faithful to God's commandments. "With G-d's help, and in the merit of my holy forebears, I have remained faithful, regardless of my shattered physical condition, to the principles governing communal activity that I was taught by my Rebbe—the great self-sacrificing leader and mentor, my father, of blessed memory. With self-sacrifice I fulfill his holy testament, by disseminating Torah study inspired by the awe of heaven, by furthering authentic Jewish education, and in general by working for the public welfare."[71]

Paradoxically, men like Ernst Bloch and Klaus Schenk or Benjamin Cohen and Louis Brandeis, whose families had drifted away from Judaism and who were described by the Rebbe as apostates or nebbich Jews, were the very people responsible for his rescue. Yet the Rebbe felt that Jews like these bore the responsibility for causing God's punishment through the Holocaust. In the Rebbe's world, it was not beyond God to use them to accomplish miracles as well.

The Rebbe also believed that observant Jews should bear some of the responsibility as they should have worked harder to make nonobservant Jews more religious. Many such beliefs of the Rebbe's are disquieting, but several Lubavitch scholars point out that his words reflect the classical Jewish approach and are rooted in Torah sources, including Maimonides, who writes that "when a calamity strikes the community we must cry out, examine our lives and correct our ways. To say that the calamity is merely a natural phenomenon and a chance occurrence is insensitive and cruel."[72]

Contemporary Lubavitchers are particularly sensitive on the subject of the Rebbe's views on the Holocaust and prefer to emphasize a radically different angle espoused by his successor, Rebbe Menachem Mendel Schneerson.[73] Rebbe Schneerson commented: "To say that those very people were deserving of what transpired, that it was a punishment for their sins, heaven forbid, is unthinkable. We cannot *explain* the Holocaust, for we are limited by the earthbound perspective of mortal understanding. As G-d says, in a prophecy of Isaiah, 'For My thoughts are not your thoughts.' No scales of judgment could ever condemn a people to such horrors." He went on to explain, "So awesome was the cruelty to which our people were subjected that Satan himself could not find sins to justify such suffering." Later he added, "To say that the Jews were punished for their sins with the Holocaust is a desecration of God's name."[74]

Ironically, the older Rebbe's view of the Holocaust turns men like Hitler into instruments of divine will. His newspaper explained in July 1941 that American Jews should realize that God ruled the world and caused all events and that they were wrong to think that only "an energetic effort on the part of the democracies can and will annihilate" Hitler. The Rebbe believed that, as the Talmud says, "God sets up a wicked ruler like Haman so that he shall make His people return to the good way." Hitler was sent as "a plague of God, in order to cause the Jews to return to the Good, and the only salvation for the Jews is to repent of their sins."[75] This view of Hitler and God is troubling for most people, needless to say.

The Rebbe's desire to rebuild his community, notes historian Michael Berenbaum, "in and of itself was a response to the destruction of European Jewry." The Rebbe believed that "the survival of the Jewish people depends on the Torah." On many occasions between 1941 and 1943, he pleaded with the Orthodox community for funds to build a central yeshiva, the Tomchei Temimim. He chastised his followers for not contributing enough to Chabad schools generally, admonishing them to "support these Yeshivahs more generously and thereby free yourselves from the shame of not paying the rightful dues which the Torah expects a Jew to honor." A central Lubavitcher yeshiva would cure many of the sicknesses that had befallen the Jews and would save Jewry from "religious annihilation." [76]

The Rebbe also rigorously defended the right to freedom of religious expression. He appealed to his followers to help Jews under the Soviets who were prevented from practicing their religion, and he attacked secular Jewish leaders in Israel for not providing a religious education for the orphaned children of Orthodox victims of the Holocaust. Such neglect was a "shameless effrontery"; teachers had "set up an 'apostasy corner' for the children entrusted in their care." [77] His language was aggressive: "In German-occupied territories Hitler set up lime-kilns in order to torture and cremate Jewish bodies; in [Israel] a certain group has set up houses of apostasy in order to torture and cremate Jewish souls. . . . These people are teaching the children to desecrate the *Shabbos,* to eat *treifah* [nonkosher] food, to eat on *Yom Kippur,* to eat *chametz* [leavened products forbidden on Passover]. They do not even allow them to say *Kaddish* [the prayer for the dead] in memory of their parents who lost their lives in sanctification of the Divine Name, and they teach them to scoff at the notion of G-d and Jewish religious observance." He asked American Jewish leaders to help in the campaign against the secular education of these children, saying that, although they had failed to rescue the Jews under Hitler, now it was time to "rescue their orphans from apostasy." Withholding a religious education was "a despicable moral violation" that had to be "utterly uprooted from the Jewish people." For the Rebbe, not following God's laws was the worst sin one could commit, and he devoted his life to making Jews observant, according to his definition.[78]

During the ten years from his rescue in 1940 until his death, in 1950, the Rebbe energetically built up the Lubavitch community in the United States from his home at 770 Eastern Parkway in Brooklyn, New York, now the headquarters of Chabad. He founded several schools for boys and girls, summer camps, and a publishing house. In 1945, after the war, he set up his Refugee Relief and Rehabilitation Organization in Paris, which helped secular and religious people in DP camps get food and eventually immigrate to Israel. He apparently stopped talking about the Holocaust as punishment for the sins of the Jews and focused strictly on his spiritual mission and the coming of the Messiah. In 1949, he became a U.S. citizen, saying on that occasion, "I recall with gratitude the humanitarian act of the American Government in those critical days in 1940, when it intervened to help rescue me from Hitler's clutches and bring me to these American shores." The Rebbe never publicly described the details of his escape. It does not appear even in his private memoirs. As one Lubavitcher explained: "It was God's work. It was a miracle. It did not need to be discussed unless the Rebbe wanted it to be discussed." Most Lubavitchers believe the mechanics of the miracle are immaterial. It allowed the Rebbe to strengthen Chabad around the world, a movement he felt God ordained for all Jews, and that was all that mattered.[79]

When the Rebbe died, his followers, under the leadership of Menachem Mendel Schneerson, prepared him for burial as if he were an ancient high priest of Israel. Menachem declared that the Rebbe had been a prophet, the Moses of his generation, and even the Messiah. He believed he was able to commune with the Rebbe even in death. Several in the community were disappointed that the Rebbe's predictions of the Messiah throughout the 1940s had not come true, a "campaign" some have argued Menachem had initiated. Some

Rebbe Joseph Isaac Schneersohn's grave in Cambria Heights, New York.
His followers leave messages asking him to pray for them in heaven.
(Author's collection)

briefly claimed that, as the Messiah, he had not really died and that they should be patient for him to reveal himself. In the meantime, Menachem took over the position of Rebbe in 1951.[80]

Joseph Isaac Schneersohn's vision to make Chabad one of the most important organizations for Yiddishkeit in the world has largely been realized, thanks to the dedication and perseverance of both the Rebbe himself and his son-in-law. Chabad is the largest Hasidic sect globally, comprising approximately 200,000 committed adherents plus hundreds of thousands of Jews who attend Chabad schools, synagogues, and study groups. There are over 3,800 emissary couples in forty-five states and sixty-one foreign countries, and the movement has 2,766 institutions worldwide and an operating budget of close to one billion dollars a year. The Rebbe's view— strengthened, and greatly enlarged on, by his son-in-law, the seventh Rebbe, Menachem Schneerson—has motivated thousands of Lubavitchers to go out and set up communities. This is in essence Chabad's mission, and it has been highly successful.

In the summer of 1994, Rebbe Menachem Schneerson died without leaving an heir apparent, and Chabad suffered a crisis of leadership. Many in the community proclaimed that Rebbe Schneerson was the Messiah and that he would soon return from the dead to lead the Jews to Israel and establish God's earthly kingdom. Large signs went up on New York's George Washington Bridge, for example, declaring him the Messiah, as if to convince the rest of the world. This controversial belief split the community, and many people thought the movement might collapse. In fact, however, a decade has passed without a resurrection, and despite the crisis, the Lubavitch movement continues to grow. If Rebbe Joseph Isaac Schneersohn could see today what his movement and disciples have created, he would be proud. He would probably say God rescued him from Poland to make Chabad one of the most influential Hasidic groups ever and to build a strong house of Torah in America.[81]

FIFTEEN

The Fates of the Rescuers

If the Rebbe never alluded to his rescue, neither did Bloch. Indeed, since he was in the secret service, he had been trained never to discuss his duties, even with his wife.[1] Had he survived the war, Bloch might have been more open. After rescuing Schneersohn, he returned to his industrial espionage work and, later in 1940, was promoted to lieutenant colonel.[2] He commanded over forty officers and staff members and dined on occasion with industrialists such as Gustav Krupp von Bohlen and Max Schlenker. He enjoyed the confidence of the executives of important German firms, including I. G. Farben, and provided the military with information on the industrial capabilities of various countries, as these companies helped him place spies abroad. His job brought him into regular contact with both Canaris and Wohlthat. Early in 1941, he attempted to assess the industrial capacities of the British Empire, the United States, and the Soviet Union—no small task. For his accomplishments in the Abwehr, he was awarded the War Merit Cross Second and First Class with Swords.[3]

Bloch was so highly skilled and respected that Field Marshal von

Ernst Bloch (far right) on the Russian front, 1943 (Author's collection)

Reichenau asked in 1941 to have him join his staff to advise the Army Group South in economic matters, but the request was denied.[4] That a staunch Nazi like Reichenau would have chosen a half Jew for such a critical job seems incredible. Obviously, he knew Bloch's work and valued his expertise.

Bloch served in the Abwehr until his petition to be sent to the Russian front as a battalion commander was granted in April 1943 and he was posted to the area around Kiev.[5] The army had categorically denied Bloch's earlier requests for a combat command because of age. His personnel file states no reason for the official change in April, but several Abwehr officers went to the front at the time. And one can assume that in the spring of 1943, as the Wehrmacht prepared for the battle of Kursk, one of the greatest battles of the war, it needed his experience more as a combat officer than as an economic spy. Also in April 1943, the Gestapo began investigating the Abwehr for antigovernment activities and arrested several of its members. Canaris himself came under suspicion, and his secret service ceased to function effectively. One of the crimes it had committed was the smuggling of Jewish refugees out of Germany. Perhaps Bloch drew the right conclusions, if he indeed knew about the charges, and tried to get away from a situation that could turn dangerous for him.[6]

During the battle of Kursk, Bloch commanded troops in the rear, keeping the lines of communication and supply open for the soldiers at the front. After the disastrous defeat at Stalingrad during the winter of 1942–43, Hitler had focused on a new offensive at Kursk. He hoped to regain the initiative and turn the tide of war. By 5 July 1943, the day the battle began, the Germans had deployed 2,700 tanks, 2,500 planes, and almost a million men against Kursk. The Russians fought them with 3,300 tanks, 2,650 planes, and almost one and a half million men. The engagement was the biggest clash of armor to date.[7] Eleven days later, on 16 July, unable despite vicious fighting to penetrate the layers of defensive works and minefields around Kursk, Hitler ordered a withdrawal.

One may wonder why Bloch left the Abwehr to take part in such horrible battles, but Bloch and many other German officers would not have found the move strange. Bloch's son and his secretaries contend that he left because his only opportunity for promotion lay on the front, where he felt he belonged.[8] Moreover, in 1943, Germany's recently expanded borders began to shrink, limiting the need for industrial espionage. Bloch apparently preferred life on the front to life in the office. One of his former subordinates wrote Bloch in September 1943: "I am happy to hear from you, Herr Lt. Colonel, that things are going well with you and can imagine that life out there is more satisfying for you than the desk work that goes on here. We I-Wi [International Economic Intelligence] people . . . often think of our former father [boss]."[9]

In November 1943, his regimental commander wrote that Bloch had quickly adjusted to life on the front. He had already been awarded the Iron Cross Second Class in October, and by December the general of the division noted that Bloch was ready to command a regiment.[10] He was well on his way to becoming an accomplished leader of men in battle.

As life under the Nazis became more difficult for Jews and Mischlinge, Canaris tried to protect Bloch by stating in his files in 1943 that Bloch was "positive about Nazism." Canaris did all he could to shield his subordinates from potentially harmful Nazi officials. In 1944, Bloch's superiors described him as a "National Socialist"; a censor, however, wrote a question mark next to this description. One of Bloch's secretaries had reported that he detested Hitler and told jokes about him.[11] Bloch never belonged to the party, and both his son and his secretary claim he detested the Nazi regime, although he served the army loyally. No conclusive evidence exists to show whether Bloch became a "positive Nazi" only on the surface to protect himself or whether he truly believed in National Socialism. Most likely, his commanders described him that way without his knowledge to shield him.

After Kursk, Bloch was given command of a regiment of the 213th Security Division with over three thousand soldiers fighting on the Russian front.[12] Frau Rotraut Nonnemann wrote to Bloch's wife on 19 July 1944 to congratulate her on his promotion: "I have heard from some old I-Wi comrades that your husband finally received a regiment. I am terribly happy for him and hope that he has enough time to familiarize himself with his new task before the Russians are inside our region." A family friend told Frau Bloch that he hoped that she had good news from her husband because "he must be having a hell of a time fighting the Russians."[13] The war was lost for all intents and purposes, and many soldiers fighting for Germany knew it. But most, including Bloch, fought on. For exemplary service, the army promoted Bloch to colonel on 1 June 1944. By 1945, Bloch's regiment had been decimated, with only a handful of men still alive, and the Russians were closing in on Germany's heartland. By then, Bloch was no longer in the army.[14]

On 2 January 1944, Hitler ordered one of his generals to put to-gether a list of active Mischling army officers and officers married to Jews or to Mischlinge who had received Hitler's *Deutschblütigkeitser-klärung* (German blood declaration).[15] Bloch was one of the seventy-seven officers on the list. After the 20 July 1944 bomb plot failed to kill Hitler, he and many of his cronies declared Mischlinge, among others, guilty.[16] Hitler no longer deemed Mischlinge worthy of living in the Reich and earmarked them for extermination. Bloch was possibly closer to death than he realized.

Martin Bormann, Hitler's right-hand man wrote on 2 November 1944 that the "event of 20 July has shown the necessity to remove all people in positions of authority who, owing to their ancestry, could be seen as a liability to the National Socialist ideology and its Welt-anschauung." Even Mischlinge declared as *deutschblütig,* Bormann believed, should be deprived of the rights of Aryans. During the war's final days, Hitler discharged several dozen battle-tested offi-cers despite their prior Aryanization.[17] The release of these officers was counterproductive at a time when Hitler needed every experi-enced soldier available.

The SS helped hunt down Mischlinge the Wehrmacht could not immediately locate, including Bloch. In September 1944, Heinrich Himmler, the Reichsführer of the SS, requested Bloch's discharge because of his Jewish ancestry even though Bloch's commander had described him on 1 March 1944 as a "National Socialist . . . who has shown himself brave in the face of the enemy." Despite such positive reports, on 15 September 1944, Obersturmbannführer Suchanek in Himmler's office wrote General Burgdorf in the Army Personnel Office requesting Bloch's dismissal and immediate deportation to a forced-labor camp.[18] On 26 September, Burgdorf confirmed that Bloch had been dismissed but noted that Bloch had previously re-ceived Hitler's "German blood" declaration and that he had asked to be "sent to the front despite his several wounds from the first World War." In spite of Burgdorf's halfhearted protest, the army relieved

Bloch of his command in October 1944. It was only on 15 February 1945, however, that Burgdorf signed an order discharging him.[19] The document read as follows: "The Führer has decided as of 31 January 1945 to discharge you from active duty. It is an honor to thank you on behalf of the Führer for your service rendered during war and peace for our people and fatherland. I wish you all the best in the future. Heil Hitler."[20]

Bloch was stunned. When ordered to leave his regiment, though, he most likely obeyed without question. Walther Brockhoff, a close friend of Bloch's, wrote to Bloch's wife on 31 October 1945 to ask why his friend had been discharged, because he still could not think of any logical reason: "One does not dismiss a brave and battle-tested officer from the front in the hour of greatest danger. There have been and will be few officers of his caliber."[21]

Returning home as a retired officer, Bloch talked to various bankers and industrialists about possible employment after the war.[22] But a few months later the Volkssturm, a paramilitary organization for civilian fighters formed toward the end of the war, drafted Bloch into its ranks. He was probably lucky to have been forced from his regiment, as its death toll was high. Bloch wrote to his wife on 10 April 1945: "Unfortunately our whole regiment is decimated. Almost all the officers are dead, wounded, or missing. . . . However, the regiment has fought bravely to the bitter end, holding its ranks excellently."[23]

It seems that in the Volkssturm Bloch trained men, then fought next to them against the Russians. The last time he saw his family was at the christening of his fourth child, Maria, on 14 January 1945. That day, he felt demoralized and worried about his future. He knew the Russians were approaching Berlin, so he arranged for his family to leave for the West, to be captured by the Americans, while he stayed in Berlin and helped defend the city. He did not think he would live to return to his family.

In late April 1945, the Russians closed in on the German capital.

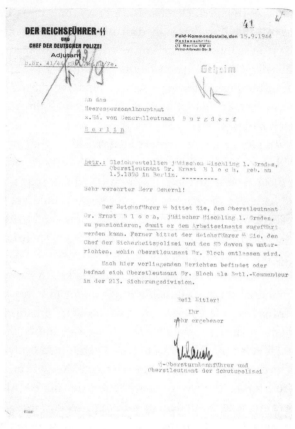

On 15 September 1944, Obersturmbannführer Suchanek in Himmler's office wrote General Burgdorf in the Army Personnel Office requesting Bloch's dismissal and immediate deportation to a forced-labor camp (Bundesarchiv/Militärarchiv)

Just a couple of weeks earlier, a comrade from Bloch's regiment in Russia, a Captain Pfeiffer, had written him an emotional letter describing the sad state of the troops facing the war's imminent end: "We have become poor and insignificant. Now it is our responsibility to clean up everything that this short-sighted government has destroyed."[24] Bloch continued to fight just outside of Berlin. After repelling several Russian attacks, he reportedly led a counterattack against Soviet lines, throwing grenades into their midst and firing his submachine gun as he advanced. A mortar shell, landing right behind him, ended his life when a piece of shrapnel blew a hole in his neck.[25] It was 30 April 1945—one day before his forty-seventh birthday and just over a week before the war would end with Germany's final defeat.

After the war, a childhood friend of Bloch's, Karl Pries, honored Sabine Bloch's wish that he find her husband's body or grave so she could obtain a pension to support her four children. He reported the results of his search in a letter on 24 October 1946: "My dear Sabine, . . . We have finally been able to find Bloch's body. . . . I believe that we can be certain that this corpse is Bloch's because of its obvious features. The corpse . . . is in unbelievably good condition. One can still see the scar on his mouth. The lower and upper jaw showed the horrible wound inflicted on his teeth with their gold crowns. The color of the hair was most definitely that of Bloch's. . . . Bloch had a large wound in the neck that certainly killed him instantly. The face was for all intents and purposes very peaceful, without any signs of trepidation, and his mouth was closed. As a result, it is my opinion that Ernst had a fast and beautiful soldier's death that many would have envied."[26] Now Frau Bloch had the evidence required to receive a widow's pension and thus had a source of income. Some of Bloch's children were upset with their father for staying in the Volkssturm when he could have escaped death with them. His actions do indeed seem strange, but, trained as an officer in the Prussian tradition, he evidently regarded his duty to his country as his highest calling. Like Canaris, he lived in a schizophrenic world, condemning Hitler and his regime but, because of his upbringing and training, serving his commander in chief and his country loyally even until death.

Canaris, unlike Bloch, continued his Abwehr activities, collecting intelligence for the Wehrmacht but also pursuing his goal of persuading high-ranking officers to oppose Hitler. His department became a haven for several men who were plotting to kill Hitler. One of them, Hans Oster, despised Hitler and the Nazi elite for their "lying demagogy" and "moral corruption." Other men in Canaris's Abwehr, like Bloch, continued to rescue Jews.

Besides the dozen and a half Jews Bloch rescued from Warsaw in 1939, Canaris's Abwehr also helped several hundred others escape the Third Reich.[27] Canaris did his best to uphold the honor of the Wehrmacht while often ordering sabotage measures against Hitler's orders. The Nazis arrested a number of Canaris's men, including Oster, in 1943 and placed Canaris himself under surveillance. In February 1944, he was dismissed from his post, and the SS eventually took over the Abwehr. Canaris was given an unimportant job with the Special Staff for Mercantile Warfare and Economic Combat Measures, where the Gestapo kept a close watch on him. After the attempt on Hitler's life in July 1944, the Nazis arrested him, although they could not prove he had any direct involvement in the bomb attack that almost killed Hitler.[28] After months of interrogations and imprisonment in the Flossenbürg concentration camp, he was convicted of treason and sentenced to death. On 9 April 1945, the SS hangmen went to his cell, stripped him naked, marched him to the gallows, and hanged him. His corpse was placed on a woodpile in the camp and incinerated.[29]

Conclusion

All too often the history of Nazi Germany is depicted as a morality play, a story of good and evil, victims and perpetrators. Such a dichotomous view fails, however, to account for the complexity of the Third Reich, not to mention that of human motivation and behavior.

On one side of the polarized view of the Rebbe's rescue stand the altruistic American liberators of oppressed Europe. Our American heroes were nevertheless reluctant to act until personally pressured. American officials failed to respond not only to thousands of desperate pleas from European Jews who wished to escape to the United States but also to Germany's own request at the Evian conference in 1938 that they be allowed to emigrate.[1] It took extremely influential politicians, including Secretary of State Cordell Hull and the assistant chief of the State Department's European Affairs Division, Robert T. Pell, together with Postmaster General James A. Farley, Justice Louis Brandeis, Senator Robert Wagner, Attorney General Benjamin Cohen, and several others, to steer Rebbe Schneersohn's case through the bureaucratic Bermuda Triangle. Without such a powerful and persistent lobby in Washington, what chance would the average European Jew have had to reach America? Even Jews in the U.S. government did not do enough for those suffering under Hitler. Most of the Jews close to Roosevelt, according to historian David Wyman, "did very little to encourage rescue action." The efforts of Brandeis, Cohen, and Philip Kleinfeld were unusual. Other American Jewish leaders in government, says Saul Friedman in his study of U.S. policy toward Jewish refugees, "opted for mendicancy rather than leadership. . . . Insecure themselves, constantly wary of raising the spectre of double-loyalty which was the grist of anti-Semites, these persons overexerted themselves to display their Americanism, their concern for this nation's welfare to the exclusion of all others, even when doing so meant the deaths of loved ones in Europe."[2] Although Roosevelt was subject to political pressure, American Jews were uncertain what they wanted him to do. The antisemitic Breckinridge Long, who as head of immigration committed himself to halting refugees to America, wrote in his diary in 1944: "The Jewish organizations are all divided amid controversies. . . . There is no cohesion or any sympathetic collaboration — rather rivalry, jealousy and antagonism." Many Jewish organizations, moreover, were, as Henry L. Feingold observes, "traumatized by domestic anti-Semitism and reluctant to accept responsibility for [their] European brethren."[3]

Although the Jewish community did not in fact unite to push through policy, many in Roosevelt's government wanted to prevent the perception that the president was controlled by Jews and doing their bidding.[4] Also, Roosevelt had to think of the labor unions, who were apt to see an influx of refugees as a threat to American jobs just as the United States was emerging from the Depression. Even if that fear may have been driven by antisemitism and not by any real threat to the job market, Roosevelt had to take the support of the unions seriously. It is also true that most Americans simply did not want the immigration quotas eased.[5]

Antisemitism seems, in large part, to have been behind Americans' desire to limit immigration. Steven Early, Roosevelt's press secretary, wrote the president in July 1941: "A very grave problem, apparently being entirely ignored, is the quiet and persistent growth of anti-Jewish feeling in our larger centers. I see it and sense it here there and elsewhere, where the plain folks are beginning to resent the pro-Jewish attitude at Washington and also locally. The great and mysterious influx of Jewish refugees, most of whom seem to have ample funds and immediately go into business. The great number of the Jewish faith placed in high position where their own lack of tolerance is immediately paraded to the masses. . . . Pray God we never have religious outrages here but it seems to me that official Washington would do well to recognize this growth, and by care and tact, calm it down."[6] Roosevelt was walking a delicate tightrope, wanting to help some Jews under Hitler but wanting also to prevent damaging criticism of his administration. Luckily for the Rebbe, he was one of those the Roosevelt administration decided to help.

For the record, Roosevelt hated antisemitism; according to Rabbi Stephen Wise, the prominent Jewish leader, Roosevelt was "genuinely free from religious prejudice and racial bigotry."[7] Certainly he had many other matters to attend to in 1939 and 1940. But none of them justifies his inaction. In 1943, Secretary of the Treasury Henry Morgenthau complained: "When you get through with it, the attitude to date is no different from Hitler's attitude."[8] To prevent the deaths of millions of Jews was not a priority in Roosevelt's government, especially after the December 1941 attack on Pearl Harbor, when the United States was thrust into global conflict. At that point, most government leaders simply focused on winning the war.

Even after receiving convincing evidence in 1942 that the Nazis were systematically killing Jews by the hundreds of thousands, Roosevelt could offer Wise only hollow words: "We shall do all in our power to be of service to your people in this tragic moment."[9] Roosevelt would not exert the necessary effort to force the immigration authorities to help the oppressed seeking refuge; moreover, he would not pursue the diplomatic and military options necessary to prevent or at least slow the killing of Jews under Hitler. In David Wyman's judgment, "Roosevelt's indifference to so momentous a historical event as the systematic annihilation of European Jewry emerges as the worst failure of his presidency." Unless a particular person like the Rebbe was brought to his attention by influential people, Roosevelt felt the best way to help Jews under Hitler was to defeat Germany as soon as possible. The nameless millions were ignored. Although "well aware of the catastrophic situation," according to Wyman, he seemed indifferent to their fate.[10]

Maybe Roosevelt and those in the State Department felt the Jews were trying to gain preferential treatment over the Russians, Poles, Slavs, Jehovah's Witnesses, and others who were also dying. After the war President Harry S. Truman, although a big supporter of the state of Israel, expressed what may have been a common attitude among American politicians: "The Jews, I find[,] are very, very selfish. They care not how many Estonians, Latvians, Finns, Poles, Yugoslavs or Greeks get murdered or mistreated as DP [displaced persons] as long as the Jews get special treatment. Yet when they have power, physical, financial or political[,] neither Hitler nor Stalin has anything on them for cruelty or mistreatment to the under dog."[11] Truman's statement makes clear why more American politicians did not take action to help the Jews suffering and dying under Hitler.

Many condemn Jewish leaders for not fighting harder against Roosevelt's apparent indifference. Elie Wiesel says, "They should have shaken heaven and earth, echoing the agony of their doomed brethren; taken in by Roosevelt's personality, they, in a way, became accomplices to his inaction."[12] A number of Jewish leaders, including the Rebbe, made mistakes in their dealings with the government on rescue issues. "Orthodox leaders and even prominent and learned rabbis, are capable of making serious, and in some cases fatal mistakes," observes historian Ephraim Zuroff. "Any attempt to portray the *gedolim* [great Jewish leaders] as perfect human beings, incapable of error, is not only inaccurate but an affront to our intelligence and an insult to the memory of those whose lives were not saved during those terrible times."[13] But why didn't the Jews pressure Roosevelt more?

American Jews greatly admired Roosevelt, some comparing him "to their great biblical heroes, Abraham, Moses, Isaiah . . . because of his concern for the common man and the poor, his optimism for the future, his hatred of all forms of exploitation, and his ever-insisting pleas for education, secular and religious, [which] indicated his conviction that democracy and humanitarianism could not function without knowledge, as well as his faith."[14] A few leaders, like Kalmanowitz and Kotler of the Vaad, and Peter Bergson, head of the Emergency Committee to Save the Jewish People of Europe, saw the urgency of the situation. Although immigrants and without significant financial resources, they got the U.S. government to move at its highest levels and helped save thousands of lives. Henry Morgenthau, the only Jew in Roosevelt's cabinet, is also a notable example, as he compiled convincing information on Breckinridge Long's crimes, confronted the president, and helped bring about the War Refugee Board (WRB) in 1944. The WRB, according to David Wyman, saved between 100,000 and 200,000 lives.[15] Unfortunately, such men were rare.

Often a lack of imagination and aggressiveness, as well as unwillingness to go against Roosevelt, prevented Jewish leaders from meeting the situation head-on. Most of them knew things were bad for the Jews under Hitler, but many could not fathom just how bad. Roosevelt could possibly have been prodded into action had they threatened him with political retaliation, which they seem not to have attempted.[16] Even Morgenthau, Kalmanowitz, Kotler, and other Vaad leaders missed opportunities to rescue people. Certainly many Jewish leaders failed to take the most radical forms of action to help mitigate or prevent the crimes being committed.

Only in late 1943, when the true scope of the Holocaust dawned on Morgenthau and the Vaad leadership, did they aggressively pursue the rescue of Jews under Hitler.[17] Yet even Kalmanowitz, who was ardent in his commitment to rescue, wrote Assistant Secretary of State Adolf A. Berle in August 1944 to send prayer books and Bibles to the Jews in the USSR when the requisite funds could have been used for lifesaving efforts.[18] For Rebbe Schneersohn, taking care of the soul was just as important as, if not more important than, saving the body, and his emphasis on learning and penance meant a failure to take many of the actions needed to save lives under Hitler. Even when there was much available information, people had a difficult time understanding that Hitler was using gas chambers to slaughter millions.

The motives of the politicians whose support was essential for the approval of the Rebbe's visa and for his rescue bear examining in the light of this history of inaction. Max Rhoade, who lobbied successfully for the Lubavitchers, explained his strategy for manipulating those politicians: "In dealing with government officials here in Washington, it is particularly important to handle the individual in accordance with his personal psychology. . . . I might add that everything here in Washington, contrary to public impression, is not done on the basis of 'getting friendly.' There are peculiar types of bureaucratic officials who are absolutely rigid, and it would ruin a matter not to harmonize with their own personalities. That is a large part of the technique of getting favorable action in Washington. You must first of all know something about your man and size him up properly. With some, the 'friendly basis' is the 'ticket,' with others, it is poison. It might be just right to use political influence with one individual and suicide to use it with another, and so on."[19] Rhoade constantly emphasized the Rebbe's significance to Jews all over the world and compared him to the pope in order to convince American officials that their intervention would benefit them on many levels. They could proudly illustrate their contribution to world Jewry, prove their humanitarian concern for the European Jews under Hitler, and gain the support of a large group of voting Lubavitchers. Even Rhoade did not let his sincere belief in the necessity of saving the Rebbe completely distract him from his financial interests.

While high-ranking American officials did not take the necessary action to help those who could have been saved, many rose to the occasion when approached about rescuing the Rebbe. Hull's intervention is remarkable since, according to Wyman, he "paid almost no attention to his department's policies concerning the destruction of the Jews."[20] Far from being interested because his wife was of Jewish descent, Hull worried that people would find out about her background and that, as Michael Beschloss writes, it "would cause controversy and keep him from the Presidential nomination he so passionately desired."[21] Nonetheless, Hull took positive action on behalf of the Rebbe in 1939 and 1940, and the Jewish leader knew it, writing to him on 25 March 1940: "We feel deeply grateful to you for your kind help in the issuance of our emigration visas to the United States, and our heartfelt thanks to you for your kindness. Blessed is this country with its famous and beloved leader President Roosevelt, the greatest and most outstanding figure of our age, famed for his humane feelings and love of peace, and its equally famous and great Secretary of State. May the Almighty bless you and grant you long life, good health and every success in your work for this country and humanity as a whole."[22] But the "famous and great" Hull acted under pressure.

Ironically, Hull summed up perfectly the verdict on America's inaction when he said at an October 1939 meeting of the Inter-Governmental Committee on Political Refugees, "I think it would be most unfortunate if future historians should be called upon to say that civilized man confessed his inability to cope with this harrowing problem and let the undertaking die at its most critical period."[23] The "inability to cope" was the very excuse used by many in the government. According to the Rescue Commission of the American Jewish Conference, "the number [of refugees with visas] amounted to about 5.9 percent of those who could have been admitted if one considered the entire quota rather than the effective one" from 1933 to 1944. What was needed was a commitment to save lives, and that commitment was absent.[24]

Sadly, America's inaction confirmed to some Nazi officials the apathy with which the Western powers observed the persecution of Jews. The lack of international response during the Evian conference and of diplomatic pressure after Kristallnacht in 1938 further demonstrated this indifference. Hitler said on 30 January 1939, "It is a shameful example to observe today how the entire democratic world dissolves in tears of pity, but then, in spite of its obvious duty to help, closes" its heart "to the poor, tortured people."[25] The failure to rescue those on the refugee ship *St. Louis* in May 1939 further evidenced the world's uncaring attitude. The Nazi paper *Der Weltkampf* wrote in August 1939, "We are saying openly that we do not want the Jews, while the democracies keep on claiming that they are willing to receive them—and then leave the guests out in the cold! Aren't we savages better men after all?"[26]

Hitler's and *Der Weltkampf*'s statements had elements of truth. The inaction of the Allies, writes Henry L. Feingold, "allowed the Nazi regime to claim that the world at large shared their revulsion to Jews as well as guilt in their death."[27] One can only speculate whether the Nazi regime would have altered its extermination plans if international pressure had been applied as early as 1939. One thing is certain: had the United States simply altered its immigration policies starting in 1938 or 1939, hundreds of thousands of Jews would have been saved by 1941. In fairness to America's leaders, most could not imagine that the alternative to not letting these refugees in would be genocide. Moreover, the United States did not have a legal obligation to these people, and most governments are amoral by definition.[28]

On the other side of the two-dimensional view stand the villainous Germans. Although the fiction that all German citizens were equally evil may have held up at a great distance, any closer interaction with German society would have shattered the illusion. Even Hitler drew a distinction between the role of the army and that of his elite SS troops. In August 1939, he informed Himmler: "Poland will be wiped off the map of nations. What will happen behind the Wehrmacht front may not meet with the approbation of the generals. The army is not to take part in the elimination of the Polish cadres and the Jews. This will be the task of the SS."[29] If Hitler did not expect all the high-ranking officers in the German military to support extermination of the Jews, why should we assume they did? Yet even if we don't, the fact that Helmut Wohlthat, chief administrator of Göring's Four Year Plan; Wilhelm Canaris, head of the Abwehr; Bloch; and others in the Wehrmacht risked their careers and lives to get a group of ultra-Orthodox Jews out of Poland, through Germany, and on to Latvia under the Gestapo's nose can only be seen as astonishing.

Wohlthat had expressed to Robert Pell after the Evian conference his willingness to intercede for particularly important Jews; saving the Rebbe suited his personal ideology and offered an opportunity to foster goodwill in Washington. Given the international climate of hostility, any goodwill toward Germany was welcomed. It was clear that the German Foreign Office was keenly interested in Roosevelt's opinions on Nazi policies and that Wohlthat was an important player in helping maintain good relations with the United States. Germany was not at war with the United States yet and still hoped to convince Britain to ignore its actions in Poland and to join it as an ally. Germany was also promoting a program of Jewish emigration at this stage, and the Rebbe and his group leaving Europe fit into this strategy. Canaris, too, had voiced reservations about Hitler's regime to Wohlthat and others long before he pursued a course of protest against the regime and before the Rebbe's case landed on his desk. He had used his office to protect several half-Jewish officers, including Bloch, and promoted them according to their abilities despite racial policies. Bloch simply followed his orders, which in the Abwehr might often have required him to do unusual things. Or did he? Thoughts of his Jewish father and other Jewish relatives might have made the order to save Rebbe Schneersohn and his followers a pleasure to carry out. Perhaps such thoughts made him refuse to give up when locating the Rebbe proved difficult. Bloch's secretary claimed that he later helped two Jewish families escape to Switzerland.[30]

Bloch does not fit neatly into the category of either hero or villain, victim or perpetrator. His motivation both for serving in the army and for helping the Rebbe bring into sharp relief the complicated and often conflicting loyalties felt by most Germans in the 1930s and 1940s. Why did Bloch want to serve Hitler's state? Bloch was a career soldier, wounded and decorated in World War I, and he found in the army his beloved calling.[31] Bloch wore the German uniform, swore an oath to Hitler and Germany, gathered valuable data on enemy countries for the Nazi war machine, and fought on the Russian front against one of Germany's archenemies. He saw Germany and the Nazi state as distinct entities; he could serve Germany without serving Hitler. Only this explanation can account for why he volunteered in 1943 for the Russian front and later fought and died in the Volkssturm when he could have escaped with his family to the West. Although perhaps self-delusional, Bloch felt bound by his oath to his nation to remain loyal to his comrades.[32]

Had Bloch known about the genocide, would he have continued to fight? As a high-ranking Abwehr and combat officer, he must have known more than the average soldier.[33] Moreover, he knew enough to help Jews escape from the Nazis. But if Bloch saw firsthand evidence of what we today call the Holocaust, he probably did not understand the full meaning of what he witnessed. He had to concentrate on surviving, and the systematic extermination of the entire Jewish population of Europe would have been unbelievable from his point of view. The paradox that Bloch fought for a regime that not only exterminated people like his father but would have eventually annihilated him and, at best, relegated his children to second-class citizenship or subjected them to sterilization is tragic in itself.[34]

Bloch was not alone. Tens of thousands of Mischlinge fought in the Wehrmacht, and many of them did so as high-ranking officers, even as generals and admirals. They served because they were drafted or were career soldiers. Some volunteered in order to survive by hiding in uniform. Some enlisted because they wanted the adventure and glory of a military career; they trained for war, and when it came, they did their duty. Most were German patriots serving their country.

Bloch was a creature of war, and his late volunteerism for a combat command, in spite of his being persecuted, attests to this fact. He knew how to save others but ultimately did not know how to save himself. The real question is whether Bloch was unable or unwilling to save himself by escaping to the West. He certainly knew the fate that awaited the Rebbe and other Jews he helped if they stayed in German-occupied territory. He knew that Hitler was aware of his Jewish past. But did he know what was ultimately going to happen to him? The answer is buried on the battlefield where Bloch gave his life defending his country. He took his paradox to the grave.

The rescue of Schneersohn represents the complexity of life in Germany, not just a curious anomaly. It suggests that American officials might have been able to rescue even more Jews, but it also reveals the enormous difficulties involved in such efforts. Yet it also shows that many Jewish leaders in the United States, even knowledgeable ones, lacked the urgency to push the government harder to help those Jews still stranded in Europe—Jews who with American help and the easing of immigration restrictions would have also been rescued from Hitler's hell. The story of Bloch and the Rebbe shows some of the moral complexity of the war.

Today what could or should have been done seems obvious.

"Nothing is easier than to apportion praise and blame, writing many years after the events," historian Walter Laqueur has observed. "It is very easy to claim that everyone should have known what would happen once Fascism came to power. But such an approach is ahistorical. . . . [F]ew come out of the story unblemished. It was a story of failure to comprehend, among Jewish leaders and communities inside Europe and outside, a story of failure among non-Jews in high positions in neutral and Allied countries who did not care, or did not want to know or even suppressed the information."[35] The Rebbe's followers worked hard to put a name, a face, a great reputation, and a large following in front of powerful politicians. Although they might ignore the faceless masses, leaving a revered leader in Hitler's clutches was unthinkable. Thus they worked tirelessly to rescue the Rebbe, while unnamed and ordinary Jews under Hitler were left to suffer and die.

The Talmud says, "If you save a life you save the world." The remarkable rescue of the Lubavitcher Rebbe saved more than a dozen lives. All it took was letter writing, a few thousand dollars, and the courage to speak up.

"The past is the teacher of the present and the guide of the future."

Rebbe Joseph Isaac Schneersohn

In 1992, I began investigating the phenomenon of soldiers of Jewish descent who fought in the Wehrmacht; the result was published as *Hitler's Jewish Soldiers: The Untold Story of Nazi Racial Laws and Men of Jewish Descent in the German Military*. During my research, I came across the story of Ernst Bloch and the Rebbe, a story that seemed too fantastic to believe.

The short section on the rescue in Rolf Vogel's *Ein Stück von Uns* particularly sparked my interest. I examined documents in the National Archives in Washington, D.C., and in the Bundesarchiv/Militärarchiv in Freiburg, and I interviewed several members of Bloch's family in the United States, France, and Germany, including his son Martin, who gave me 250 pages of primary documents and almost 200 photos. In 1996, I received a copy of Winfried Meyer's *Unternehmen Sieben* from Martin, who directed my attention to the pages on which his father and the rescue were mentioned. Although Meyer devotes only a few pages to the rescue, his research proved most helpful. One of Bloch's secretaries, Ursula Cadenbach, in Hamburg, offered valuable background on Bloch's character. With her help, I located his subordinate Klaus Schenk. To examine Helmut Wohlthat's denazification file, I visited the Hauptstaatsarchiv in Düsseldorf. Shortly thereafter, I asked the Lubavitchers in Latvia for information about Mordechai Dubin, the Latvian diplomat who was a key informant about the Rebbe for U.S. officials. They led me to the Chabad headquarters in the United States.

Lubavitcher Rabbi Avraham Laber of Troy, New York, provided me with documents about the Lubavitcher community's interactions with lawyers and politicians in Washington and about its religious activities in 1939–40. From Gershon Jacobson, editor in chief of the *Algemeiner's Journal* in New York City, I obtained information about Dubin. With the help of Rabbi Shalom Dovber Levine and Rabbi Leib Altein, I found additional documents in the Lubavitcher Library in Brooklyn. A number of Lubavitchers gave eyewitness accounts, in particular the Rebbe's grandson Barry Gourary and one of the Rebbe's students, Joseph Wineberg, who were both in Poland when Hitler invaded. I spent many hours discussing the rescue with Lubavitch historians Simon Jacobson, Yosef Jacobson, Avraham Laber, and Eliezer Zaklikovsky. In addition to being generous with their time, they also provided several documents about Chabad and the Rebbe. In 2003, I met Milton Kramer, the son of Hyman Kramer and the historian of the family, and Debby Kramer Neumark, the daughter of Sam Kramer. To learn more about the Lubavitchers' interaction with the Roosevelt administration as well as about U.S. policy toward refugees, I visited the Roosevelt Institute and Library in Hyde Park, New York. I also used the Agudah Archives of Orthodox Judaism and the Vaad collection at Yeshiva University, both in New York City.

Eliezer Zaklikovsky and Rachel Altein's *Out of the Inferno,* a compilation, without commentary, of documents and eyewitness accounts, was a wonderful resource, even if it does not tell the story in full. Historians and journalists, too, have touched on the rescue of Rebbe Schneersohn from various angles, but to the best of my knowledge mine is the only historical study that synthesizes into a single account sources from the Lubavitchers and from German and

American archives, as well as oral and written testimonies. Much of the information in this book appears here for the first time.

The Lubavitchers and their documents were essential to researching the Rebbe's rescue. Although I respect the Lubavitchers, my experience with them was complex and sometimes frustrating, not unlike the experiences of Susan Fishkoff and Avrum Ehrlich.[1] Working with the Lubavitcher community on interpreting the documents is frustrating because they are an ahistorical group. Chabad Rabbi Manis Friedman says, "History is not an exact science and its interpretation of the events is not always correct. Charting the history of Judaism, which the Rebbe is part of, is very different than charting the history of the Jews. It is exploring the divine plan of humanity and this is very different than exploring history of people and countries." Lubavitcher Rabbi Heschel Greenberg explains, "Religious Jews look at history as a secondary matter to the primacy of belief. The Torah and Talmud come before history." Although one can respect these beliefs, the Lubavitchers' ahistorical approach to their movement reveals itself dramatically when the record detracts from the image of their organization or their Rebbe. When something might be construed as negative, they often say it is false, or an incorrect interpretation of the documents, or the explanation of those who hate them, or simply an indication of inadequate understanding of their movement. For many of them, to question the Rebbe is unthinkable. Moreover, when they do not like something in the documents about their group, they often censor the material or alter it. They have even been known, according to Avrum Ehrlich, to fabricate documents to prove a point or hide an unpleasant fact about their history.[2] One Lubavitch rabbi explains that finding their sources "is easier said than done since Lubavitch looks to the future much more than to the past. This is also why much of what you've learned by speaking to me (and others?) has been hard to document."[3] Moreover, as the historian David Myers observes, modern critical thought has challenged traditional Judaism by encouraging

Orthodox Jews to depart from the "tenets of inherited faith. The more one knew about the past, the more reasons there were for abandoning it."[4]

Even though some Lubavitchers could be difficult, there were many others who took time to speak with me, feed me, and read my manuscript. I am deeply thankful for all their help and kindness. Occasionally someone who thought I might end up saying something critical would withhold further help. Nevertheless, there were a few who embraced criticism and engaged in open debate, especially Rabbi Simon Jacobson and Rabbi Yosef Y. Jacobson, who explained: "Rebbe Menachem Mendel Schneerson said, 'Love Socrates, love Plato, love Aristotle, but above all else, love the truth.'" Yosef Jacobson believes the Rebbe wanted people to embrace controversy and explore every angle of an argument. He believes Chabad teaches that God prefers the ugly truth over beautiful lies.[5] Yet his voice and sentiment seem to be those of the minority.

Most Lubavitchers resist the task of documenting the past. "One can accomplish more with honey than with a stick," observes Rabbi David Edelman of the task of critical assessment.[6] Although his point is well taken, my job as a historian requires me to explore both the good and the bad about any historical event. Lubavitchers live in a sacred time, celebrating sacred events, and at least some of them believe they are living at the end of history. My work as a historian is to interpret documents and to tell the story they reveal. Some of my conclusions may be incompatible with the core of Lubavitcher beliefs. By its very nature, history situates a people in time; Lubavitch Hasidism wants to situate the Rebbe outside of time, in the belief that his teaching endures forever. As a historian, I want to see the Rebbe as a man of his time, and thus again we may clash. Lubavitchers are what they are—worthy of our respect and admiration, though not uncritically. And I am what I am—a scholar working in faithfulness to his task and his discipline, and perhaps worthy of their respect and admiration, though not uncritically.

CHAPTER ONE: THE INVASION

1. Bethell, *War Hitler Won*, 13, 140.

2. Höhne, *Canaris*, 338–39; Bethell, *War Hitler Won*, 2–3; Gutman, *Jews of Warsaw*, 3; Madej and Zaloga, *Polish Campaign*, 106–7; Gilbert, *Second World War*, 1; Brissaud, *Canaris*, 141.

3. Bethell, *War Hitler Won*, 2; Höhne, *Canaris*, 353.

4. Interview with Karin Falencki, BMRS. The story about the planes fighting above Warsaw is confirmed by other accounts as well. See Warfield and Warfield, *Call Us to Witness*, 25. See also Altein and Zaklikovsky, *Out of the Inferno*, 305; Gutman, *Jews of Warsaw*, 4; Bethell, *War Hitler Won*, 4.

5. Kershaw, *Nemesis*, 190, 200; Rossino, *Hitler Strikes Poland*, 5–7, 225; Manstein, *Lost Victories*, 24.

6. Kershaw, *Nemesis*, 190–200, 240; Rossino, *Hitler Strikes Poland*, 27; Mayer, *Why Did the Heavens*, 183.

7. Keegan, *Second World War*, 44–47; Churchill, *Gathering Storm*, 443–45; Bethell, *War Hitler Won*, 27–28; Cooper, *German Army*, 169–71.

8. Gutman, *Jews of Warsaw*, 4; Friedman, *No Haven*, 39, 43; Medoff and Wyman, *Race against Death*, 1; Bauer, *American Jewry*, 39. Even Roosevelt was somewhat prejudiced against Jews. See Morgan, *FDR*, 508–9; Goodwin, *No Ordinary Time*, 102; Wyman, *Abandonment of the Jews*, 6.

9. Friedman, *No Haven*, 174; Bauer, *American Jewry*, 39; Lipstadt, *Beyond Belief*, 92–93, 129; Wyman, *Paper Walls*, 10.

10. Burns, *Lion and the Fox*, 394; Kennedy, *Freedom from Fear*, 425; McJimsey, *Presidency of Franklin Delano Roosevelt*, 193–94, 203.

11. Kaplan, *Scroll of Agony*, 19.

12. Kershaw, *Nemesis*, 240–44; Rossino, *Hitler Strikes Poland*, 1. See also Gilbert, *Holocaust*, and Mayer, *Why Did the Heavens*.

13. Bauer, *History of the Holocaust*, 142–43; Bauer, *American Jewry*, 31, 67; interview with Karin Falencki, BMRS; Levin, *Holocaust*, 207. See also Bethell, *War Hitler Won*, 13.

14. Gilbert, *Holocaust*, 84; Brewster and Jennings, *Century*, 213; Benz, *Holocaust*, 61; Kershaw, *Nemesis*, 152–53; Gutman, *Jews of Warsaw*, 11; Johnson, *History of the Jews*, 492; Wyman, *Abandonment of the Jews*, 4, 19; Bethell, *War Hitler Won*, 13.

15. Kaplan, *Scroll of Agony*, 20–21, 28.

16. Hoffman, *Despite All Odds*, 15; Huberband, *Kiddusch Hashem*, 178; Levin, *Holocaust*, 150; Aschheim, *Brothers and Strangers*, 143–45, 150–51; Matthäus, "German *Judenpolitik*," 162–64; Maurer, *Ostjuden in Deutschland*, 26–28.

17. Aschheim, *Brothers and Strangers*, 3–5, 13–14, 152; Peter Noa file, 9, BMRS.

18. Rheins, "Verband nationaldeutscher Juden," 255; Aschheim, *Brothers and Strangers*, 15.

19. Levin, *Holocaust*, 149–50; Gilbert, *Holocaust*, 87–108; Mayer, *Why Did the Heavens*, 182; Sydnor, *Soldiers of Destruction*, 39–40.

20. Huberband, *Kiddush Hashem*, xii–xiii. The Torah means "instruction."

21. Brissaud, *Canaris*, 157; Sydnor, *Soldiers of Destruction*, 42–43.

22. Levin, *Holocaust*, 154–55; *Von Hassell Diaries*, 79; Below, *Als Hitlers Adjutant*, 72–73; Brissaud, *Canaris*, 157; Kershaw, *Nemesis*, 248.

23. Brissaud, *Canaris*, 157; Kershaw, *Nemesis*, 247.

24. Rossino, *Hitler Strikes Poland*, 62, 124–28, 203; Mayer, *Why Did the Heavens*, 181. Kershaw believes 4,000 ethnic Germans were killed. Accurate figures are yet to be determined (Kershaw, *Nemesis*, 241–42).

25. Bethell, *War Hitler Won*, 9–15, 61, 84, 101, 119–20, 123; Weinberg, *World at Arms*, 51, 65–66; Kaplan, *Scroll of Agony*, 23; Warfield and Warfield, *Call Us to Witness*, 27; interview with Karin Falencki, BMRS; Madej and Zaloga, *Polish Campaign*, 122; Craig, *Germany*, 716.

26. Kaplan, *Scroll of Agony*, 25; Bethell, *War Hitler Won*, 27, 169; Craig,

Germany, 716; House, *Combined Arms Warfare,* 113–14; Corum, *Roots of Blitzkrieg,* 203; Watts and Murray, "Military Innovation," 372. The Allies had a superior ratio of 1.2 to 1 in manpower and 3,000 tanks to the Germans' 2,200–2,800. Corum states that in 1940, the French Char B tank was probably the best in the world. Special thanks to Lieutenant Colonel Jeffrey Scott of American Military University for these sources.

27. Madej and Zaloga, *Polish Campaign,* 158; Brewster and Jennings, *Century,* 215.

28. See Rossino, *Hitler Strikes Poland;* Sydnor, *Soldiers of Destruction,* 37–40. "Aryan," as Raul Hilberg notes, "is not even a race designation. At best, it is a term for a linguistic-ethnic group" (Hilberg, *Destruction of the Jews,* 45n.6). The Nazis used the term to describe a people they believed were Germanic, blond, and blue-eyed.

CHAPTER TWO: THE LUBAVITCHERS AND THEIR REBBE

1. The traditionalists, the *Mitnagdim,* according to Rabbi Eli S. and Rabbi Zalman Posner, were responsible for giving the name of Hasidim to the followers of the Besht. Interview with Eli S., BMRS; Zalman to Rigg, 8 January 2004, Schneersohn folder 6, BMRS. On the name Besht, see Ehrlich, *Leadership,* 22; Johnson, *History of the Jews,* 295; *Likkutei Dibburim,* 1:71–72.

2. Ehrlich, *Leadership,* 21–26, 113–14; Fishkoff, *Rebbe's Army,* 17–18; Eliach, *Hasidic Tales,* xv–xvi; Robinson, *Essential Judaism,* 384–91; Hoffman, *Despite All Odds,* 15, 17; Dimont, *Jews, God, and History,* 244–45, 279–91; Johnson, *History of the Jews,* 260–63, 267–72, 295–97, Jacobs, *Jewish Religion,* 456; Ehrlich, *Messiah of Brooklyn,* 14–15. Special thanks to Rabbi Yosef Jacobson and Rabbi Simon Jacobson for information about the Besht and help with the phraseology.

3. Ehrlich, *Leadership,* p. 12, 73, 93, 113–17; Rabinowicz, *Hasidism,* 90; Loewenthal, *Communicating the Infinite,* 9; interview with Zaklikovsky, 4 June 2003; Hoffman, *Despite All Odds,* 18–19; *Likkutei Dibburim,* 2:104–7. *Tanya* means "It has been taught." Rebbe Joseph I. Schneersohn writes that "Chabad Chassidus, especially, is a Divine philosophy that opens the portals of wisdom and understanding, to know and recognize with intellectual comprehension 'Him Who spoke and the world came into being.' It indicates the path for every individual, according to his capabilities, to approach Holiness and to serve God with his heart and mind" (*On the Teachings,* 18).

4. Ehrlich, *Leadership*, 27–33, 46, 51, 87, 95, 100, 160–61, 202, 232, 239, 241; Laber to Rigg, 22 April 2001, Schneersohn folder 6, BMRS; interview with Bernhard Klein; interview with Avraham Laber; Hoffman, *Despite All Odds*, 20, 24; interview with David Kranzler, 23 January 2004; J. I. Schneersohn, *"Tzemach Tzedek,"* 3; Rabinowicz, *Hasidism*, 90; Wertheim, *Law and Custom*, 27; *Hasidism Reappraised; Likkutei Dibburim*, 1:x, 33, 35; *Tanya*, chs. 2, 10, 37. Lubavitch is not unique in the Hasidic world in believing that if the Messiah comes, it will be its Rebbe. Other Hasidic groups also believe this about their rebbes.

5. Quoted in Ehrlich, *Leadership*, 31.

6. *Likkutei Dibburim*, 4:21; 1:105, 116–17; 2:92.

7. Hoffman, *Despite All Odds*, 29. For Chabad's ancestor worship, see Ehrlich, *Leadership*, 106–11.

8. Rebbe Schneersohn is also called Maharyatz, the acronym for "Moreinu HaRav Rebbe Yosef Yitzchak," or Our Master, the Rabbi, Rebbe Yosef Yitzchak. He is also known as the Frierdiker Rebbe, or the Previous Rebbe, since he is the sixth Rebbe out of seven.

9. *Likkutei Dibburim*, 1:31, 91, 128, 194, 307; 2:48; Ehrlich, *Leadership*, 261–62.

10. Kaminetzky, *Days in Chabad*, 218; *Rebbes*, 16–17 (the quote has been changed slightly to reflect the original Hebrew); Ehrlich, *Leadership*, 108, 242. Arthur Green of Brandeis University points out that many of the stories about the Rebbe's childhood "are Hasidic legends, not historical accounts" (Green to Rigg, 27 July 2003, Schneersohn folder 6, BMRS). *The Rebbes* is written for a young audience and does not list sources so it too must be read skeptically. Nonetheless, it tells the story that most Lubavitchers accept.

11. Armstrong, *Battle for God*, 148; *Likkutei Dibburim*, 4:255; Ehrlich, *Leadership*, 244–45; S. D. Schneersohn, *Ahavas Yisrael*, 1–72.

12. *Likkutei Dibburim*, 4:244–55.

13. Interview with Zalman Posner, 3 May 2003; Metzger, *Heroic Struggle*, 189; interview with Manis Friedman, 4 March 2004; Zaklikovsky, *America*, 69.

14. *Sichot Kodesh*, 282.

15. *Likkutei Dibburim*, 1:179–80; *Challenge*, 49; Meyer, *Unternehmen Sieben*, 128; Zaklikovsky, *America*, 74.

16. *Challenge*, 49; Ehrlich, *Leadership*, 247–48.

17. *Challenge*, 50; Hoffman, *Despite All Odds*, 23–24, 31; *Rebbes*, 12; Meyer,

Unternehmen Sieben, 128; Hosking, *Russia*, 395; Zaklikovsky, *America*, 68; Ehrlich, *Leadership*, 252, 257.

18. News clipping attached to telegram from Riga to Secretary of State Hull, 18 March 1940, visa case files 1933–40, 811.111, Joseph Schneersohn, itinerary 705, General Records of Department of State, RG 59, NAR (hereafter file 811.111, Joseph Schneersohn, itinerary 705, GRDOS, RG 59, NAR); Metzger, *Heroic Struggle*, 144; Zaklikovsky, *America*, 68; Posner to Rigg, 8 January 2004, Schneersohn folder 6, BMRS; Ehrlich, *Leadership*, 248, 252; interview with David Kranzler, 24 January 2004. For information on the Yevsektzia, see *Jews and Jewish Life in Russia* and *Likkutei Dibburim*, 1:144. More than two million Jews immigrated to the United States from Russia, Romania, and the Austro-Hungarian Empire from 1881 to 1924.

19. Hoffman, *Despite All Odds*, 23; Metzger, *Heroic Struggle*, 307–8; Ehrlich, *Leadership*, 263–65; Solomon, *Educational Teachings*, 6.

20. Bauer, *American Jewry*, 31, 67; Gutman, *Jews of Warsaw*, xv.

21. Hoffman, *Despite All Odds*, 23; Ehrlich, *Leadership*, 254–58, 262; *Jews and Jewish Life in Russia;* according to David E. Fishman, "Judaism in the USSR, 1917–1930," 253–58, the Lubavitchers have censored some information about the criticism leveled at the Rebbe for using JDC funds principally for Lubavitchers.

22. Metzger, *Heroic Struggle*, 34, 35; Interview with Eli S., 31 December 2003; Zaklikovsky, *America*, 7, 10, 23; Ehrlich, *Leadership*, 262, 266. For information about the Rebbe's defense of his actions in Russia, see *Igrois Koidesh*, 1:618–20, 6:196–97.

23. *Challenge*, 52; Metzger, *Heroic Struggle*, 19, 53–54, 105–7, 111, 146–47; interview with Barry Gourary, BMRS.

24. Interview with Eli S., 31 December 2003; Metzger, *Heroic Struggle*, 138; interview with Heschel Greenberg, 23 February 2004; J. I. Schneersohn, *Lubavitcher Rabbi's Memoirs*, 1. After his death, many of the Rebbe's followers spoke of his being with them. One of his translators, Uri Kaploun, writes that the Rebbe "is present with us here and now" (*Likkutei Dibburim*, 1:xii). The belief that the Rebbes are together in spirit is important in Chabad. A painting in the Chabad Society in New York called *March to the Redemption* depicts Rebbes marching in a straight line symbolizing their common purpose and unified front.

25. Hoffman, *Despite All Odds*, 37. See also Metzger, *Heroic Struggle*, 167n3. According to Barry Gourary, this account is revisionist history. He

claims that Menachem was not active in Hasidic causes at the time. Rather, he was studying for a career in electrical engineering, something his father-in-law disapproved of, feeling it would pollute his mind with secular interests (Gourary to Rigg, 4 August 2003, Schneersohn folder 6, BMRS). See also Ehrlich, *Leadership*, 274, 297, 315–16.

26. Metzger, *Heroic Struggle*, 104–5, 131–33, 139–40; Zaklikovsky, *America*, 23.

27. Propaganda tract given out by the Lubavitchers, file 811.111, Joseph Schneersohn, itinerary 705, GRDOS, RG 59, NAR; Special Agent Tubbs to Fitch, 10 January 1940, file 811.111, Joseph Schneersohn, itinerary 705, GRDOS, RG 59, NAR; Metzger, *Heroic Struggle*, 143–44; *Kramers*, 15, 68; Zaklikovsky, *America*, 10; Ehrlich, *Leadership*, 258, 262, 266; Edelman to Rigg, 23 February 2004, Schneersohn folder 6, BMRS.

28. Mindel, *Lubavitcher Rabbi*; Records of the United States Theaters of War, World War II, 360 C.60P, 15/1, WNRC; interview with Rabbi Meir Greenberg, BMRS; Hoffman, *Despite All Odds*, 24; Meyer, *Unternehmen Sieben*, 128; "This Is Your Life"; *Likkutei Dibburim*, 1:vii; Metzger, *Heroic Struggle*, 153; Posner to Rigg, BMRS; Ehrlich, *Leadership*, 258; J. I. Schneersohn, *Saying Tehillim*, 1n1. "Even if an ordinary person is imprisoned," the Rebbe observes, "he becomes refined by the experience" (*Likkutei Dibburim*, 1:94).

29. Metzger, *Heroic Struggle*, 325, 328.

30. Hoffman, *Despite All Odds*, 25; Bauer, *History of the Holocaust*, 285; interview with Eli S., 31 December 2003; Eli S. to Rigg, BMRS. The following list of sixty-six Lubavitchers murdered by the Soviets is by no means comprehensive: Yitzchak Alperovich, Pinchas Althaus, Eliyohu Balkind, Mordechai Brusin, Avraham Budnav, Shmuel Chanin, Yekutiel Chanin, Yona Cohen, Shmuel Aba Dulitzky, Feivish Estrin, Meir Friedman, Shaul Friedman, Yehosua Friedman, Hendel Galprin, Meir Gansburg, Yosef Garfinkel, Eliyohu Gitlin, Yehoshua Gold, Dober Grinpes, Yehoshuah Gurary, Nateh Hanzburg, Eliezer Katz, Michoel Katzeneleboigen, Sarah Katzeneleboigen, Dovber Kuznitzav, Zalman Kuznitzav, Dovid Labak, Shimon Lazarov, Menachem Mendel Lein, Yehoshua Lein, Dober Levertov, Simcha Levin, Elchanan Dovber Marazov, Pinchas Marazov, Shmuel Marazov, Yehuda Medalia, Yaakov Zecharya Meskolik, Shmuel Natik, Shmuel Nimotin, Avrahamn Baruch Pevsner, Nachum Yitzchak Pinson, Nason Nateh Rabinov, Yaakov Yosef Raskin, Yehuda LeibRaskin, Yitzchak Raskin, Ben Tzion Chaim Raskin,

Yitzchak Rivkin, Shmuel Rozenbaum, Schnuer Zalman Schneerson, Yochanan Schneerson, Yitzchak Elchonan Shagalov, Skveerki, Avraham Levik Slavin, Chaim Sosonkin, Itah Sosonkin, Moshe Sosonkin, Aryeh Spaznikov, Betzalel Spivack, Kherson, Avraham Swerdlov, Aaron Eliezer Tzeitlin, Meir Tzinman, Yaakov Wangreen, Shneur Zalman Weinshtak, Feivel Zalmanav, and Hershel Zuben.

31. *Likkutei Dibburim*, 1:58, 66, 89, 91, 173, 176; 5:10; Jacobs, *Jewish Religion*, 464, interview with Heschel Greenberg, 29 February 2004.

32. Jacobson, *ZiKoron*, 97–125; Zaklikovsky, *America*, 41; Ehrlich, *Leadership*, 268.

33. Jacobson, *ZiKoron*, 150–51; "This Is Your Life"; Metzger, *Heroic Struggle*, 166.

34. Interview with Barry Gourary, BMRS.

35. Hoffman, *Despite All Odds*, 37; Dalfin, *Seven Chabad-Lubavitch Rebbes*, 114; Ehrlich, *Leadership*, 257.

36. The pogroms of 1929 broke out in several cities, including Hebron and Jerusalem. They occurred for many reasons, but mainly as a result of the nationalist antagonism between the Arabs and the Jews. The anger the Palestinians felt was fueled by false rumors that the Jews wanted to build a place of worship at the Wailing Wall. Some Jews were killed and several thousands had to leave their homes in the old city of Jerusalem. A few days before these events, the Rebbe had spent several hours at the Wailing Wall praying.

37. About the Rebbe's 1929 visit, file 811.111, Joseph Schneersohn, itinerary 705, GRDOS, RG 59, NAR; Ehrlich, *Leadership*, 266, 277; Zaklikovsky, *America*, 6, 7n1, 8, 10, 17, 20. Many have asked why his other son-in-law, the future seventh Rebbe, Menachem Mendel Schneerson, did not accompany him. Menachem was head of all Chabad affairs in Europe at the time, a very important position (Zaklikovsky, *America*, 29). Yet it does seem that it was Gourary who was being groomed to be the next Rebbe. He had been the Rebbe's aide for almost forty years. See Ehrlich, *Leadership*, 253–57, 325.

38. Propaganda tract prepared by the Lubavitchers, file 811.111, Joseph Schneersohn, itinerary 705, GRDOS, RG 59, NAR; Jacobson, *ZiKoron*, 205–6; 360 C.60P, 15/1, WNRC; *Challenge*, 53; Jacobson, "Journey to America," 3; Meyer, *Unternehmen Sieben*, 128; *Kramers*, 15, 68; Zaklikovsky, *America*, 11, 13, 15–16, 18, 34–35; Ehrlich, *Leadership*, 269–71.

39. *Likkutei Dibburim*, 5:10, 27–28, 33, 46, 50, 94. The Rebbe often talked

about the Messiah. See *Likkutei Dibburim,* 1:13, 82, 87, 93, 149–50; 2:1, 16–18, 131, 227, 266–73, 275–76, 279–80, 288–90, 296–98; J. I. Schneersohn, *Saying Tehillim,* 47. For a Chabad perspective on the Messiah, see Boteach, *Wolf.*

40. *Challenge,* 53; interview with Eliezer Zaklikovsky, 4 June 2003.

41. Interview with Barry Gourary, interview with Joseph Wineberg, BMRS; Hoffman, *Despite All Odds,* 24; Zaklikovsky, *America,* 41.

CHAPTER THREE: POLAND UNDER THE GERMANS

1. Altein and Zaklikovsky, *Out of the Inferno,* 298, 303; interview with Joseph Wineberg, BMRS; interview with Barry Gourary, BMRS; Jacobson, "Journey to America," 3–4.

2. Interview with Meir Greenberg, BMRS; Zaklikovsky, *America,* 49.

3. Interview with Shmuel Fox, 14 January 2003.

4. Interview with Meir Greenberg, BMRS.

5. Altein and Zaklikovsky, *Out of the Inferno,* 303; interview with Avraham Laber, 6 January 2004; Zaklikovsky, *America,* 49.

6. Interview with Mordechai Dov Altein, 14 January 2003.

7. Interview with Meir Greenberg, BMRS; Jacobson, "Journey to America," 4; Zaklikovsky, *America,* 50.

8. *Challenge,* 53; interview with Hirsch Kotlarsky, 3 January 2003; interview with Joseph Wineberg, BMRS; interview with Eli S., 31 December 2003; interview with Adam Boren, 9 December 2003; *Hakreah Vehakedusha* [Reading and Holiness] 2, no. 13 (October 1941), 1; 2, no. 15 (December 1941), 2; interview Kranzler, 8 February 2004; interview S. Jacobson, 24 June 2004.

9. Interview with Joseph Wineberg and Barry Gourary, BMRS.

10. Kee, *1939,* 310; Gutman, *Jews of Warsaw,* 7; Kaplan, *Scroll of Agony,* 26; Warfield and Warfield, *Call Us to Witness,* 29; Bethell, *War Hitler Won,* 102; Madej and Zaloga, *Polish Campaign,* 139; Altein and Zaklikovsky, *Out of the Inferno,* 298.

11. Interview with Barry Gourary, BMRS; Jacobson, "Journey to America," 4.

12. Altein and Zaklikovsky, *Out of the Inferno,* 298; *Rebbes,* 149; Pell to Rhoade, 13 November 1939, Schneersohn folder 1, BMRS; interview with Zalman Gourary, BMRS; Jacobson, "Journey to America," 4; Chabad vs. Barry and Hanna Gourary, U.S. District Court, CV-1985-

2909, 6, Schneersohn folder 6, Kramer files, BMRS; Zaklikovsky, *America*, 49.

13. Gutman, *Jews of Warsaw*, 4–5; Altein and Zaklikovsky, *Out of the Inferno*, 298–99; Madej and Zaloga, *Polish Campaign*, 116, 122; Warfield and Warfield, *Call Us to Witness*, 31–32; Gilbert, *Second World War*, 2.

14. Warfield and Warfield, *Call Us to Witness*, 32. See also Bethell, *War Hitler Won*, 27.

15. Bethell, *War Hitler Won*, 27, 122; Rossino, *Hitler Strikes Poland*, 1; Shirer, *Berlin Diary*, 209.

16. Interview with Barry Gourary, BMRS; Altein and Zaklikovsky, *Out of the Inferno*, 298; *Rebbes*, 149.

17. Interview with Barry Gourary, BMRS; Zuroff, *Response*, 44–45, 47; Bauer, *History of the Holocaust*, 283. Zuroff says there were forty-three Lubavitcher yeshiva students in Vilna at the time. He puts the number of Orthodox refugees at around 2,100 and Bauer at 2,611—hence my figure of 2,500.

18. Altein and Zaklikovsky, *Out of the Inferno*, 298; Madej and Zaloga, *Polish Campaign*, 138; Kaplan, *Scroll of Agony*, 26; Bethell, *War Hitler Won*, 113.

19. Altein and Zaklikovsky, *Out of the Inferno*, 298; Kaplan, *Scroll of Agony*, 27; Interview with Joseph Wineberg, BMRS; Solomon, *Jewish Book*, 55, 103.

20. Altein and Zaklikovsky, *Out of the Inferno*, 298–299; interview with Joseph Wineberg, BMRS.

21. Kaplan, *Scroll of Agony*, 20; Altein and Zaklikovsky, *Out of the Inferno*, 304.

22. Kee, *1939*, 310.

23. Altein and Zaklikovsky, *Out of the Inferno*, 299; interview with Meir Greenberg, BMRS.

24. Altein and Zaklikovsky, *Out of the Inferno*, 306.

25. Ibid., 299; Jacobson, "Journey to America," 4; *Likkutei Dibburim*, 1:119. On angels and Hasidim, see Lamm, *Religious Thought*, 202, 522. The Rebbe frequently spoke of angels. See *Likkutei Dibburim*, 1:5–7, 20, 118–19, 159; 2:29, 42, 178, 214, 283.

26. Altein and Zaklikovsky, *Out of the Inferno*, 303, 305; Jacobson, "Journey to America," 4.

27. Gutman, *Jews of Warsaw*, 6; interview with Joseph Wineberg, BMRS.

28. Altein and Zaklikovsky, *Out of the Inferno*, 304; interview with Joseph Wineberg, BMRS; interview with Barry Gourary, BMRS.

29. Altein and Zaklikovsky, *Out of the Inferno*, 299, 304–5; interview with Joseph Wineberg, BMRS; Zaklikovsky, *America*, 50.

30. Interview with Joseph Wineberg, BMRS.

31. Zaklikovsky, *America*, 49; Altein and Zaklikovsky, *Out of the Inferno*, 299–300, 303.

32. Kaplan, *Scroll of Agony*, 29.

33. *Rebbes*, 151; *Complete Artscroll Siddur*, 90–91; Altein and Zaklikovsky, *Out of the Inferno*, 300–301.

34. Interview with Joseph Wineberg, BMRS; Altein and Zaklikovsky, *Out of the Inferno*, 304; Zaklikovsky, *America*, 50.

35. Cooper, *German Air Force*, 101; Altein and Zaklikovsky, *Out of the Inferno*, 300–01; Kaplan, *Scroll of Agony*, 29; *Von Hassell Diaries*, 79.

36. *Rebbes*, 150–51.

37. Altein and Zaklikovsky, *Out of the Inferno*, 302.

38. Interview with Joseph Wineberg, BMRS.

39. Weinberg, *World at Arms*, 56.

40. Churchill, *Gathering Storm*, 392–95; Madej and Zaloga, *Polish Campaign*, 152–53; Weinberg, *World at Arms*, 51–52, 55.

41. Kee, *1939*, 316.

42. Interview with Joseph Wineberg, BMRS; *Rebbes*, 149; Kaplan, *Scroll of Agony*, 35; Kershaw, *Nemesis*, 236.

43. Huberband, *Kiddusch Hashem*, 46–48; Altein and Zaklikovsky, *Out of the Inferno*, 301; *Likkutei Dibburim*, 1:5–7, 20; 2:42, 48.

44. Levin, *Holocaust*, 152; interview with Shmuel Fox, 14 January 2003.

45. Altein and Zaklikovsky, *Out of the Inferno*, 301–2; Kaplan, *Scroll of Agony*, 35–36.

46. Manstein, *Lost Victories*, 58; Kaplan, *Scroll of Agony*, 36; Cooper, *German Air Force*, 101; Gilbert, *Second World War*, 13; Madej and Zaloga, *Polish Campaign*, 140; Altein and Zaklikovsky, *Out of the Inferno*, 290, 300–301; Gutman, *Jews of Warsaw*, 7; Strzetelski, *Where the Storm*, 87.

47. Levin, *Holocaust*, 150; Gilbert, *Second World War*, 8; Sydnor, *Soldiers of Destruction*, 39; Huberband, *Kiddusch Hashem*, xvi; Altein and Zaklikovsky, *Out of the Inferno*, 295; interview with Chaskel Besser, BMRS.

48. Meyer, *Unternehmen Sieben*, 136; "1,000 Rabbis Greet Rabbi Schneersohn"; "Rabbi from Warsaw"; interview with Barry Gourary, BMRS. Most Lubavitchers questioned about this event deny the Rebbe had any mental weakness. Manis Friedman admits that the Rebbe could suffer from emotional pain but believes he could not have had a nervous

breakdown, as Meyer writes. If he had, Friedman notes, the community would have known about it. He claims that such weakness would reveal a crisis of faith, something impossible for a Rebbe (interview Friedman, 17 June 2004). Shalom Dovber Levine claims the Rebbe probably had become "heartbroken" over killings in Warsaw, and that was interpreted as a nervous breakdown (interview Levine, 16 June 2004). I believe that had the Rebbe had such a show of mental "weakness," Lubavitch scholars would not have documented it. Lubavitchers have falsified records they want forgotten (Ehrlich, *Messiah of Brooklyn*, 9).

49. Altein and Zaklikovsky, *Out of the Inferno*, 301.

50. Gutman, *Jews of Warsaw*, 7; Kaplan, *Scroll of Agony*, 27, 35, 38; Altein and Zaklikovsky, *Out of the Inferno*, 306; interview Karin Falencki, BMRS.

51. Madej and Zaloga, *Polish Campaign*, 141; Cooper, *German Air Force*, 103; Brewster and Jennings, *Century*, 215; Kaplan, *Scroll of Agony*, 39; Mayer, *Why Did the Heavens*, 183.

52. Kaplan, *Scroll of Agony*, 38; Gutman, *Jews of Warsaw*, 8; Madej and Zaloga, *Polish Campaign*, 141.

53. Madej and Zaloga, *Polish Campaign*, 156; Cooper, *German Army*, 169; Gilbert, *Holocaust*, 91; Weinberg, *World at Arms*, 57; Mayer, *Why Did the Heavens*, 178; Kershaw, *Nemesis*, 236; Bullock, *Hitler*, 556.

54. Churchill, *Gathering Storm*, 443; file 811.111, Joseph Schneersohn, itinerary 705, GRDOS, RG 59, NAR; 360 C.60P, WNRC; Keegan, *Second World War*, 44–47.

55. Kershaw, *Nemesis*, 243–45; Strzetelski, *Where the Storm*, 107–27; Segal, *New Order in Poland*, 56–58; Bethell, *War Hitler Won*, 147; Rossino, *Hitler Strikes Poland*, 141; Gilbert, *Second World War*, 6; Kaplan, *Scroll of Agony*, 10, 43.

56. Kaplan, *Scroll of Agony*, 38, 43.

57. Interview with Barry Gourary; BMRS.

CHAPTER FOUR: A PLAN TAKES SHAPE

1. Interview with Joseph Wineberg, BMRS; *Igrois Koidesh*, 5:5; Jacobson, "Journey to America," 4–5.

2. Interview with Meir Greenberg, BMRS.

3. Wyman, *Abandonment of the Jews*, 184; Friedman, *No Haven*, 225; Beschloss, *Conquerors*, 53; Feingold, *Politics of Rescue*, 19; Gellman, *Secret Affairs*, 98; Wagner to Hull, 22 September 1939, 360 C.60P, 15/1,

WNRC; Kleinfeld to Wagner, 24 September 1939, Schneersohn folder 3, Chabad Library Documents (hereafter CLD), BMRS.

4. *Kramers*, 76; Wagner to Hull, 22 September 1939 and 26 September 1939, 360 C.60P, 15/1, WNRC; Dept. of State to American Legation in Riga, 13 January 1940, file 811.111, Joseph Schneersohn, itinerary 705, GRDOS, RG 59, NAR.

5. Kramer to Rabinovitz, 24 September 1939, and Kramer to Rhoade, 25 September 1939, Schneersohn folder 3, CLD, BMRS; interview with Joseph Wineberg, BMRS.

6. Wagner to Hull, 26 September 1939, and Hull to American legation in Riga (John C. Wiley), 360 C.60P, 15/2, WNRC; Packer to Hull, 30 September 1939, 360 C.60P, 15/7, WNRC.

7. Johnson, *History of the Jews*, 460; Burns, *Lion and the Fox*, 230.

8. Rabinovitz to Brandeis, 29 September 1939, 360 C.60P, 15/2 and 15/6, WNRC; Jacobson, "Journey to America," 3.

9. Cohen to Pell, 2 October 1939, 360 C.60P, 15/3, WNRC; Lasser, *Benjamin V. Cohen*, 7–8, 26–27.

10. Pell, memorandum about his telephone conversation with Cohen, 2 October 1939, 360 C.60P, 15/4, 1, WNRC.

11. Wistrich, *Hitler*, 57; Wyman, *Paper Walls*, xiii, 45, 48; Wise, *Challenging Years*, 221.

12. Wistrich, *Hitler*, 57; Wyman, *Paper Walls*, 50; Friedman, *No Haven*, 56, 60; Feingold, *Bearing Witness*, 77.

13. Wyman, *Paper Walls*, 49.

14. Friedman, *Dare to Survive*, 144, 154; Feingold, *Politics of Rescue*, 280–83.

15. 360 C.60P, 15/4, 2, WNRC; Wyman, *Paper Walls*, 51, 56; Feingold, *Politics of Rescue*, 54, 58–63, 71; Meyer, *Unternehmen Sieben*, 130–32; Feingold, *Bearing Witness*, 76.

16. Interview with Chaskel Besser, BMRS; discussion with Leib Altein, September 1997; interview with Rachel Altein, 14 January 2003; interview with David Edelman, 8 March 2004.

17. Klein, *Kennedy Curse*, 15; interview with Eliezer and Chanie Zaklikovsky, 25 December 2003 (the Zaklikovskys verify that this story circulates but they deny the truth of it); interview with Heschel Greenberg, 29 February 2004. Although not often used, curses are a part of Judaism; the Rebbe, for example, cursed Soviet officials who dared harm Torah students (*Likkutei Dibburim*, 5:10; see also Jacobs, *Jewish Religion*, 55).

18. Department of State, Office of Special Agent Charge, 360 C.60P, 15/6, WNRC; file 811.111, Joseph Schneersohn, itinerary 705, GRDOS, RG 59, NAR; Kleinfield to Farley, 27 September 1939, and Irwin S. Chanin to Bloom, 27 September 1939, Schneersohn folder 3, CLD, BMRS; Schneersohn to Roosevelt, 12 September 1941, box 7, OF 76c, FDRL. Rabbi Avraham Laber, a historian of the Lubavitcher movement, regards these numbers as a conservative estimate, since they reflect those who considered the Rebbe their leader and one did not have to be a Lubavitcher to follow the Rebbe. Rabbi Eliezer Zaklikovsky agrees. See also affidavit of Rabbi Israel Jacobson, January 1940, Schneersohn folder 3, CLD, BMRS; Hoffman, *Despite All Odds*, 23; Meyer, *Unternehmen Sieben*, 129. Paula Hyman, professor of history and head of Judaic Studies at Yale University, believes that the 160,000 figure is very inflated and that it was probably more likely 40,000. Bernhard Klein of Kingsborough Community College of Brooklyn concurs with Hyman's estimate. Henry Feingold, director of the Jewish Resource Center of Baruch College in New York, puts the figure even lower, at probably no more than 20,000. According to Lubavitcher sources, the population was 40,000 in 1929 (see Zaklikovsky, *America*, 19). If Zaklikovsky's source is correct, 110,000 Lubavitchers would have had to have entered the United States between 1929 and 1939. Lubavitcher Rabbi Zalman Posner agrees with scholars like Hyman, Klein, and Feingold and calls the 160,000 figure "nonsense." David Kranzler estimates Chabad membership as 10,000; Rabbi Moshe Kolodny, director of the Agudath Israel of America Archives in New York, says 2,000 (Posner to Rigg, 8 January 2004, Schneersohn folder 6, BMRS; interview with Kranzler, 23 January 2004; interview with Kolodny, 21 January 2004). Even today, however, the Lubavitchers do not keep records of their membership.

19. Affidavit of Rabbi Israel Jacobson, January 1940, Schneersohn folder 3, CLD, BMRS; Lipstadt, *Beyond Belief,* 2.

20. Feingold, *Politics of Rescue,* 139, 330n44; Hull to Farley, 2 October 1939, Schneersohn folder 3, CLD, BMRS.

21. Telephone conversation with Mr. Smits from the Latvian embassy, 2 October 1939, Division of European Affairs, State Department, 360 C.60P, 15/6, WNRC; interview with Joseph Wineberg, BMRS; Kramer to Rabinovitz, 24 September 1939, Schneersohn folder 3, BMRS.

22. 360 C.60P, 15/3, WNRC.

23. Brissaud, *Canaris*, 158; Abshagen, *Canaris*, 150; Meyer, *Unternehmen Sieben*, 134; Geist and Kirck to Hull, 360 C.60P, 15/5, WNRC.

24. Hull to Robert Wagner, 26 September 1939, and Hull to James Farley, 2 October 1939, 360 C.60P, 15/6, WNRC; Herzstein, *Roosevelt and Hitler*, 233; Kershaw, *Profiles in Power*, 149; Rossino, *Hitler Strikes Poland*, 90; Feingold, *Politics of Rescue*, 19, 42–43; Wyman, *Paper Walls*, 56; 360 C.60P, 15/4, 2, WNRC.

CHAPTER FIVE: THE NAZI CONNECTION

1. "War Front"; Metzmacher, "Deutsche-englische," 407; Abshagen, *Canaris*, 45–47, 57; Meyer, *Unternehmen Sieben*, 130–31; testimony by Jews whom Wohlthat helped in the 1930s, 100021/49193, HHSAD; interview by Rolf Vogel with Helmut Wohlthat. Some of the men in the resistance whom Wohlthat was in touch with were Ulrich von Hassell, Carl Goerdeler, and General Ludwig Beck.

2. Hilberg, *Destruction*, 76–80; Meyer, *Unternehmen Sieben*, 128–39.

3. Jacobson, "Journey to America," 3; Höhne, *Canaris*, 411; Abshagen, *Canaris*, 99.

4. Abshagen, *Canaris*, 150; Generalfeldmarschall von Mackensen to Generaloberst von Blomberg, 11 January 1936, RW 6/73, BA-MA; Reichsminister und Chef der Reichskanzlei Lammers to Generalfeldmarschall von Mackensen, 3 February, 1939, N 39/62, BA-MA.

5. Höhne, *Canaris*, 7, 15, 167–69, 362; Brissaud, *Canaris*, 5–6; Abshagen, *Canaris*, 19–20, 23, 44.

6. Kahn, *Hitler's Spies*, 226, 229; Abshagen, *Canaris*, 12, 21, 71, 73, 229; lecture by Canaris at a conference of the military high command, 3 March 1938, RW 6/56, BA-MA. Höhne, *Canaris*, 34, 45–47, 51–52, 131–34, 213, 216, 247; Brissaud, *Canaris*, 7, 10.

7. Kahn, *Hitler's Spies*, 231–32; Abshagen, *Canaris*, 75; Meyer, *Unternehmen Sieben*, 14; Höhne, *Canaris*, 86, 162, 177–78; Brissaud, *Canaris*, 12–13, 50.

8. Kahn, *Hitler's Spies*, 234–35; Meyer, *Unternehmen Sieben*, 134; Höhne, *Canaris*, 212.

9. Höhne, *Canaris*, 212; Brissaud, *Canaris*, 28; Abshagen, *Canaris*, 25–36, 74, 76, 83, 94, 157. Historian Alexander Rossino notes that the Geheime Feldpolizei (Secret Field Police) were linked to both the Abwehr and the SS.

10. Vogel, *Ein Stück*, 306–7; *Die Nachhut* 11 (15 February 1971), 12, Msg

3-22/1, BA-MA; Bar-Zohar, *Hitler's Jewish Spy*. See also Meyer, *Unternehmen Sieben*.

11. Brissaud, *Canaris*, 89, 155; Meyer, *Unternehmen Sieben*, 134; Höhne, *Canaris*, 250, 258, 276, 360; Clark, *Barbarossa*, 14; Craig, *Politics*, 495; *Reichgesetzblatt*, 4 February 1938, BA-MA; Militärgeschichtliches Forschungsamt, *Build-Up*; Kershaw, *Nemesis*, 57, 188. See also O'Neill, *German Army*, 72.

12. Brissaud, *Canaris*, 156; Kahn, *Hitler's Spies*, 235; Höhne, *Canaris*, 364.

13. Brissaud, *Canaris*, 156; Meyer, *Unternehmen Sieben*, 26, 30, 31.

14. Bürkner to Wohlthat, 15 January 1948, 100021/49193, Bl. 55F, HHSAD; Brissaud, *Canaris*, 158; Abshagen, *Canaris*, 150.

15. Höhne, *Canaris*, 296, 298, 303–4, 331–32, 335, 352; Wheeler-Bennett, *Nemesis*, 455; Brissaud, *Canaris*, 151. See also *Von Hassell Diaries*, 75. After witnessing one of Hitler's outbursts against Britain in spring 1940, Canaris declared that Hitler was "mad" (Höhne, *Canaris*, 331).

16. Brissaud, *Canaris*, 153; Frei, *National Socialist Rule*, 125; Lauren, *Power and Prejudice*, 126–27; Victor, *Hitler*, 196; Bauer, *History of the Holocaust*, 147; Kershaw, *Profiles in Power*, 152; Gutman, *Jews of Warsaw*, 12–15; Wistrich, *Hitler*, 73; Levin, *Holocaust*, 150, 204; Rossino, *Hitler Strikes Poland*, 10, 14, 22; Höhne, *Canaris*, 363.

17. Meyer, *Unternehmen Sieben*, 134; Abshagen, *Canaris*, 197; Bürkner to Wohlthat, 15 January 1948, 100021/49193, 55, HHSAD; interview with Martin Bloch, BMRS; Pers 6/9887, BA-MA; Brissaud, *Canaris*, 23.

CHAPTER SIX: BLOCH'S SECRET MISSION

1. Pers 6/9887, Bl. 1a, BA-MA; Ernst Bloch file, Bl. 96–99, BMRS; Rigg, *Hitler's Jewish Soldiers*, 56–57.

2. Interview with Martin Bloch, BMRS; Bloch file, BMRS.

3. Interview with Ursula Cadenbach, BMRS; interview with Martin Bloch, BMRS; Pers 6/9887, BA-MA; Bloch file, BMRS.

4. First Draft of a Collection of Materials for the Bloch Family History by Martin Bloch, 3 November 1962, Bloch file, BMRS.

5. Margarete Bloch to Ernst Bloch, 8 February 1921, Bloch file, BMRS.

6. Ibid.

7. Doctorate, 2 August 1924, Bloch file, BMRS; Hans von Bosse to Bloch, 29 April 1930, Bloch file, BMRS.

8. Interview with Ursula Cadenbach, BMRS; Kahn, *Hitler's Spies*, 90; Höhne, *Canaris*, 200; Pers 6/9887, BA-MA; silver plate given to Bloch

by Japanese industrialists "in commemoration of our trip throughout Greater Germany May/June 1939" and photo album documenting "trip of the German armed forces high command with German business leaders through Belgium and France from 16 to 21 November 1940," Bloch file, BMRS.

9. Verordnung zum Reichsbürgergesetz, 14.11.1935, *Reichgesetzblatt*, part 1, no. 135, 1333–36, BA-MA; Hilberg, *Destruction*, 48; *Legalizing the Holocaust*, 31; Adler, *Verwaltete Mensch*, 280. If a Jewish woman had a child out of wedlock and the father's identity could not be determined, the Nazis classified the child as a full Jew. See *Akten der Parteikanzlei der NSDAP: Rekonstruktion eines verlorengegangenen Bestandes*, microfiche, 107-00404, BA-B; *Heeresadjutant bei Hitler*, 32. If a person was "3/8 Jewish," he or she was most often classified as a quarter Jewish. Countless men and women documented in my book *Hitler's Jewish Soldiers* were actually "37.5% Jewish," and most were classified as quarter Jews. See *Akten-NSDAP*, 107-00389-390. When a person was more than 37.5% Jewish but not 50% Jewish, he or she was usually classified as a half Jew. Likewise, when somebody was more than 12.5% Jewish—say, 18.75 Jewish—the person was usually classified as a quarter Jew.

10. Kammer and Bartsch, *Nationalsozialismus*, 39–40; Kershaw, *Nemesis*, 572; Rich, *Hitler's War Aims*, 1–2; Stoltzfus, *Resistance*, xxv; Kaplan, *Between Dignity and Despair*, 191.

11. Gilbert, *Holocaust*, 45–47; Vogel, *Ein Stück*, 238; Meyer, *Unternehmen Sieben*, 128; Bloch file, BMRS; Kahn, *Hitler's Spies*, 91.

12. Rigg, *Hitler's Jewish Soldiers*, 186–87; Pers 6/9887, BA-MA; Bloch file, BMRS; Vogel, *Ein Stück*, 308–9; Kahn, *Hitler's Spies*, 91.

13. Martin Bloch to Rigg, 29 August 1996, Bloch file, BMRS; Pers 6/9887, report by Canaris about Bloch, 14 March 1937, 13, Pers 6/9887, BA-MA; certificate of award from Hitler to Bloch, 19 October 1938, Bloch file, BMRS.

14. "Johannes Hamburger" is a pseudonym. At the request of his family, their name and whereabouts have been kept secret.

15. Interview with Johannes Hamburger's widow, December 1996, BMRS.

16. Interview with Klaus Schenk (pseudonym), BMRS.

17. Interview with Klaus Schenk, BMRS; Gilbert, *Holocaust*, 824. Donald Niewyk, a renowned Holocaust historian, disputes Gilbert's claim that tens of thousands of homosexuals were killed. According to his files, around 10,000 were murdered by the Nazis. See also Rigg, *Hitler's Jew-*

ish Soldiers, 26. For an interesting case study, see Tent, *In the Shadow,* 128–30.

18. Meyer, *Unternehmen Sieben,* 135–36; Höhne, *Canaris,* 361.
19. Meyer, *Unternehmen Sieben.* See also Höhne, *Canaris,* 265–66.
20. Höhne, *Canaris,* 489, 507; Abshagen, *Canaris,* 101. See also Meyer, *Unternehmen Sieben.*
21. Rigg, *Hitler's Jewish Soldiers,* 51–67.
22. Bauer, *History of the Holocaust,* 54; Rigg, *Hitler's Jewish Soldiers,* 72.
23. For more information on Mischlinge in the Wehrmacht, see Rigg, *Hitler's Jewish Soldiers.*

CHAPTER SEVEN: THE SEARCH BEGINS

1. *Challenge,* 53.
2. Interview with Joseph Wineberg, BMRS.
3. *Likkutei Dibburim,* 1:120. In the Rebbe's form of Judaism, women are not allowed to dance with the Torah. The *Hakkafos,* as the dancing is known, was deeply spiritual for the Rebbe; "During the *Hakkafos* the doors of heaven are open, because the Torah's happiness throws open the doors and gates of all the chambers of heaven" (*Likkutei Dibburim,* 2:81). See also *Likkutei Dibburim,* 2:89, 172–73.
4. Huberband, *Kiddusch Hashem,* 53–54; Kaplan, *Scroll of Agony,* 45.
5. Kaplan, *Scroll of Agony,* 44, 46, 48, 54, 55, 56, 59.
6. Jacobson to Kramer, 30 October 1939, Schneersohn folder 3, CLD, BMRS. See also Rhoade to Kramer, 27 October 1939, Schneersohn folder 1, BMRS; Rhoade to Hull, 2 November 1939, file 811.111, Samarius Gourary, itinerary 705, GRDOS, RG 59, NAR; Rhoade to Kramer, 4 November 1939, Schneersohn folder 1, BMRS.
7. See Rhoade to Hull, 2 November 1939, and letter to American consular officer in Warsaw, 14 January 1939, file 811.111, Samarius Gourary, and Hodgdon to Yellen, 21 May 1940, file 811.111, Rubin Halberpsohn, itinerary 705, GRDOS, RG 59, NAR.
8. Memorandum in Visa Department about Mr. Rhochkind, secretary to Senator Borah, who called about Rabbi Gourary's case, 12 January 1939, file 811.111, Samarius Gourary, itinerary 705, GRDOS, RG 59, NAR.
9. See Cases Bernhard Hamburger, Rubin Halberpsohn, Moses Rokach, Yoel Halpern, and Joseph Isaac Schneersohn, file 811.111, itinerary 705, GRDOS, RG 59, NAR.
10. Tubbs to Fitch, 10 April 1939, file 811.111, Bernhard Hamburger; Kinsey

to Fitch, 1 September 1938, file 811.111, David Rokeach; file 811.111, Joseph E. Gottlieb; Kinsey to Fitch, 1 September 1938, file 811.111, David Rokeach; Kinsey to Burr, 11 July 1934, file 811.111, Mosche Levin; file 811.111, Rabbi David Cohen, itinerary 705, GRDOS, RG 59, NAR.

11. Jacobson to Lieberman, 24 October 1939, Schneersohn folder 3, CLD, BMRS; Pell to Cohen, 28 October 1939, 360 C.60P, 15/9, WNRC.

12. Pell to Cohen, 28 October 1939, and Kirck to Pell, 19 November 1939, 360 C.60P, 15/9, WNRC.

13. Levin, *Holocaust*, 206; Gutman, *Jews of Warsaw*, 29; Warfield and Warfield, *Call Us to Witness*, 117; Kaplan, *Scroll of Agony*, 71, 73, 78-79; Mayer, *Why Did the Heavens*, 189.

14. Kaplan, *Scroll of Agony*, 78-79.

15. *Likkutei Dibburim*, 4:73, 5:314; interview with Paula Hyman, September 2003; interview with Heschel Greenberg, 5 March 2004.

16. Interview with Klaus Schenk, BMRS.

17. Interview with Mrs. Hamburger, BMRS.

18. Höhne, *Canaris*, 250-52, 364; interview with Barry Gourary, 8 May 2003, BMRS; interview with Klaus Schenk, BMRS. Photographs in the Bloch family archive confirm that, when on assignment, Bloch was often in civilian clothes.

19. Rigg, *Hitler's Jewish Soldiers*, 11-14, 109-10; Aschheim, *Brothers and Strangers*, 143-45, 150-51; Matthäus, "German *Judenpolitik*," 162-64; Maurer, *Ostjuden*, 26-28; interview with Heinz Günter Angress, BMRS; Hans Mühlbacher file, BMRS; interview with Friedrich Schlesinger, BMRS.

20. Interviews with Robert Braun, Michael Günther, Hans B. (Bernheim), Hermann Aub, BMRS. See also Gilbert, *Holocaust*, 90; Huberband, *Kiddusch Hashem*, xiii; Kaplan, *Scroll of Agony*, 54, 60.

21. Rigg, *Hitler's Jewish Soldiers*, 40-45.

CHAPTER EIGHT: A LAWYER'S WORK

1. Schneersohn folder 7, Kramer file, BMRS; file 811.111, Joseph Schneersohn, itinerary 705, GRDOS, RG 59, NAR. Some of the other people who helped put the event together were Mr. William Fischman and Mr. and Mrs. Lou G. Siegel. See also Special Agent Tubbs in Dept. of State to Fitch, 10 January 1940, file 811.111, Joseph Schneersohn, itinerary 705, GRDOS, RG 59, NAR.

2. "This Is Your Life."

3. Jacobson to Rhoade, 8 October 1939, Schneersohn folder 7, Kramer file, BMRS; Jacobson, "Journey to America," 3; Rhoade to Jacobson, 28 October 1939, Schneersohn folder 1, BMRS.

4. Rhoade to Kramer, 30 October 1939, 9 November 1939, and 13 November 1939, and Rhoade to Brandeis, 30 October 1939, Schneersohn folder 1, BMRS; Zuroff, *Response*, 93, 128.

5. Rhoade to Kramer, 28 October 1939, Rhoade to Kramer, 30 October 1939, and Rhoade to Kramer, 9 November 1939, Schneersohn folder 1, BMRS.

6. Jacobson, "Journey to America," 5.

7. Rhoade to Jacobson, 25 October 1939, Schneersohn folder 3, CLD, BMRS.

8. Interview with two Lubavitchers who wish to remain anonymous, 4 May 2003; interview with Rabbi Avraham Laber, 8 May 2003; Laber to Rigg, 23 September 2003, Schneersohn folder 6, BMRS.

9. Wyman, *Abandonment of the Jews*, 103, 130.

10. Jacobson to Kramer, 30 October 1939, Schneersohn folder 7, Kramer file, BMRS; Rhoade to Kramer, 4 November 1939, Schneersohn folder 1, BMRS.

11. Rhoade to Cohen, 4 November 1939, Schneersohn folder 1, BMRS; interview with Joseph Wineberg, BMRS.

12. Rhoade to Cohen, 4 November 1939, Schneersohn folder 1, BMRS.

13. Ibid.

14. Wyman, *Paper Walls*, 3–5; Kranzler, *Thy Brother's Blood*, 128.

15. Rhoade to Cohen, 4 November 1939, Schneersohn folder 1, BMRS.

16. Interview with Mordechai Dov Altein, 14 January 2003.

17. Rhoade to Jacobson, 4 November 1939, and Rhoade to Kramer, 6 December 1939, Schneersohn folder 1, BMRS; Avtzon, *Day to Recall*, 196.

18. Rhoade to Pell, 1 December 1939, 360 C.60P, 15/23, WNRC.

19. Rhoade to Kramer, 6 November 1939, Schneersohn folder 1, BMRS. Rabbi Yosef Jacobson speculates that Israel Jacobson wanted to keep as much money in reserve as possible lest it be needed for bribes to the Soviets—or, for that matter, the Germans (interview, 3 March 2004). Rabbi Heschel Greenberg concurs (interview, 5 March 2004).

20. Rhoade to Jacobson, 8 November 1939, Schneersohn folder 1, BMRS; affidavit of Rabbi Israel Jacobson, January 1940, Schneersohn folder 3, CLD, BMRS.

21. Rhoade to Kramer, 6 November 1939, Schneersohn folder 1, BMRS.

22. Ibid.
23. Pell to Kirck, 10 November 1939, and Rhoade to Pell, 9 November 1939, 360 C.60P, 15/12, WNRC.
24. Rhoade to Gwinn, 8 November 1939, Schneersohn folder 1, BMRS.
25. 360 C.60P, 15/12, WNRC.
26. Levin, *Holocaust*, 150; interview with Shmuel Fox, 14 January 2003; 360 C.60P, 15/10, WNRC.
27. Rhoade to Kramer, 27 October 1939, and Rhoade to Bilmanis, 8 November 1939, Schneersohn folder 1, BMRS; Friedman, *No Haven*, 41.
28. Telegram to Riga from Secretary of State Hull, 18 March 1940, file 811.111, Joseph Schneersohn, itinerary 705, GRDOS, RG 59, NAR. The files show eighteen people in the group, including the Rebbe. Rhoade to Bilmanis, 8 November 1939, Rhoade to Kramer, 8 November 1939 and 9 November 1939, and Rhoade to Pell, 9 November 1939, Schneersohn folder 1, BMRS.
29. Rhoade to Kramer, 9 November 1939, 360 C.60P, 15/11, WNRC.
30. Interview with Meir Greenberg, BMRS.
31. Kaplan, *Scroll of Agony*, 68.
32. Rhoade to Kramer, 9 November 1939, 360 C.60P, 15/11, WNRC. Rhoade to Kramer, 11 November 1939, Schneersohn folder 1, BMRS.
33. Rhoade to Kramer, 9 November 1939, Schneersohn folder 1, BMRS.
34. Rhoade to Kramer, 9 November 1939 and 13 November 1939, Schneersohn folder 1, BMRS.
35. Rhoade to Kramer, 11 November 1939, Schneersohn folder 1, BMRS.
36. Pell to Rhoade, 15 November 1939, and Rhoade to Kramer, 21 November 1939, Schneersohn folder 1, BMRS.
37. Rhoade to Kramer, 16 November 1939, and Rhoade to Bilmanis, 8 November 1939, Schneersohn folder 1, BMRS.
38. Rhoade to Kramer, 16 November 1939, Schneersohn folder 1, BMRS.
39. Rhoade to Kramer, 20 November 1939, Schneersohn folder 1, BMRS.
40. Rhoade to Kramer, 21 November 1939, Schneersohn folder 1, BMRS.
41. Rhoade to Kramer, 21 November 1939, Schneersohn folder 1, BMRS; Rhoade to Pell, 30 November 1939, 360 C.60P, 15/22, WNRC; Rhoade to Pell, 30 November 1939, Schneersohn folder 1, BMRS; Kranzler, *Brother's Blood*, 128.
42. Rhoade to Kramer, 25 November 1939, Schneersohn folder 1, BMRS; Kramer to Rhoade, 16 October 1939, Schneersohn folder 3, CLD, BMRS.

CHAPTER NINE: THE ANGEL

1. Interview with Klaus Schenk, BMRS; Vogel, *Ein Stück*, 308–9; Bürkner to Wohlthat, 15 January 1948, Bl. 56, HHSAD; Cohen, *Shmuos*, 235; Jacobson, "Journey to America," 5.
2. Interview with Barry Gourary, BMRS.
3. Interview with Meir Greenberg, BMRS.
4. Interview with Klaus Schenk, BMRS; interview with Barry Gourary, BMRS.
5. Kirck to Pell, 25 November 1939, 360 C.60P, 15/13, WNRC; Rhoade to Kramer, 27 November 1939, Schneersohn folder 1, BMRS.

CHAPTER TEN: THE ESCAPE ROUTE

1. Rhoade to Kramer, 27 November 1939, Schneersohn folder 1, BMRS.
2. Jacobson to Kramer, 19 December 1939, Schneersohn folder 3, CLD, BMRS. The Rebbe came by his love of books naturally. Both his father and his grandfather seem to have placed a great deal of emphasis on collecting them. See *Likkutei Dibburim*, 2:139–40. Most of the Rebbe's books were not sacred, but there were other manuscripts relating to the Chabad called *ksovim* and they were as sacred as lives, according to the Rebbe. *Chabad v. Barry and Hanna Gourary*, U.S. District Court, CV-1985-2909, 6–9, Schneersohn folder 6, Kramer files, BMRS.
3. Stulman to American consul, 15 November 1939, 360 C.60P, WNRC; Jacobson to Stulman, 15 October 1939, Schneersohn folder 7, Kramer file, BMRS.
4. Rhoade to Kramer, 27 November 1939, Schneersohn folder 1, BMRS.
5. Rhoade to Kramer, 1 December 1939, Schneersohn folder 1, BMRS; Joseph Schneersohn, Kleinfeld to Coulter, 17 January 1940, file 811.111, itinerary 705, GRDOS, RG 59, NAR.
6. Rhoade to Kramer and Kleinfeld, 17 January 1940; Kramer to Troutman, 11 March 1940, Kleinfeld to Troutman, 17 January 1940, Coulter to Bannerman, 3 January 1940, Kleinfeld to Coulter, 12 January 1940, file 811.111, Joseph Schneersohn, itinerary 705, GRDOS, RG 59, NAR.
7. Bauer, *American Jewry*, 51; Feingold, *Politics of Rescue*, 140.
8. File 811.111, Hans Jacobsohn; file 811.111, Mayer Jacobsohn; Simmons to Drew, 17 November 1937, file 811.111, Anna Schmucker; file 811.111, Israel Cohen (under Cohen, Brajna) and Izrael Cohen, itinerary 705, GRDOS, RG 59, NAR.

9. Rhoade to Pell, 28 November 1939, Schneersohn folder 1, BMRS.
10. 360 C.60P, 15/21, WNRC; Rhoade to Kramer, 30 November 1939, Schneersohn folder 1, BMRS.
11. Gutman, *Jews of Warsaw*, 12–15.
12. Rhoade to Pell, 30 November 1939, 360 C.60P, 15/21, WNRC; Rhoade to Kramer, 27 November 1939, Schneersohn folder 1, BMRS.
13. Special Agent Tubbs in Dept. of State to Fitch, 10 January 1940, file 811.111, Joseph Schneersohn, itinerary 705, GRDOS, RG 59, NAR; Jacobson and Levitin to Kramer, 6 December 1939, Schneersohn folder 3, CLD, BMRS.
14. Rhoade to Kramer, 1 December 1939, Schneersohn folder 1, BMRS.
15. Rhoade to Pell, 1 December 1939, 360 C.60P, 15/23, WNRC.
16. Rhoade to Pell, 2 December 1939 and 4 December 1939, Schneersohn folder 1, BMRS; Kee, *1939*, 318.
17. Rhoade to Pell, 2 December 1939, and Rhoade to Kramer, 1 December 1939, Schneersohn folder 1, BMRS.
18. Rhoade to Pell, 4 December 1939, 360 C.60P, 15/25, WNRC.
19. Ibid.
20. Rhoade to Pell, 2 December 1939, and Rhoade to Kramer, 3 December 1939, Schneersohn folder 1, BMRS.
21. Memorandum from Pell about his conversation with Rhoade, 29 November 1939, 1–2, 360 C.60P, 15/18, WNRC.
22. Ibid.

CHAPTER ELEVEN: FLIGHT

1. Interview with Klaus Schenk, BMRS.
2. Memorandum of conversation between Rhoade and Pell, 29 November 1939, 2, 360 C.60P, 15/18, WNRC.
3. Interview with Barry Gourary, BMRS.
4. Kirck to Pell, 13 December 1939, 360 C.60P, 15/17, WNRC; Kramer to Pell, 8 December 1939, Schneersohn folder 3, CLD, BMRS.
5. Kirck to Pell, 22 December 1939, 360 C.60P, 15/19, WNRC; Levinson, *Untold Story*, 121.
6. Interview with Klaus Schenk, BMRS.
7. Ibid.
8. *Rebbes*, 154; interview with Klaus Schenk, BMRS.
9. Interview with Klaus Schenk, BMRS; interview with Heschel Greenberg, 5 March 2004.

10. The account of the roadblock is from the interview with Schenk.

11. Cohen, *Shmuos*, 235; *Rebbes*, 155. My thanks to Rabbi Avraham Laber for the translation of the Cohen source.

12. Rabbi Heschel Greenberg describes the experience and beliefs of Rabbi Nisson Mengel, a survivor of Auschwitz, as paralleling those of the Lubavitchers in 1939. As the war was nearing its end in 1945, Mengel was forced on a death march with hundreds of other inmates. Giving up and wanting to die, he started to step out of line, knowing he would be shot. A Nazi soldier encouraged him not to and even gave him water. Over the course of the march, the soldier repeated his encouragement and, according to Mengel, enabled him to survive. The soldier must have been the prophet Elijah in German disguise, he felt. And if the man was merely a Nazi soldier and not Elijah, how much greater the miracle (interview with Heschel Greenberg, 29 February 2004).

13. Interview with Barry Gourary, BMRS.

14. *Rebbes*, 154.

15. Meyer, *Unternehmen Sieben*, 137; *Rebbes*, 155; Vogel, *Ein Stück*, 311.

16. Interviews with Joseph Wineberg and Barry Gourary, BMRS.

CHAPTER TWELVE: WAITING IN RIGA

1. Jacobson, "Journey to America," 6; interview with Rachel Altein, 14 January 2003; Zaklikovsky, *America*, 50.

2. NARWDC, GR. 59, GRDOS, 705, VISA CASE FILES 1933–1940, Rhoade to Pell, 20 December 1939, file 811.111, Joseph Schneersohn, itinerary 705, GRDOS, RG 59, NAR.

3. Rhoade to Kramer, 28 November 1939, Schneersohn folder 1, BMRS. Before one received a visa, one had to have an affidavit, an affirmation from a U.S. citizen that the immigrant would not become a public charge (interview with David Kranzler, 23 January 2004).

4. Rhoade to Jacobson, 21 December 1939, Schneersohn folder 1, BMRS.

5. Rhoade to Kramer, 22 December 1939, Schneersohn folder 1, BMRS.

6. Altein and Zaklikovsky, *Out of the Inferno*, 296.

7. Dept. of State Legal Adviser to Mr. Hackworth, 12 January 1940, and Dept. of State to American Legation in Riga, 13 January 1940, file 811.111, Joseph Schneersohn, itinerary 705, GRDOS, RG 59, NAR.

8. Rhoade to Hull, 23 December 1939, Rhoade to Kramer, 22 December 1939, Rhoade to Kramer, 27 December 1939, Schneersohn folder 1, BMRS.

9. Rhoade to Pell, 23 December 1939, Schneersohn folder 3, CLD, BMRS.

10. Pell to Rhoade, 26 December 1939, and Schneersohn to Jacobson, 26 December 1939, Schneersohn folder 3, CLD, BMRS; Meyer, *Unternehmen Sieben*, 139; Jacobson, "Journey to America," 6. The Rebbe's personal possessions were deemed sacred. Hence, great effort was probably made to rescue them (private viewing of several of his possessions with Shalom Dovber Levine, 31 December 2003).

11. Schneersohn to Jacobson, 26 December 1939, Schneersohn folder 3, CLD, BMRS.

12. Interview with Arthur Green of Brandeis University, 25 January 2003; Hoffman, *Despite All Odds*, 178.

13. Interview with Eli S., 31 December 2003; Dimont, *Jews, God, and History*, 107–9; Johnson, *History of the Jews*, 149; Rebbe Menachem Schneerson said it was a mitzvah to have books in the home (interview with Heschel Greenberg, 5 March 2004).

14. Interview with Arthur Green, 25 January 2003; Hoffman, *Despite All Odds*, 183; *Chabad v. Barry and Hanna Gourary*, U.S. District Court, CV-1985-2909, 6–13; Schneersohn folder 6, Kramer files, BMRS; Ehrlich, *Leadership*, 274. Thousands of the Rebbe's books were viewed by the author in a private tour of the Chabad library on 31 December 2003. Special thanks to Rabbi Dovber Levine for this viewing.

15. *Igrois Koidesh*, 5:322; interview with Barry Gourary, BMRS; interview with David Kranzler, 25 January 2004.

16. Zuroff, *"Out of the Inferno."* Heschel Greenberg says the Rebbe did many things the Lubavitchers do not understand but that they consent to be baffled by because he was a spiritual giant (interview, 5 March 2004).

17. Levine to Rigg, 31 July 2003, Schneersohn folder 4, BMRS.

18. Walsh to Hull, 29 December 1939, Schneersohn folder 1, BMRS.

19. Wagner to Warren, 29 December 1939, and Coulter to Wagner, 5 January 1940, file 811.111, Joseph Schneersohn, itinerary 705, GRDOS, RG 59, NAR.

20. Rhoade to Cohen, 29 December 1939, and Rhoade to Kramer, 22 December 1939, Schneersohn folder 1, BMRS; Rhoade to Cohen, 2 January 1940, and memo prepared by Coulter received by Farley, 3 January 1940, Schneersohn folder 2, BMRS.

21. Rhoade to Sabath, 3 January 1940, Rhoade to Miss Ruppert, 3 January 1940, Rhoade to Latimar, assistant to Farley, 3 January 1940, Farley to

Wiley, 5 January 1940, Walsh to Hull, 29 December 1939, Schneersohn folder 2, BMRS.

22. Coulter to Rhoade, 4 January 1940, Rhoade to Coulter, 6 January 1940, Schneersohn folder 3, BMRS.

23. Weinberg, *World at Arms*, 135.

24. Rhoade to Kramer, 4 January 1940, Schneersohn folder 2, BMRS.

25. Wyman, *Abandonment of the Jews*, 47; Rhoade to Kramer, 4 January 1940, 2, Schneersohn folder 2, BMRS.

26. Bauer, *History of the Holocaust*, 136; Wyman, *Abandonment of the Jews*, 153; Rhoade to Kramer, 4 January 1940, 4, Schneersohn folder 2, BMRS; Feingold, *Politics of Rescue*, 186; Feingold, *Bearing Witness*, 67.

27. Rhoade to Kramer, 4 January 1940, 6, Schneersohn folder 2, BMRS; Rhoade to Kramer, 8 January 1940, Schneersohn folder 3, CLD, BMRS.

28. Wiley to Hull, 28 December 1939, file 811.111, Joseph Schneersohn, itinerary 705, GRDOS, RG 59, NAR.

29. Rhoade to Troutman, 4 January 1940, file 811.111, Joseph Schneersohn, itinerary 705, GRDOS, RG 59, NAR.

30. Special Agent Tubbs in Dept. of State to Fitch, 10 January 1940, file 811.111, Joseph Schneersohn, itinerary 705, GRDOS, RG 59, NAR.

31. Jacobson, "Journey to America," 6; U.S. Post Office to Mr. T. F. Fitch, 21 March 1940, Coulter to Bannerman, 3 January 1940, Rhoade to Troutman, 11 January 1940, file 811.111, Joseph Schneersohn, itinerary 705, GRDOS, RG 59, NAR.

32. Special Agent Tubbs in Dept. of State to Fitch, 10 January 1940, file 811.111, Joseph Schneersohn, itinerary 705, GRDOS, RG 59, NAR.

33. Rhoade to Paul Rissman, 9 January 1940, Schneersohn folder 2, BMRS.

34. Rhoade to Rissman, 13 January 1940, Schneersohn folder 2, BMRS; Wiley in Riga to Secretary of State Hull, 26 January 1940, file 811.111, Joseph Schneersohn, itinerary 705, GRDOS, RG 59, NAR.

35. Wyman, *Paper Walls*, 209–12; Feingold, *Politics of Rescue*, 15, 17–18, 38, 135–36, 209; Gellman, *Secret Affairs*, 232.

36. Goodwin, *No Ordinary Time*, 101, 102; Wyman, *Paper Walls*, viii; Kennedy, *Freedom from Fear*, 417–18; Feingold, *Politics of Rescue*, 66; Bauer, *History of the Holocaust*, 130; Feingold, *Bearing Witness*, 63, 78–79.

37. Feingold, *Politics of Rescue*, 204; Coulter to Cooper, 6 July 1940, Biddle to Roosevelt, 14 June 1940, Holden to Early, 27 May 1940, box 2, OF 3186, FDRL.

38. Feingold, *Politics of Rescue,* 148, 154.
39. Friedman, *No Haven,* 225.
40. Medoff and Wyman, *Race against Death,* 6–7; Wyman, *Paper Walls,* 146; Feingold, *Politics of Rescue,* 286.
41. Joseph Schneersohn, Affidavit from Rabbi Israel Jacobson, 22 December 1939; Dept. of State to American Legation in Riga, 13 January 1940; Wiley to Hull, 26 January 1940; Coulter to Bannerman, 3 January 1940, file 811.111, Joseph Schneersohn, itinerary 705, GRDOS, RG 59, NAR. Schneersohn had accounts with Chase National Bank and American National Bank and Trust Company of Chicago, with sums of $3,000 and $2,000, respectively. See also Rhoade to Pell, 30 November 1939, Schneersohn folder 1, BMRS.
42. 360 C.60P, 15/20, WNRCSM; Kleinfeld to Hull, 17 January 1940, Schneersohn folder 3, CDC, BMRS.
43. Rhoade to Kramer, 22 January 1940, Schneersohn folder 3, CLD, BMRS.
44. Schneersohn to Blum, 7 February 1940, Schneersohn folder 3, CLD, BMRS.
45. Meyer, *Unternehmen Sieben,* 139; Jacobson, "Journey to America," 6.
46. NARWDC, GR. 59, GRDOS, 705, VISA CASE FILES 1933–1940, Rhoade to Warren, 8 February 1940, file 811.111, Joseph Schneersohn, itinerary 705, GRDOS, RG 59, NAR. Rhoade to Butler, 29 January 1940, Schneersohn folder 3, CLD, BMRS; NARWDC, GR. 59, GRDOS, 705, VISA CASE FILES 1933–1940, 811.111, Rhoade to Visa Dept., 8 February 1940, file 811.111, Joseph Schneersohn, itinerary 705, GRDOS, RG 59, NAR. Jacobson to Butler, 14 February 1940, Schneersohn folder 7, Kramer file, BMRS.
47. Rhoade to Kramer, December 1939, Schneersohn folder 1, BMRS; Rhoade to Kramer, 8 January 1940, Schneersohn folder 3, CLD, BMRS. As the Rebbe immediately started repaying those in Riga who had loaned him money, one might assume he made sure Rhoade got his money, but the documents are unclear on this point. On the Riga loans, see *Igros Koidesh,* vol. 12, letters 4414, 4364, 4435, 4444.
48. Labor to Rigg, 19 May 1997, Bloch file, BMRS; Rhoade to Pell, 26 December 1939, Schneersohn folder 3, CLD, BMRS; interview with Barry Gourary, BMRS.
49. Friedman, *No Haven,* 134.

CHAPTER THIRTEEN: CROSSING A PERILOUS OCEAN

1. Keegan, *Second World War*, 49.
2. Jacobson, "Journey to America," 6; American legation in Riga to Secretary of State Hull, 18 March 1940, file 811.111, Joseph Schneersohn, itinerary 705, GRDOS, RG 59, NAR; Edelman to Rigg, 23 February 2004.
3. American legation in Riga to Secretary of State Hull, 18 March 1940, and handwritten note entitled "Schneersohn et al.," file 811.111, Joseph Schneersohn, itinerary 705, GRDOS, RG 59, NAR; interview with Barry Gourary, BMRS; Jacobson, "Journey to America," 6; Zaklikovsky, *America*, 61.
4. Jacobson, "Journey to America," 6; 360 C.60P, 15/20, WNRC; Meyer, *Unternehmen Sieben*, 138; interview with Alex Weisfogel, 20 January 2004.
5. Churchill, *Gathering Storm*, 436, 423, 434, 491; Kee, *1939*, 307, 320; Rowlands, *HMS Royal Oak;* Stott, "Four Generations"; Blair, *Hitler's U-Boat War*, 67–68.
6. Blair, *Hitler's U-Boat War*, 118, 120, 124, 138–39, 141; McInnis, *War*, 67; Stott, "Four Generations."
7. Interview with Mordechai Dov Altein, 14 January 2003.
8. McInnis, *War*, 67.
9. Zaklikovsky, *America*, 51.
10. Clair, 146, 148.
11. Zaklikovsky, *America*, 53; Lubavitch HQ PR (Lubavitch News Service), 1 March 1965; Wyman, *Paper Walls*, 152; interview with Barry Gourary, BMRS; interviews with Alex Weisfogel, 20 January 2004, 23 February 2004. Weisfogel, a passenger, regards as exaggerated the number of encounters purported in Chabad sources, which, according to him, wish to emphasize divine intervention. Weisfogel remembers only one German U-boat stopping the ship, southwest of Iceland.
12. Memorandum to the President from Warren and McDonald, 8 October 1940, box 3, OF 3186, FDRL; Lamm, *Religious Thought*, 458–59; H. Rabinowicz, *Hasidism*, 303.

CHAPTER FOURTEEN: THE REBBE IN AMERICA

1. Zaklikovsky, *America*, 50–51; interview with Eliezer Zaklikovsky, 4 June 2003.
2. Wyman, *Paper Walls*, 126; Blair, *Hitler's U-Boat War*, 771.

3. Jacobson, "Journey to America," 7. It seems Bloch got seventeen people out of Warsaw in 1939, but only eleven of them traveled to the United States in March 1940 (Zaklikovsky, *America*, 58, 63). The Rebbe's secretary and his family and a few other Lubavitchers did not get out of Riga (Edelman to Rigg, 23 Feb. 2004, Schneersohn Folder 6, BMRS).

4. Jacobson, "Journey to America," 7; interviews with Meir Greenberg and Barry Go}\ury, BMRS; Posner to Rigg, 8 January 2004, Schneersohn folder 6, BMRS.

5. *Challenge*, 54; Zaklikovsky, *America*, 6, 54, 56, 58; "Rabbi from Warsaw," 46–48; "Lubawitzer Rabbi," 31–32; Meyer, *Unternehmen Sieben*, 138; Ehrlich, *Leadership*, 101.

6. Interview with Zalman Posner, 3 May 2003; Zaklikovsky, *America*, 63.

7. Zaklikovsky, *America*, 55, 57, 61, 63; *Rebbes*, 157; Lubavitch HQ PR (Lubavitch News Service), 1 March 1965. In the quotation, the Rebbe uses the word *holocaust*. Since this source came out in 1965, it is unclear what exact Yiddish or Hebrew word the Rebbe used during the war for Hitler's extermination, but it was clear that he meant the Holocaust. The "communal sin offering" is a Talmudic expression used as a metaphor, a way of saying that all people in the world are part of one organism; what happens in one part of the "organism" affects the entire "body."

8. Lubavitch HQ PR, 1 March 1965; *Likkutei Dibburim*, 3:222.

9. Interview with Shalom Dovber Levine, 15 June 2004.

10. Altein and Zaklikovsky, *Out of the Inferno*, 290. When the Rebbe arrived in Riga, he wrote a letter addressing world Jewry about the horrific situation of Polish Jews under the Nazis. He asked Jewish people "regardless of sect of affiliation" to create a fund for Polish Jewry and give the funds to the Joint (*Igrois Koidesh*, 5:4–5). The Rebbe stayed at the Greystone Hotel for several months until he moved to his headquarters in Brooklyn.

11. NARWDC, GR. 59, GRDOS, 705, VISA CASE FILES 1933–1940, 811.111, Schneersohn to Hull, 25 March 1940, file 811.111, Joseph Schneersohn, itinerary 705, GRDOS, RG 59, NAR.

12. Memorandum for the President from Edwin M. Watson, Secretary to the President, 20 August 1940, box 7, OF, FDRL. David Rabinovitz, who was involved with the rescue, gives the most credit for it to Brandeis (*Igrois Koidesh*, 12:19).

13. Schneersohn to Roosevelt, 12 September 1941, and Rebbe's prayer at-

tached to letter from Kaufman to Roosevelt, 2 December 1941, box 7, OF 76c, FDRL. Many Jewish synagogues offered prayers for the president.

14. Schneersohn to Roosevelt, 1 September 1942, box 8, OF 76c, FDRL. Throughout the war, the Rebbe continued to send food to Russia (interview with Heschel Greenberg, 5 March 2004).

15. *Toldois Chabad*, 323; *Hakreah Vehakedusha* [Reading and Holiness], June 1941, 15; Medoff and Wyman, *Race against Death*, 193; *Igrois Koidesh*, 5:44; interview with David Kranzler, 8 February 2004.

16. Lubavitch HQ PR, 1 March 1965; *Igrois Koidesh*, vol. 5, letters 1133, 1136.

17. *Igrois Koidesh*, vol. 5, letter 1237. This letter refers to about 52 visas. Since most of the other documents talk about 30 visas, the 30 figure is probably correct. *Igrois Koidesh*, vol. 5, letters 1212, 1272, 1335–36, 1391, 1420; Schneersohn to Jacobson, 26 December 1939, Schneersohn folder 3, CLD, BMRS; *Hakreah Vehakedusha*, March 1941, 15; interview with David Kranzler, 8 February 2004.

18. *Hakreah Vehakedusha*, June 1941, 15; Medoff and Wyman, *Race against Death*, 193. For information about the Rebbe's fund, see Ehrlich, *Leadership*, 64.

19. Zuroff, *Response*, xvii. Interview Heschel Greenberg, 5 March 2004.

20. Feingold, *Politics of Rescue*, 131, 160, 164–65; BA-MA, BMRS, Posner to Rigg, 8 January 2004, Schneersohn folder 6, BMRS. It seems that this was the plight of many. See Vaad Memorandum for the State Department, box 20, folder 123, YU-VHC.

21. *Hakreah Vehakedusha*, February 1942, 12.

22. *Hakreah Vehakedusha*, June 1941, 5; August 1941, 2; December 1941, 1; December 1942, 1; October 1944, 1; December 1944, 1; January 1945, 1; April 1945, 1. The Rebbe wrote that American Jews were "nurtured with the sole hope that the Jewish people will be saved through a victory of world-democracy," something he felt was entirely wrong. See also *Hakreah Vehakedusha*, January 1942, 1–2. What happened to the Jews under Haman was also democracy and it could change quickly, the Rebbe's newspaper said. The best thing for Jews to do was to rely on God (*Hakreah Vehakedusha*, March 1942, 3).

23. *Igrois Koidesh*, vol. 5, letter 1498. For more information on the Jewish experience in Shanghai during the war, see Freyeisen, *Shanghai*.

24. *Hakreah Vehakedusha*, February 1942, 40–41; interview with Joseph Wineberg, BMRS. One student died in China, many believe because of the unwillingness of the Vaad, the U.S. Orthodox rescue organization, to

help Lubavitchers (interview with Avraham Laber, 8 May 2003). Rabbi
Laber is quick to add that this is many Lubavitchers' version but that he
should not be used as the source for its legitimacy. A number of Chabad
rabbis interviewed for this book, like Shalom Dovber Levine and Eliezer
Zaklikovsky, have heard similar stories. Whether there is documentation or not, in other words, most Lubavitchers blame the Vaad. Rabbi
Eli S. claims, indeed, that some in Chabad firmly believe that the Vaad
was responsible for the deaths of several Lubavitcher students in China
(interview with Eli S., 31 December 2003).

25. Interview with Barry Gourary, BMRS. The brothers-in-law disliked each
other intensely, according to Barry Gourary, because they knew they
were both candidates for the position of Rebbe. Gourary describes their
relationship in 1940 as resembling that of Cain and Abel, without the
murder. He claims that after Samarius, his father, initiated the rescue of Menachem, his mother, Chana, asked, "Why are you doing this?
Don't you know Menachem hates you?" Samarius replied, "Yes, I know
he probably will do me [political] harm if he comes to the U.S., but I
have been given my orders." Although Samarius disliked Menachem,
he would not leave his brother-in-law, or any other Jew for that matter, to die under the Nazis. Thus, he obeyed the Rebbe and rescued
Menachem, who, according to Barry Gourary, was conducting "under-
handed dealings" to become the next Rebbe. Soon after Menachem was
indeed named the Rebbe, Samarius became a strong supporter of his
brother-in-law.

Chana is a difficult person to understand. According to Rabbi Eli S.,
she was driven by considerable resentment, convinced that the Rebbe
valued her sister and brother-in-law more than her and Samarius. At
her marriage, for example, there were only a few guests; at her sister's,
there were hundreds, and it was a great celebration. She never got over
what she thought a painful display of favoritism (interview with Eli S.,
31 December 2003).

The candidacy of Rabbi Menachem was not a forgone conclusion
until 1951, and, in fact, Samarius seemed to have been groomed for
the position, traveling with the Rebbe on most of his important trips
throughout the 1920s and 1930s. See Ehrlich, Leadership, 3.

Rabbi Heschel Greenberg cites Rabbi Zelig Slonim as recounting
that a few years after Menachem became the Rebbe, Samarius approached him for advice not as a Rebbe but just as a fellow rabbi. Unable

to give any, Menachem went to the grave of their father-in-law to ask him. He returned with an answer that impressed Samarius and convinced him to accept his brother-in-law as the Rebbe. Greenberg feels that Menachem never felt anything but love for his brother-in-law and that the whole conflict was caused by Barry and Chana's jealousy and resentment (interviews, 23 February and 5 March 2004).

26. Feingold, *Politics of Rescue*, 143; Hoffman, *Despite All Odds*, 25.

27. Altein and Zaklikovsky, *Out of the Inferno*, 328–31; interviews with David Kranzler, 24 January and 8 February 2004.

28. Jacobson, *Toward a Meaningful Life*, xxiv. The only other candidate was Samarius Gourary, but according to Rabbi Eliezer Zaklikovsky, "He could not sustain the movement . . . and, in comparison to Menachem, was sub-standard. It was clear that Menachem was the only one with the skills to be a world leader of Lubavitch" (interview with Zaklikovsky, 4 June 2003). According to Rabbi Eli S., the Rebbe had actually written in a section of his unpublished memoirs that he felt Samarius unfit for Chabad leadership (interview with Eli S., 31 December 2003). Avrum Ehrlich says there was more competition than many Lubavitchers like to admit but that Menachem was indeed the best candidate (*Leadership*, 340–50).

29. Interviews with Eliezer Zaklikovsky, 4 June 2003 and 4 March 2004. Yosef Jacobson has looked through some of the scattered archive of Samarius Gourary and has not found much because it "has not been preserved properly." If there are documents proving the Rebbe's efforts with the politicians, they should be in this archive.

30. Kranzler, *Brother's Blood*, 12–13, 34, 36–37, 92–93, 134–38; Zuroff, *Response*, 69; Bauer, *American Jewry*, 308; Feingold, *Politics of Rescue*, 178; Beschloss, *Conquerors*, 65, 251; interview with Moshe Kolodny, 4 September 2003; Bunin, *Fire in His Soul*, 126; Penkower, *Jews Were Expendable*, 204; box 3; box 20, folder 123; and box 21, folders 130, 132, YU-VHC; interview with David Kranzler, 8 February 2004.

31. Zuroff, *"Out of the Inferno"*; Penkower, *Jews Were Expendable*, 249; Feingold, *Politics of Rescue*, 270.

32. Altein and Zaklikovsky, *Out of the Inferno*, 244; interview with Chaskel Besser, BMRS. On 11 October 1939, Dr. Jonas Simon, chairman of the Jewish Community of New York, wrote Wagner about the Gerer Rebbe and the famous rabbis Ben Zion Halberstam of Bobov and Aaron Rokeach of Belz. Wagner immediately forwarded Simon's letter to Warren,

who advised Wagner to look into the nonquota visas allowed for "ministers of religion" under section 4(d) of the Immigration Act of 1924. He told Wagner that the Visa Division could do nothing for the moment but that, as soon as the men applied to the general consuls where they resided, their cases would be accorded "every consideration consistent with the restrictive features of the immigration laws." Besides the efforts of Wagner, the Gerer Rebbe also had the assistance of Bloom, Brandeis, and even Hull. Eventually, the politicians, with the help of German officials, were able to facilitate an escape plan. Through diplomatic channels, two German officers (one of them possibly Bloch) accompanied the Gerer Rebbe and his family to Italy, where they boarded a ship for Palestine. Simon to Wagner, 11 October 1939, and Wagner to Warren, 12 October 1939, file 811.111, Mordechai Alter, itinerary 705, GRDOS, RG 59, NAR; Zuroff, *Response*, 246; Klugman, *Light Is Sown*. Many thanks to Professor Roseanne Schnoll for her analysis of *Light Is Sown*. Yosef Jacobson says the Rebbe wrote on behalf of the Belz Rebbe (interview, 3 March 2004).

33. Walter Laqueur, "The Failure to Comprehend," in *Holocaust*, ed. Niewyk, 266; Wyman, *Abandonment of the Jews*, xiv, xiii; Feingold, *Bearing Witness*, 2–3, 226, 269; Feingold, *Politics of Rescue*, 10, 12–13, 15, 21, 218–21, 298–99, 301.

34. *Hakreah Vehakedusha*, October 1940, 12, and November 1940, 16; interview with Levine, 16 June 2004. See also *Toldot Chabad in Soviet Russia*, 223–24.

35. Interview with Meir Greenberg, BMRS; Levinson, *Untold Story*, 121; Dina Porat, "The Holocaust in Lithuania," in *Final Solution*, ed. Cesarini, 167; Seaton, *Russo-German War*, 10–11; interview with Avraham Laber, 8 May 2003; Ehrlich, *Leadership*, 284n3.

36. Memorandum for Eleanor Roosevelt, 18 March 1941, Papers of Eleanor Roosevelt, ER box 359, FDRL; *Hakreah Vehakedusha*, June 1941, 15; *Toldois Chabad*, 324; Pickett to Roosevelt, 5 March 1941, Secretary to Mrs. Roosevelt to Pickett, 15 March 1941, Pickett to Roosevelt, 17 March 1941, Papers of Eleanor Roosevelt, ER box 359, FDRL; interviews with David Kranzler, 31 December 2003 and 8 February 2004. In defense of Chabad, Simon Jacobson explains, "Spiritual integrity was not Chabad's 'own mission,' as Kranzler states," but was the mission of the entire Jewish people and has maintained Jewish continuity for over 3,000 years.

37. Interview with Barry Gourary, BMRS.

38. Welles to Roosevelt, 31 March 1941, and Prickett to Roosevelt, 22 April 1941, Papers of Eleanor Roosevelt, ER box 359, FDRL. Welles did bring the refugee problem to Roosevelt's attention on several occasions. See, for example, Welles to Roosevelt, 21 December 1940, and Counselor of Polish Embassy Jan Drohojowski, 2 December 1940, OF 3186, box 3, FDRL; Warren to Besser, 31 January 1939, file 811.111, Lotte Jacoby, itinerary 705, GRDOS, RG 59, NAR. Mrs. Roosevelt seems to have been in regular contact with Warren. Roosevelt to Warren, 21 September 1940, Papers of Eleanor Roosevelt, ER box 347, FDRL; file 811.111, Hermann Gottlieb, itinerary 705, GRDOS, RG 59, NAR; Blum, *V Was for Victory*, 11, 174; Black, *Courage*, 109.

39. Interview with Holger Herwig, 10 January 2004.

40. Levine to Rigg, 9 March 2003, Schneersohn folder 4, BMRS; Kranzler to Rigg, 9 March 2004, and Kramer to Rigg, 11 March 2004, Schneersohn folder 6, BMRS; interviews with Moshe Kolodny, 13 August 2003 and March 2004; David Kranzler, 8 February 2004; David Edelman, 8 March 2004; Alex Weisfogel, 8 March 2004; Yosef Jacobson, 3 March 2004. Weisfogel says, "With Chabad, it was always a one-way street, always favoring them." Milton Kramer, president of Chabad's National Committee for the Furtherance of Jewish Education, maintains that Weisfogel's and Kolodny's claims are untrue. He asks how they can say Chabad would not work with the Vaad when it was clear the Vaad considered Lubavitchers pariahs. Obviously, the two groups had problems with one another. Simon Jacobson feels Kolodny and people like him simply do not understand Chabad, which strives to ignite in the souls of all Jews "a belief that through our spiritual activities today we can create a better world tomorrow."

41. Zuroff, *Response*, 244; interview with David Kranzler, 31 December 2003. Problems often arose between secular and Orthodox groups. See Bunin, *Fire in His Soul*, 105; Memorandum on Why the Joint Cannot Take Care of Orthodox Jew, box 20, folder 123, YU-VHC.

42. Kranzler, *Thy Brother's Blood*, 12–13, 34, 36–42, 71, 92–93, 135, 136, 137, 138; Bunin, *Fire in His Soul*, 100, 126; Zuroff, *Response*, 39, 134, 195–97, 221, 251, 254, 286; Beschloss, *Conquerors*, 251; interview with Moshe Kolodny, 4 September 2003; Penkower, *Jews Were Expendable*, 204; box 3 and box 21, folders 120, 123, 132, YU-VHC. According to Rabbi Schochet, the Rebbe would have "worked with the devil" to save lives, but at the time he was doing what other religious leaders were: focus-

ing on spiritual action necessary to counterbalance the horrible events in the world (interview Schochet, 23 June 2004).

43. *Likkutei Dibburim*, 4:80–81.

44. The phraseology at the end of this paragraph is taken from Zuroff, "Orthodox Rescue Revisited," which expresses the same sentiment about several other Orthodox Jewish leaders (36); *Hakreah Vehakedusha*, September 1941, 2; December 1942, 1; August 1943, 1; March 1945, 1; April 1945, 1. Simon and Yosef Jacobson deny the Rebbe would have been hard to work with, stating he would have done anything to save Jews, just as he would use non-observant doctors to save a life, as dictated by Halacha.

45. Friedman, *No Haven*, 129; *Likkutei Dibburim* 4:79–80; *Hakreah Vehakedusha*, June 1, 6; August 1941, 1; December 1941, 4.

46. Blum, *V Was for Victory*, 178; Wise, *Challenging Years*, 22; Kranzler, *Thy Brother's Blood; Igrois Koidesh*, 7:33–35 (letter 1893); interview with Simon Jacobson, 4 March 2004. There are numerous documents about the Rebbe's religious crusade in America between 1940 and 1945, but few about his political activism in that period—something many Lubavitchers claim was just as important. Rabbi Eliezer Zaklikovsky maintains that documents exist but have not yet been found. He also says, with sadness, that many of the documents were taken from the file cabinets in the yeshiva in Brooklyn by students and rabbis. But having looked through thousands of documents in numerous archives in the United States, I conclude that more would have been found if the Rebbe was indeed as active as many claim (interview with Eliezer Zaklikovsky, 4 March 2004).

47. *Hakreah Vehakedusha*, February 1942, 4.

48. *Hakreah Vehakedusha*, June 1, 1941, 6–8; July 1941, 1; August 1941, 2–3; November 1941, 1–3; December 1941, 1, 4–5; January 1942, 1–2; February 1942, 1; April 1942, 4; August 1942, 1–2; July 1943, 1; August 1943, 1.

49. Zaklikovsky, *America*, 36.

50. Levine to Rigg, 9 March 2003, Schneersohn folder 4, BMRS.

51. Wyman, *Abandonment of the Jews*, 78; Friedman, *No Haven*, 130.

52. Zuroff, *Response*, 257–60; Medoff and Wyman, *Race against Death*, 11, 43, 113–14, 144, 154–56; Kranzler, "Orthodoxy's Finest Hour," 34–35; David Kranzler, "Stephen S. Wise and the Holocaust," in *Reverence, Righteousness, and Rahamanut*, ed. Schacter, 158, 186; Kranzler, *Thy Brother's Blood*, 71, 100–101, 141.

53. *Igrois Koidesh*, 7:187–95 (letter 1988).

54. Ibid.

55. Ibid., Rebbe Schneersohn to Klatzkin, 31 March 1943, Agudath Archives of New York. Thanks to Professor Roseanne Schnoll and Rabbi Avraham Laber for translating the letter. See also *Hakreah Vehakedusha*, June 1941, 1–8, and July 1941, 1–4; *Likkutei Dibburim*, 3:56–57, 62–64, 81, 85–86, and 5:317–18; Medoff and Wyman, *Race against Death*, 34; interview with Eli S., 31 December 2003.

56. *Likkutei Dibburim*, 5:311; Jacobson, "Journey to America," 7; Zaklikovsky, *America*, 61, 65; *Hakreah Vehakedusha*, January 1942, 1; interview with Heschel Greenberg, 6 March 2004. In the Rebbe's worldview, divine punishments could be stopped by pleading with God (Schneersohn, *On the Teachings of Chassidus*, 41).

57. Ehrlich, *Leadership*, 102, 266, 285n17. Rabbi Heschel Greenberg notes that the Rebbe did not have other options because, had he stayed with his flock, he would have died in Warsaw and been unable to save a single soul (interview, 6 March 2004).

58. *Hakreah Vehakedusha*, April 1941, 16; July 1941, 2, 6; August 1941, 2; September 1941, 3; December 1941, 4; January 1942, 1; August 1942, 1; May 1943, 1; July 1943, 1; August 1945, 1.

59. *Likkutei Dibburim*, 5:255–57; *Hakreah Vehakedusha*, May 1941, 4; October 1941, 2–4; December 1942, 1; interview with Eliezer Zaklikovsky, 4 June 2003; Levine to Rigg, 9 March 2003, Schneersohn folder 4, BMRS; Meyer, *Unternehmen Sieben*, 138-39. Sending emissaries throughout the world to make Jews more observant had been a tradition since Chabad's founding. See *Likkutei Dibburim*, 1:67.

60. *Likkutei Dibburim*, 3:291 and 1:111; interview with Zalman Posner, 3 May 2003; *Hakreah Vehakedusha*, June 1941, 4; Ehrlich, *Leadership*, 281; interview with David Kranzler, 23 January 2004; Wertheim, *Law and Custom*, 432n53.

61. *Hakreah Vehakedusha*, October 1940; April 1941, 16; October 1941, 1–4; June 1941, 1–2, 5–6; July 1941, 2; August 1941, 2; September 1941, 1, 6; March 1942, 1; July 1942, 1, 4; September 1942, 1–2; December 1942, 1; June 1943, 1; September 1943, 1; December 1943, 1; January 1944, 1; July 1944, 1; February 1945, 1; Levine to Rigg, 9 August 2003, Schneersohn folder 6, BMRS. Since the Lubavitchers spoke Yiddish, which has its roots in thirteenth-century German (see Johnson, *History of the Jews*, 338), and wore seventeenth-century Polish garb, it is difficult to follow

their argument that Jews should not abandon their language and dress, when they seem already to have done so. The concept that the Jews were being punished for their sins was held by other Jewish religious leaders as well. Interviews with Heschel Greenberg, 23 February 2004; Eliezer Zaklikovsky, 13 January 2004; Yosef Jacobson, 3 March 2004.

62. *Likkutei Dibburim*, 3:101 and 5:313–14. For more on politics, see *Hakreah Vehakedusha*, May 1941.

63. *Hakreah Vehakedusha*, June 1941, 6.

64. Isaiah 2:4, 11:4–9, 50, 52, 53, 66:6–8; Ezekiel 4:16, 33:11, 37, 38:18–23; interview with Moshe Kolodny, 4 September 2003; Black and Rowley, *Peake's Commentary*, 586–87; *Hakreah Vehakedusha*, September 1941, 4; *Likkutei Dibburim*, 3:56–57, 62–64, 81, 85–86, and 4:317–18.

65. *Hakreah Vehakedusha*, July 1941, 6–7; June 1941, 1; January 1945, 1; interview with Moshe Kolodny, 4 September 2003; *Igrois Koidesh*, 7:187–95 (letter 1988).

66. *Hakreah Vehakedusha*, June 1941, 7–8. Although this article is not signed by the Rebbe, it is obvious that he is the principal author. Besides, nothing made it into the Chabad newspaper without the Rebbe's approval.

67. *Likkutei Dibburim*, 3:40–42, 56–57–62–63; 4:71; 5:315; Dalfin, *Seven Chabad-Lubavitch Rebbes*, 109; *Hakreah Vehakedusha*, July 1941, 2–4, and October 1943, 1. The view that American Jews were responsible for the Holocaust was held by others. See Alice Lyons Eckardt, "Suffering, Theology, and the Shoah," in *Contemporary*, ed. Jacobs, 46–47.

68. *Hakreah Vehakedusha*, August 1941, 2.

69. The Rebbe was especially horrified that so many American Jews did not go to the synagogue on the Sabbath, did not take ritual baths, shaved their beards, and failed to wear religious garments. He was also disturbed that they worshiped in services with mixed seating. "In a word, in America one is allowed to do whatever is forbidden in the rest of the world" (*Likkutei Dibburim*, 3:83).

70. *Likkutei Dibburim*, 3:56–57, 62–64, 81, 85–86, and 5:317–18; *Hakreah Vehakedusha*, October 1944, 1; J. I. Schneersohn, *"Tzemach Tzedek,"* 99, 105. For the Rebbe's thoughts on *teshuvah*, see *Likkutei Dibburim*, 2:1–2, 65; J. I. Schneersohn, *Saying Tehillim*, 31.

71. *Likkutei Dibburim*, 3:229; Altein and Zaklikovsky, *Out of the Inferno*, 308.

72. Despite numerous requests, the Chabad community has been unable

to provide documents that would present a different picture. Around 1,500 pages of the Rebbe's speeches printed in *Likkutei Dibburim*, hundreds of pages of articles in his newspaper from 1941 to 1945, several of his letters translated by Lubavitchers, and numerous books about Lubavitch present the Rebbe's theological beliefs as they are rendered in this chapter. Rabbi Eli Shmotkin is reputed to have documents that show the Rebbe's beliefs in another light, but he has refused to provide them (discussion with Eli Shmotkin, 30 January 2004). Zalman Posner claims the English translation of *Likkutei Dibburim* used here is a poor rendition of the Rebbe's "profound insights" and thus unreliable (interview Posner, 18 June 2004). Since the translated volumes of the *Dibburim* are printed by the official Chabad publishing house Kehot, I find this argument unconvincing. Even if the translation is weak, the Rebbe's basic message is indeed preserved, and his thoughts also mirror those in his letters and newspaper.

73. Interview with Eliezer Zaklikovsky, 4 May 2003.

74. *Every Jew Has a Silver Lining*, 3; interview with Yosef Jacobson, 3 March 2004. Rabbi Jacobson transcribed hundreds of M. M. Schneerson's talks. The last quotation is from a talk Jacobson heard in 1990. Many Lubavitchers do not see the two Rebbes' views as contradictory. Since Lubavitchers believe that the Rebbe knows what his society and age is ready for, he may have different responses than his predecessors or successors; in essence, though, they all think the same. For the modern reader, this seems an apologetic way of looking at their leaders' philosophies. Ehrlich, *Leadership*, 54–55; interviews with Eli S., 31 December 2003, and Milton Kramer, 31 December 2003. For more insight into Chabad's views of pain and suffering, see Jacobson, *Meaningful Life*, 125–33. The complicated topic of the Holocaust and why it happened has many nuances. Both of the rebbes' views, that the Holocaust is a punishment and that we cannot know why it is happening, are compatible beliefs in the Orthodox world, but to understand this, notes Simon Jacobson, takes time and a lot of study (interview S. Jacobson, 25 June 2004).

75. *Hakreah Vehakedusha*, July 1941, 2, 6; April 1944, 1; April 1945, 1.

76. Jacobson, "Journey to America," 10; *Likkutei Dibburim*, 3:57, 80, 225, and 5:276, 305–7, 311; Berenbaum to Rigg, 28 February 2003, Schneersohn folder 6, BMRS.

77. *Likkutei Dibburim*, 3:174, 203; see also 5:316.

78. Ibid., 3:125–26, 219–25, 230–32.

79. Ibid., 3:219–25; *Rebbes*, 14; Hoffman, *Despite All Odds*, 26; *Kramers*, 71; Zaklikovsky, *America*, 88; H. Rabinowicz, *Hasidism*, 399; J. I. Schneersohn, *Lubavitcher Rabbi's Memoirs*, xi; interviews with Meir Greenberg and Joseph Wineberg, BMRS; interviews with Heschel Greenberg, 23 February 2004, and Simon Jacobson, 4 March 2004. Rabbi Shalom Dovber Levine, an expert on the Rebbe's writings, says the Rebbe never mentioned the escape in his writings (interview, 5 March 2004).

The headquarters in Brooklyn were purchased by the Kramer brothers. They had been used as an abortion clinic (interview with Milton Kramer, 31 December 2003).

80. Ehrlich, *Leadership*, 82, 84, 87, 108, 115–16, 373–74, 387–88; Zaklikovsky, *America*, 93.

81. Ehrlich, *Leadership*, 3, 12, 108–9, 117, 259, 359; Fishkoff, *Rebbe's Army*, 10–16, 261–84; Lenowitz, *Jewish Messiahs*, 215–23. Rabbi Zalman Shmotkin, director of the Lubavitch News Service, says he and others believe that messianism is on the wane (Fishkoff, *Rebbe's Army*, 275). Rabbi Heschel Greenberg disagrees, claiming that most Lubavitchers believe Rebbe Schneerson is the Messiah but keep their view to themselves (interview, 6 March 2004). For a critical take on the Lubavitch community's response to the Rebbe's death, see Berger, *Rebbe*. Milton Kramer, former president of Chabad, regards Berger's book as unscholarly, as does Heschel Greenberg (Kramer to Rigg, 29 February 2004, BMRS; interview with Heschel Greenberg, 6 March 2004).

CHAPTER FIFTEEN: THE FATES OF THE RESCUERS

1. Interview with Martin Bloch, BMRS.

2. Pers 6/9887, Blatt 19, BA-MA. Bloch's military files say he did not become a lieutenant colonel until 1941, but during a trip in November 1940, his office already referred to him as that rank. There must have been a mistake in communication with the OKW.

3. Mader, *Hitler*, 57–66; BA-MA, interview with Ursula Cadenbach, BMRS; Pers 6/9887, Blatt 62, 72, BA-MA.

4. Pers 6/9887, Blatt 25, BA-MA; Lt. Col. Bloch to Commander of Abwehr I, Oberst G. Piekenbrock, 7 January 1943, Bloch file, BMRS.

5. Pers 6/9887, Blatt 27, 35, 42, BA-MA; interviews with Martin Bloch and Ursula Cadenbach, BMRS.

6. Höhne, *Canaris*, 515–17, 527; Abshagen, *Canaris*, 223.

7. Keegan, *Second World War*, 468; Cooper, *German Army*, 458–59; Glantz and House, *Battle of Kursk*, 344–45.

8. Interviews with Martin Bloch and Ursula Cadenbach, BMRS; interview with Brigitte Motz, 8 March 2004. See Abshagen, *Canaris*, 223.

9. Adolf Ratjen to Bloch, 2 September 1943, Bloch file, BMRS.

10. Pers 6/9887, Blatt 35, BA-MA.

11. Abshagen, *Canaris*, 92; Pers 6/9887, Blatt 35, 39, BA-MA; interview with Ursula Cadenbach, BMRS.

12. Hans Eduard Meyer to Sabine Bloch, 20 March 1950, BMRS. Pers 6/9887, Blatt 25, BA-MA.

13. Rotraut Nonnenmann to Sabine Bloch, 19 July 1944, BMRS; H. W. von Goerschen to Sabine Bloch, 26 July 1944, BMRS.

14. Lt. Col. Bloch to Sabine Bloch, 10 April 1945, Bloch file, BMRS; BA-MA, Pers 6/9887.

15. Pers 6/9887, Blatt 41, BA-MA.

16. Adam, *Judenpolitik*, 331–32; Meyer, *Jüdische Mischlinge*, 100, 108, 153.

17. Absolon, *Wehrgesetz*, 119; Bormann to Lammers, 2 November 1944, R 43II/599, BA-B; 43II/603b, BA-B.

18. Suchanek to Burgdorf, 15 September 1944, Pers 6/9887, Blatt 41, BA-MA.

19. Burgdorf to Suchanek, 26 September 1944, Pers 6/9887, Blatt 42, BA-MA.

20. Pers 6/9887, Blatt 44, BA-MA.

21. Walther Brockhoff to Sabine Bloch, 31 October 1945, Bloch file, BMRS; interview with Martin Bloch, BMRS.

22. Interview with Martin Bloch, BMRS.

23. Bloch to Sabine Bloch, 10 April 1945, Bloch file, BMRS.

24. Pfeiffer to Bloch, 6 April 1945, Bloch file, BMRS.

25. Interviews with Martin Bloch and Ursula Cadenbach, BMRS; Register's Officer, Berlin, to Karl Preis, 1 November 1946, Bloch file, BMRS.

26. Karl Preis to Sabine Bloch, 24 October 1946, Bloch file, BMRS.

27. Höhne, *Canaris*, 465, 466, 489, 524; Abshagen, *Canaris*, 84, 90, 108, 122–23. For information about the number of Jews rescued, Dept. of State to American Legation in Riga, 13 January 1940, file 811.111, Joseph Schneersohn, itinerary 705, GRDOS, RG 59, NAR. See also Gilbert, *Righteous*, 184–85. For an excellent work about Canaris's efforts to help people of Jewish descent in the Abwehr, see Meyer, *Unternehmen Sieben*.

28. Höhne, *Canaris*, 557–63, 569; Abshagen, *Canaris*, 11, 191, 238–39, 240.
29. Höhne, *Canaris*, 571, 583–84, 594, 596–98; Bürkner to Wohlthat, 15 January 1948, 100021/49193, Blatt 55F, HHSAD; Kahn, *Hitler's Spies*, 235–36; Abshagen, *Canaris*, 246–57; Brissaud, *Canaris*, 2.

CONCLUSION

1. Rhoade to Kramer, 17 January 1940, Schneersohn folder 2, BMRS.
2. Wyman, *Abandonment of the Jews*, 315; Friedman, *No Haven*, 50.
3. Blum, *V Was for Victory*, 176–77; Feingold, *Politics of Rescue*, 15.
4. Unsigned letter to Roosevelt, 1 September 1941, OF 76c, box 7, FDRL.
5. Lipstadt, *Beyond Belief*, 2, 91–93, 97, 115.
6. Barringer to Roosevelt, 30 June 1941, and Early to Roosevelt, 29 July 1941, OF 76c, box 7, FDRL.
7. Wise, *Challenging Years*, 228.
8. Wyman, *Abandonment of the Jews*, 183.
9. Goodwin, *No Ordinary Time*, 396.
10. Wyman, *Abandonment of the Jews*, xv, 103.
11. Safire, "Truman on Underdogs."
12. Friedman, *No Haven*, 143.
13. Zuroff, "Orthodox Rescue Revisited," 37.
14. Kranzler, "Stephen S. Wise," 170.
15. Medoff and Wyman, *Race against Death*, 12; Wyman, *Abandonment of the Jews*, 285; Pehle to Kalmanowitz, 8 December 1944, and Pehle to Kalmanowitz, 19 December 1944, box 21, folder 132, YU-VHC; Feingold, *Politics of Rescue*, 269–70. William D. Rubinstein regards Wyman's figures as exaggerated by "at least 90 per cent" but does not present supporting data ("The Myth of Rescue," *Holocaust*, ed. Niewyk, 237). See also Morgenthau to Vaad, 8 July 1944, box 130, YU-VHC; George Warren to Vaad, 2 November 1944, box 20, folder 123, YU-VHC; Lipstadt, *Beyond Belief*, 263.
16. Kranzler, "Stephen S. Wise," 182–83.
17. Zuroff, "Orthodox Rescue Revisited," 36–37; Beschloss, *Conquerors*, 53.
18. Kalmanowitz to Berle, 4 August 1944, box 20, folder 123, YU-VHC.
19. Rhoade to Kramer, 17 January 1940, Schneersohn folder 2, BMRS.
20. Wyman, *Abandonment of the Jews*, 184–85, 191. Jan Ciechanowski, ambassador of the Polish government-in-exile, delivered a white paper to Hull in June 1941 "charging the Nazis with 'compulsory euthanasia' against the Jews," yet Hull still did not act (Friedman, *No Haven*, 135).

Often he would even have files on the refugee issues "routed away" from his office (Gellman, *Secret Affairs*, 346).

21. Beschloss, *Conquerors*, 53.
22. Schneersohn to Hull, 25 March 1940, file 811.111, Joseph Schneersohn, itinerary 705, GRDOS, RG 59, NAR.
23. Meeting of Officers of the Inter-Governmental Committee on Political Refugees, 17 October 1939, 5, OF 3186, box 2, FDRL.
24. Feingold, *Politics of Rescue*, 166, 233, 295–96.
25. Friedman, *No Haven*, 83. See also Lipstadt, *Beyond Belief*, 95.
26. Bauer, *History of the Holocaust*, 281.
27. Feingold, *Politics of Rescue*, 49.
28. Feingold, *Bearing Witness*, 68, 78.
29. Brissaud, *Canaris*, 153.
30. Browning, *Origins*, 65; Cadenbach to Martin Bloch, 16 November 1996, Bloch file, BMRS. Another of Bloch's secretaries tells of approaching her boss about a delicate issue. She had a friend who was a half Jew and she was unsure whether she should maintain the relationship, given the political situation. Bloch assured her that she was not breaking any laws and that it was all right to continue having contact with the person. Only later did she discover, to her great embarrassment, that Bloch himself was a Mischling (interview with Brigitte Motz, 8 March 2004).
31. Nonnenmann to Sabine Bloch, 24 February 1950, Bloch file, BMRS.
32. Interview with Martin Bloch, BMRS.
33. Abshagen, *Canaris*, 92.
34. Rigg, *Hitler's Jewish Soldiers*, 272.
35. Laqueur, "The Failure to Comprehend," *Holocaust*, ed. Niewyk, 260–62.

AFTERWORD

1. Fishkoff, *Rebbe's Army*, 7; Ehrlich, *Leadership*, 6, 61. Adding to this frustration is that Chabad has frequently given mixed messages about its movement's philosophy and beliefs. Lubavitchers sometimes claim in public that they do not think Rebbe Menachem Mendel Schneerson is the Messiah but in private believe he is. They have differing private and public views about non-Jews, too. Although many in Chabad today distance themselves from the belief that Gentile souls are inferior to those of Jews, their philosophy teaches that they are. As the Rebbe's newspaper wrote in December 1941, "In general and as a na-

tion, as a whole, we are always better than the other nations." The newspaper further explained in June 1942 that antisemitism often arose because people "begrudged the Jew his enviable higher position." According to Chabad, Jews have both "animal" and "divine" souls, whereas Gentiles have only an animal soul. According to historian Roman Foxbrunner, Lubavitchers view Gentile souls as of an "inferior order" and "totally evil with no redeeming qualities whatsoever." These souls "were created only to test, to punish, to elevate, and ultimately to serve Israel (in the Messianic Era)." Lubavitch philosophy teaches that having a divine soul brings man closer to God, while the animal soul drags him down. Only Jews, said the founder of Chabad, Rebbe Schneur Zalman, have a divine soul since they are the "descendants of the righteous patriarchs." Gentile souls die with the bodies, while Jewish souls are eternal. Most of these ideas are articulated in Zalman's *Tanya*, which, according to Rabbi Eli S., "is quoting the Talmud, basic Jewish law. It's not a question against Chabad, but against Judaism, as a whole. As is often the case, Chabad is now defending normative Jewish thought, a position it is comfortable with but which requires a fair chance and adequate time to achieve properly" (Eli S. to Rigg, 6 January 2004, Schneersohn folder 6, BMRS). Rabbi Eliezer Zaklikovsky contends that the claim that Gentiles have only animal souls "is absolutely absurd" (Zaklikovsky to Rigg, 4 January 2004, Schneersohn folder 6, BMRS). Zaklikovsky's view seems to be the prevalent one among many Lubavitchers today. To call Gentiles bad contradicts Jewish writings that maintain that everyone is created in the image of God, observes Rabbi Yosef Jacobson. Even Rebbe Menachem Schneerson explained that a rock has a godly soul (interview with Yosef Y. Jacobson, 3 March 2004). Rabbi Simon Jacobson adds that this topic about Jewish philosophy and Gentiles is a very complicated matter and the sources used in this note give a literal but distorted view of the issues. Jacobson claims that the Bible is full of references to the Jews being the "Chosen People," and thus, God recognizes their special role in the world. However, Jacobson also notes that every nation has a role in God's plan and that Gentiles can definitely have a divine spark in their souls. Also, if they honor God and keep some of his commandments, they can also have a share in the world to come (interview S. Jacobson 25 June 2004).

2. Ehrlich, *Leadership*, 5–6, 292–95; interviews with Heschel Greenberg, 23 February 2004, and Manis Friedman, 4 March 2004. Ehrlich writes

of Chabad: "Some editing and intentional deletion of unpleasant information, especially in published sources, has been carried out deliberately" (*Messiah of Brooklyn*, 9).

3. Elie S. to Rigg, 6 January 2004, Schneersohn folder 6, BMRS. Eli Shmotkin, a Lubavitch rabbi who at first helped me a lot, is an example of someone who made researching Chabad's past difficult. Rabbis like Avraham Laber, Simon Jacobson, Yosef Jacobson, and Eliezer Zaklikovsky, although they may not have approved of all my conclusions, still engaged in debate and did their best to help me find documents. Once Shmotkin realized he disagreed with some of the facts in my work, he was unwilling to show me any documents that might give a different picture of what I was presenting. When my book came out, he indicated he would use them to defend his movement (discussion with Eli Shmotkin, 30 January 2004). Had he shown me the documents and proved their merits, I would have willingly used them.

4. Samuel Moyn, "History's Revenge." Moyn's piece is a review of Myers's *Resisting History.*

5. Interview with Yosef Y. Jacobson, 3 March 2004.

6. Interview with David Edelman, 8 March 2004.

BIBLIOGRAPHY

PRIMARY SOURCES

Archives
Bundesarchiv, Berlin (BA-B)
Bundesarchiv/Militärarchiv, Freiburg (BA-MA)
Hessisches Hauptstaatsarchiv, Düsseldorf (HHSAD)
Institut für Zeitgeschichte, Munich
National Archive Records, Washington, D.C. (NAR)
Bryan Mark Rigg Sammlung, Bundesarchiv/Militärarchiv, Freiburg (BMRS)
Franklin D. Roosevelt Library, Hyde Park, New York (FDRL)
Washington National Records Center, Suitland, Maryland (WNRC)
Yeshiva University Archives–Vaad Hatzala Collection, 1939–63 (YU-VHC)

Recorded Interviews (BMRS)
Heinz Günter Angress, 10 December 1994
Hermann Aub, 14 December 1996
Hans B. (Bernheim), 29 October 1998
Chaskel Besser, 15 July 2003
Martin Bloch, 13 October 1996
Robert Braun, 10–14 August 1994, 7 January 1996
Ursula Cadenbach, 15 October 1996

Karin Falencki, 3 January 2003
Werner Goldberg, 17 October 1994
Barry Gourary, 8 May 2003
Meir Greenberg, 18 August 1996
Michael Günther, 19 February 1997
Zalman Gurary, 19 January 1997
Mrs. Johannes Hamburger (pseudonym), December 1996
Helmut Krüger, 27–31 August 1994
Klaus Schenk (pseudonym), 18 November 1996
Friedrich Schlesinger, 10 December 1994
Joseph Wineberg, 4 May 2003
Helmut Wohlthat (interviewed by Rolf Vogel), 17 December 1974

Unrecorded Interviews
Mordechai Dov Altein, 14 January 2003
Rachel Altein, 14 January 2003
Adam Boren, 9 December 2003
David Edelman, 8 March 2004
Shmuel Fox, 14 January 2003
Manis Friedman, 4 March 2004
Arthur Green, 25 January 2003
Heschel Greenberg, 23 and 29 February, 4–6 March 2004
Herwig Holger, 10 January 2004
Paula Hyman, September 2003
Simon Jacobson, 4 March 2002
Yosef Y. Jacobson, 3 March 2004
Bernhard Klein, 9 September 2003
Moshe Kolodny, 13 August 2003, 4 September 2003, 21 January 2004,
    8 March 2004
Hirsch Kotlarsky, 3 January 2003
Milton Kramer, 31 December 2003
David Kranzler, 31 December 2003, 23–26 January 2004, 8 February 2004
Avraham Laber, 8 May 2003, 6 January 2004, 8 March 2004
Shalom Dovber Levine, 5 March 2004
Brigitte Motz, 8 March 2004
Zalman Posner, 3 May 2003
Eli S., 31 December 2003
Immanuel Schochet, 23 June 2003

Alex Weisfogel, 20 January 2004, 8–9 March 2004
David Woolner, 18 September 2003
Eliezer Zaklikovsky, 3 May 2003, 4 June 2003, 25 December 2003, 13 January 2004, 4 March 2004

SECONDARY SOURCES

Abrams, Alan. *Special Treatment*. Secaucus, 1985.

Abshagen, Karl Heinz. *Canaris*. London, 1956.

Absolon, Rudolf. *Wehrgesetz und Wehrdienst, 1935–1945: Das Personalwesen in der Wehrmacht*. Boppard, 1960.

Adam, Uwe. *Judenpolitik im Dritten Reich*. Düsseldorf, 1972.

Adler, H. G. *Der Verwaltete Mensch: Studien zur Deportation der Juden aus Deutschland*. Tübingen, 1974.

Adolf Hitler: Monologe im Führerhauptquartier, 1941–1944. Ed. Werner Jochmann. Hamburg, 1980.

Aly, Götz, and Susanne Hein. *Vordenker der Vernichtung*. Frankfurt, 1993.

Altein, Rachel, and Eliezer Zaklikovsky, eds. *Out of the Inferno: The Efforts That Led to the Rescue of the Rabbi Yosef Y. Schneersohn of Lubavitch from War-Torn Europe in 1939–1940*. New York, 2002.

Anti-Defamation League. "Rev. Falwell's Statement That the Antichrist Is a Jew Borders on Antisemitism and Is Rooted in Christian Theological Extremism." Press release, 19 January 1999.

Armstrong, Karen. *The Battle for God*. New York, 2000.

———. *A History of God: A 4,000-Year Quest of Judaism, Christianity, and Islam*. New York, 1993.

Aschheim, Steven E. *Brothers and Strangers: The East European Jew in German and German Jewish Consciousness, 1800–1923*. Madison, 1982.

Avtzon, Sholom D. *Tishrei-Adar*. Vol. 2 of *A Day to Recall, a Day to Remember*. New York, 1998.

Bar-Zohar, Michel. *Hitler's Jewish Spy: The Most Extraordinary True Spy Story of World War II*. London, 1985.

Bauer, Yehuda. *American Jewry and the Holocaust: The American Jewish Joint Distribution Committee, 1939–1945*. Detroit, 1981.

———. *A History of the Holocaust*. New York, 1982.

Below, Nicolaus von. *Als Hitlers Adjutant, 1937–1945*. Mainz, 1980.

Benz, Wolfgang. *The Holocaust: A German Historian Examines the Genocide*. New York, 1999.

Berger, David. *The Rebbe, the Messiah, and the Scandal of Orthodox Indifference*. London, 2001.

Beschloss, Michael. *The Conquerors: Roosevelt, Truman, and the Destruction of Hitler's Germany, 1941–1945*. New York, 2002.

Bethell, Nicholas. *The War Hitler Won: The Fall of Poland, September 1939*. New York, 1972.

Black, Allida M., ed. *Courage in a Dangerous World: The Political Writings of Eleanor Roosevelt*. New York, 1999.

Black, Matthew, and H. H. Rowley, eds. *Peake's Commentary on the Bible*. New York, 1963.

Blair, Clay. *Hitler's U-Boat War: The Hunters, 1939–1942*. New York, 1996.

Blum, John Morton. *V Was for Victory: Politics and American Culture during World War II*. New York, 1976.

Boteach, Shmuel. *The Wolf Shall Lie with the Lamb: The Messiah in Hasidic Thought*. Northvale, 1993.

Brewster, Todd, and Peter Jennings. *The Century*. New York, 1998.

Brissaud, André. *Canaris*. London, 1986.

Broszat, Martin, and Norbert Frei, eds. *Das Dritte Reich im Überblick*. Munich, 1989.

Browning, Christopher. *The Origins of the Final Solution: The Evolution of Nazi Jewish Policy, September 1939–March 1942*. Lincoln, 2004.

Buber, Martin. *The Way of Man: According to the Teaching of Hasidism*. Secaucus, 1966.

Bullock, Alan. *Hitler: A Study in Tyranny*. New York, 1983.

Bunin, Amos. *A Fire in His Soul: Irving M. Bunin, 1901–1980. The Man and His Impact on American Orthodox Jewry*. New York, 1989.

Burns, James MacGregor. *The Lion and the Fox*. Vol. 1 of *Roosevelt*. Norwalk, 1956.

Cesarini, David, ed. *The Final Solution: Origins and Implementation*. New York, 1994.

Challenge: An Encounter with Lubavitch-Chabad. Ed. Charles Rader. New York, 1970.

Churchill, Winston S. *The Gathering Storm*. Vol. 1 of *The Second World War*. Boston, 1983.

Citino, Robert M. *Quest for Decisive Victory: From Stalemate to Blitzkrieg in Europe, 1899–1940*. Lawrence, 2002.

Clark, Alan. *Barbarossa: The Russian-German Conflict, 1941–1945*. New York, 1965.

Cohen, Rabbi Raphael N. *Shmuos Vsipurim*. Israel, 1977.

The Complete Artscroll Siddur. Ed. Rabbi Nosson Scherman and Rabbi Meir Zlotowitz. New York, 1984.

Contemporary Christian Religious Responses to the Shoah. Ed. Steven L. Jacobs. Lanham, 1993.

Cooper, Matthew. *The German Air Force, 1933–1945*. New York, 1981.

———. *The German Army, 1933–1945: Its Political and Military Failure*. New York, 1978.

Cordevero, Moses. *Tomer Debora*. Jerusalem, 1985.

Corum, James S. *The Roots of Blitzkrieg: Hans von Seeckt and German Military Reform*. Lawrence, 1992.

Craig, Gordon A. *Germany, 1866–1945*. New York, 1978.

Dalfin, Chaim. *The Seven Chabad-Lubavitch Rebbes*. Northvale, 1998.

Deroshos HaRan.

Dimont, Max I. *Jews, God, and History*. New York, 1964.

Ehrlich, Avrum M. *Leadership in the Habad Movement: A Critical Evaluation of Habad Leadership, History, and Succession*. Northvale, 2000.

———. *The Messiah of Brooklyn: Understanding Lubavitch Hasidim Past and Present*. Ktav, 2004.

Eliach, Yaffa. *Hasidic Tales of the Holocaust*. New York, 1982.

Every Jew Has a Silver Lining: An Adaptation of the Public Addresses of the Luba-vitcher Rebbe Rabbi Menachem M. Schneerson, on the Tenth of Teves and on Shabbos Parshas Vayechi. Ed. David Feldman, Simon Jacobson, Yosef Jacobson, and Joel Kahn. Vol. 47. New York, 1990.

Feingold, Henry L. *Bearing Witness: How America and Its Jews Responded to the Holocaust*. Syracuse, 1995.

———. *The Politics of Rescue: The Roosevelt Administration and the Holocaust, 1938–1945*. New Brunswick, 1970.

Fischel, Jack R. *The Holocaust*. Westport, 1998.

Fishkoff, Sue. *The Rebbe's Army: Inside the World of Chabad-Lubavitch*. New York, 2003.

Foxbrunner, Roman A. *Habad: The Hasidism of R. Shneur Zalman of Lyady*. Tuscaloosa, 1992.

Freedman, Samuel G. *Jew vs. Jew: The Struggle for the Soul of American Jewry*. New York, 2000.

Frei, Norbert. *National Socialist Rule in Germany*. Cambridge, 1993.

Freyeisen, Astrid. *Shanghai und die Politik des Dritten Reiches*. Würzburg, 2000.

Friedländer, Saul. *The Years of Persecution, 1933–1939.* Vol. 1 of *Nazi Germany and the Jews.* New York, 1997.

Friedman, Chaim Shlomo. *Dare to Survive.* New York, 1991.

Friedman, Saul S. *No Haven for the Oppressed: United States Policy toward Jewish Refugees, 1938–1945.* Detroit, 1973.

Gay, Ruth. *The Jews of Germany.* New Haven, 1992.

Gellman, Irwin. *Secret Affairs: Franklin Roosevelt, Cordell Hull, and Sumner Welles.* Baltimore, 1995.

Gilbert, Martin. *The Holocaust.* New York, 1985.

———. *The Righteous: The Unsung Heroes of the Holocaust.* New York, 2003.

———. *The Second World War: A Complete History.* New York, 1989.

Glantz, David M., and Jonathan M. House. *The Battle of Kursk.* Lawrence, 1999.

The Goebbels Diaries. Ed. Louis P. Lochner. New York, 1948.

Goodwin, Doris Kearns. *No Ordinary Time. Franklin and Eleanor Roosevelt: The Home Front in World War II.* New York, 1994.

Gordon, Sarah. *Hitler, Germans, and the "Jewish Question."* Princeton, 1984.

Gutman, Yisrael. *The Jews of Warsaw, 1939–1943: Ghetto, Underground, Revolt.* Bloomington, 1982.

Harris, Lis. *Holy Days: The World of a Hasidic Family.* New York, 1985.

Hasidism Reappraised. Ed. Ada Rapoport-Albert. London, 1996.

Hakreah Vehakedusha [Reading and Holiness]. Chabad's official newspaper.

Hebrew Union College–Jewish Institute of Religion at One Hundred Years. Ed. Samuel E. Karff. Detroit, 1976.

Heeresadjutant bei Hitler, 1938–1943: Aufzeichnungen des Majors Gerhard Engel. Ed. Hildegard von Kotze. Schriftenreihe der Vierteljahreshefte für Zeitgeschichte 29. Stuttgart, 1974.

Herzstein, Robert Edwin. *Roosevelt and Hitler: Prelude to War.* New York, 1989.

Hilberg, Raul. *The Destruction of the European Jews.* New York, 1961.

Hitlers Tischgespräche im Führerhauptquartier. Ed. Henry Picker. Stuttgart, 1976.

Hoffman, Edward. *Despite All Odds: The Story of Lubavitch.* New York, 1991.

Höhne, Heinz. *Canaris.* New York, 1979.

The Holocaust: Problems and Perspectives of Interpretation. Ed. Donald L. Niewyk. New York, 2003.

Hosking, Geoffrey. *Russia: People and Empire, 1552–1917.* Cambridge, Mass., 1997.

House, Jonathan M. *Combined Arms Warfare in the Twentieth Century.* Lawrence, 2001.

Huberband, Shimon. *Kiddusch Hashem: Jewish Religious and Cultural Life in Poland during the Holocaust.* New York, 1987.

Igrois Koidesh. Vols. 5, 6, 7, 12, and 19. New York, 1983–1993.

Jacobs, Louis. *The Jewish Religion: A Companion.* New York, 1995.

Jacobs, Steven L., ed. *Contemporary Christian Religious Responses to the Shoah.* Lanham, 1993.

Jacobson, Israel. "Journey to America." *Di Yiddishe Heim,* 1956.

———. *ZiKoron L'Beis Yisrael: Memories of Rabbi Israel Jacobson, 1907–1939.* New York, 1996.

Jacobson, Simon. *Toward a Meaningful Life: The Wisdom of the Sages.* New York, 2002.

Jews and Jewish Life in Russia and the Soviet Union. Ed. Yaacov Ro'i. Essex, 1995.

Johnson, Paul. *A History of the Jews.* New York, 1987.

Kahn, David. *Hitler's Spies: German Military Intelligence in World War II.* New York, 1977.

Kaminetzky, Yosef Y. *Days in Chabad.* New York, 2002.

Kammer, Hilde, and Elisabet Bartsch, eds. *Nationalsozialismus: Begriffe aus der Zeit der Gewaltherrschaft, 1933–1945.* Hamburg, 1992.

Kaplan, Chaim A. *Scroll of Agony: The Warsaw Diary of Chaim A. Kaplan.* New York, 1965.

Kaplan, Marion A. *Between Dignity and Despair: Jewish Life in Nazi Germany.* New York, 1998.

Kee, Robert. *1939: In the Shadow of War.* Boston, 1984.

Keegan, John. *The Second World War.* New York, 1990.

Kennedy, David M. *Freedom from Fear: The American People in Depression and War, 1929–1945.* New York, 1999.

Kershaw, Ian. *Hitler, 1889–1936: Hubris.* New York, 1999.

———. *Hitler, 1936–1945: Nemesis.* New York, 2000.

———. *The Nazi Dictatorship.* New York, 1985.

———. *Profiles in Power: Hitler.* New York, 1991.

Klein, Edward. *The Kennedy Curse: Why America's First Family Has Been Haunted by Tragedy for 150 Years.* New York, 2003.

Klugman, Ben Zion. *The Light Is Sown for the Righteous (Ohr Zoruah la Tzadik).* Jerusalem, 2001.

The Kramers: The Next Generation. Ed. Milton Kramer. New York, 1995.

Kranzler, David. *The Man Who Stopped the Trains to Auschwitz: George Mantello, El Salvador, and Switzerland's Finest Hour.* Syracuse, 2000.

———. "Orthodox Rescue Revisited." *Jewish Action* 63, no. 3 (Spring 2003).

———. "Orthodoxy's Finest Hour: Rescue Efforts during the Holocaust." *Jewish Action* 63, no. 1 (Fall 2002).

———. *Thy Brother's Blood: The Orthodox Jewish Response during the Holocaust.* New York: 1987.

Krüger, Helmut. *Der Halbe Stern: Leben als deutsch-jüdischer "Mischling" im Dritten Reich.* Berlin, 1992.

Kushner, Harold. *When Bad Things Happen to Good People.* New York, 1981.

Lamm, Norman. *The Religious Thought of Hasidism: Text and Commentary.* New York, 1999.

Lasser, William. *Benjamin V. Cohen: Architect of the New Deal.* New Haven, 2002.

Lauren, Paul Gordon. *Power and Prejudice.* London, 1988.

Legalizing the Holocaust: The Early Phase, 1933–1939. Introd. John Mendelsohn. Vol. 1 of *The Holocaust.* New York, 1982.

Lenowitz, Harris. *The Jewish Messiahs: From the Galilee to Crown Heights.* Oxford, 1998.

Levin, Nora. *The Holocaust: The Destruction of European Jewry, 1933–1945.* New York, 1973.

Levinson, Isaac. *The Untold Story.* Johannesburg, 1958.

Likkutei Dibburim: An Anthology of Talks by Rabbi Yosef Yitzchak Schneersohn of Lubavitch. 5 vols. Ed. Uri Kaploun. New York, 1987–2000.

Lipstadt, Deborah E. *Beyond Belief: The American Press and the Coming of the Holocaust, 1933–1945.* New York, 1986.

Loewenthal, Naftali. *Communicating the Infinite: The Emergence of the Habad School.* Chicago, 1990.

"Lubawitzer Rabbi." *Newsweek,* 1 April 1940.

Madej, Victor, and Steven Zaloga. *The Polish Campaign, 1939.* New York, 1985.

Mader, Julius. *Hitlers Spionagegenerale Sagen Aus.* Berlin, 1971.

Manstein, Erich von. *Lost Victories: The War Memoirs of Hitler's Most Brilliant General.* Novato, 1982.

Matthäus, Jürgen. "German *Judenpolitik* in Lithuania during the First World War." *Leo Baeck Yearbook* 43 (1998).

Maurer, Trude. *Ostjuden in Deutschland, 1918–1933.* Hamburg, 1986.

Mayer, Arno J. *Why Did the Heavens Not Darken? The "Final Solution" in History.* New York, 1988.

McInnis, Edgar. *The War: First Year.* New York, 1940.

McJimsey, George. *The Presidency of Franklin Delano Roosevelt.* Lawrence, 1999.

Medoff, Rafael, and David Wyman. *A Race against Death: Peter Bergson, America, and the Holocaust.* New York, 2002.

Melson, Robert. *False Papers: Deception and Survival in the Holocaust.* Champaign, 2000.

Metzger, Alter B. *The Heroic Struggle: The Arrest and Liberation of Rabbi Yosef Y. Schneersohn of Lubavitch in Soviet Russia.* New York: 1999.

Metzmacher, Helmut. "Deutsch-englische Ausgleichsbemühungen im Sommer 1939." *Vierteljahrshefte für Zeitgeschichte* 14, no. 4 (1966).

Meyer, Beate. *Jüdische Mischlinge: Rassenpolitik und Verfolgungserfahrung, 1933–1945.* Hamburg, 1999.

Meyer, Winfried. *Unternehmen Sieben: Eine Rettungsaktion für vom Holocaust Bedrohte aus dem Amt Ausland-Abwehr im Oberkommando der Wehrmacht.* Frankfurt, 1993.

Militärgeschichtliches Forschungsamt, ed. *The Build-Up of German Aggression.* Vol. 1 of *Germany and the Second World War.* Oxford, 1998.

Millet, Allan R., and Williamson Murray, eds. *Military Innovation in the Interwar Period.* New York, 1998.

Mindel, Nissan. *Rabbi Joseph I. Schneersohn, the Lubavitcher Rabbi.* New York, 1947.

Morgan, Ted. *FDR: A Biography.* New York, 1985.

Morison, Samuel Eliot. *The Oxford History of the American People.* New York, 1965.

Moyn, Samuel. "History's Revenge: What Happened to Jewish Faith When a New Attitude toward the Past Emerged?" *Forward,* 9 January 2004.

Myers, David N. *Resisting History: Historicism and Its Discontents in German-Jewish Thought.* Princeton, 2003.

Niemöller, Wilhelm. *Die Synode zu Steglitz.* Göttingen, 1970.

"1,000 Rabbis Greet Rabbi Schneersohn, Exiled Polish Leader." *New York Herald Tribune,* 20 March 1940.

O'Neill, Robert J. *The German Army and the Nazi Party, 1933–1939.* London, 1966.

Padfield, Peter. *War beneath the Sea: Submarine Conflict during World War II.* New York, 1996.

Pehle, Walter H., ed. *Der Judenpogrom 1938: Von der "Reichskristallnacht" zum Völkermord.* Frankfurt, 1988.

Penkower, Monty Noam. *The Jews Were Expendable: Free World Diplomacy and the Holocaust.* Chicago, 1983.

Plitnick, Mitchell. "Reclaiming Antisemitism." *Jews for Global Justice,* 20 July 2003.

"Rabbi from Warsaw." *Time,* 1 April 1940.

Rabinowicz, Harry. *Hasidism: The Movement and Its Masters.* Northvale, 1988.

Rabinowicz, Tzvi. *Hasidism in Israel: A History of the Hasidic Movement and Its Masters in the Holy Land.* Northvale, 2000.

Rashi. *The Torah: With Rashi's Commentary Translated, Annotated, and Elucidated.* Vol. 1. Ed. Yisrael Isser Zvi Herczeg. New York, 1995.

The Rebbes: Rabbi Yosef Yitzchak Schneersohn of Lubavitch. Vol. 2. Kfar Chabad, 1994.

Rheins, Carl J. "The Verband nationaldeutscher Juden, 1921–1933." *Leo Baeck Yearbook* 25 (1980).

Rich, Norman. *Hitler's War Aims.* New York, 1974.

Rigg, Bryan Mark. *Hitler's Jewish Soldiers: The Untold Story of Jews and Men of Jewish Descent Who Served in the German Military.* Lawrence, 2002.

Robinson, George. *Essential Judaism: A Complete Guide to Beliefs, Customs, and Rituals.* New York, 2000.

Rossino, Alexander B. *Hitler Strikes Poland: Blitzkrieg, Ideology, and Atrocity.* Lawrence, 2003.

Rowlands, Peter. *HMS Royal Oak.* http://www.hmsroyaloak.co.uk/index.htm.

Rubenstein, Richard. *After Auschwitz: History, Theology, and Contemporary Judaism.* Baltimore, 1992.

Safire, William. "Truman on Underdogs." *New York Times,* 14 July 2003.

Schacter, Jacob J., ed. *Reverence, Righteousness, and Rahamanut: Essays in Memory of Rabbi Dr. Leo Jung.* Northvale, 1992.

Schleunes, Karl A. *The Twisted Road to Auschwitz: Nazi Policy toward German-Jews, 1933–1939.* Champaign, 1970.

Schmidl, Erwin A. *Juden in der K.(u.) K. Armee, 1788–1918.* Studia Judaica Austriaca 11. Eisenstadt, 1989.

Schneersohn, Joseph I. *Lubavitcher Rabbi's Memoirs: The Memoirs of Rabbi Joseph I. Schneersohn, the Late Lubavitcher Rabbi.* 2 vols. New York, 1961.

————. *On the Teachings of Chassidus (Kuntres Toras Hachassidus)*. New York, 1965.

————. *Saying Tehillim: Selected from Letters by the Late Lubavitcher Rebbe Rabbi Yoseph Yitzhak Schneersohn on the Subject of Reciting Psalms*. New York, 1975.

————. *The "Tzemach Tzedek" and the Haskala Movement (Ha "Tzemach Tzedek" Utenaus Hahaskolo)*. New York, 1962.

Schneersohn, Shalom Dovber. *Oh Ahavas Yisrael: Heichaltzu*. Brooklyn, 1996.

Seaton, Albert. *The Russo-German War, 1941–1945*. London, 1971.

Segal, Simon. *The New Order in Poland*. New York, 1942.

Shirer, William L. *Berlin Diary: The Journal of a Foreign Correspondent, 1934–1941*. New York, 1941.

Sichot Kodesh. Unpublished transcript of Rebbe Menachem Mendel Schneerson's talks from 1958.

Solomon, Aryeh. *The Educational Teachings of Rabbi Menachem M. Schneerson*. Northvale, 2000.

Solomon, Lewis D. *The Jewish Book of Living and Dying*. Northvale, 1999.

Stoltzfus, Nathan. *Resistance of the Heart: Intermarriage and the Rosenstrasse Protest in Nazi Germany*. New York, 1996.

Stott, Greg. "Four Generations of 18th-Century Stotts, including Endnotes and Sources." *The Stott Family Tree*. http://168.144.123.218/18thCentury StottsEndnots.htm.

Strzetelski, Stanislaw. *Where the Storm Broke: Poland from Yesterday to Tomorrow*. New York, 1942.

Stuckart, Wilhelm, and Hans Globke. *Kommentare zur Deutschen Rassengesetzgebung*. Munich, 1936.

Sydnor, Charles W. *Soldiers of Destruction: The SS Death Head's Division, 1933–1945*. Princeton, 1990.

Tent, James F. *In the Shadow of the Holocaust: Nazi Persecution of Jewish-Christian Germans*. Lawrence, 2003.

"This Is Your Life." Unpublished essay by Melvin Neumark and Debby Kramer Neumark to commemorate the sixtieth birthday of Sam Kramer. Schneersohn folder 6, BMRS.

Toland, John. *Adolf Hitler*. New York, 1976.

Toldois Chabad B-Artzois Ha'Bris: History of Chabad in the USA, 1900–1950. New York, 1988.

Toldot Chabad in Soviet Russia. New York, 1989.

Toras Menachem Hisva'Aduyos. New York, 1992.

Troyer, John. "Hatemongers Try to Cleanse History. Gays: Forgotten Heroes of 9/11," *CounterPunch*, 3 May 2002.

Tull, Charles J. *Father Coughlin and the New Deal*. Syracuse, 1965.

Victor, George. *Hitler: The Pathology of Evil*. Washington, 1998.

Vital, David. *A People Apart: The Jews in Europe, 1789–1939*. Oxford, 1999.

Vogel, Rolf. *Ein Stück von Uns*. Bonn, 1973.

The Von Hassell Diaries, 1938–1944: The Story of the Forces against Hitler inside Germany as Recorded by Ambassador Ulrich von Hassell, a Leader of the Movement. New York, 1947.

"War Front: Capitalism in Germany." *Time*, 7 April 1941.

Warfield, Hania, and Gaither Warfield. *Call Us to Witness: A Polish Chronicle*. New York, 1945.

Watt, Richard M. *Bitter Glory: Poland and Its Fate, 1918–1939*. New York, 1979.

Watts, Barry, and Williamson Murray. "Military Innovation in Peacetime." In *Military Innovation in the Interwar Period*. Ed. Allan R. Millet and Williamson Murray. New York, 1998.

Weinberg, Gerhard L. *A World at Arms: A Global History of World War II*. New York, 1994.

Wertheim, Aaron. *Law and Custom in Hasidim*. Hoboken, 1992.

Wheeler-Bennett, John. *The Nemesis of Power*. New York, 1980.

Wise, Stephen. *Challenging Years: The Autobiography of Stephen Wise*. New York, 1949.

Wistrich, Robert. *Hitler and the Holocaust*. New York, 2001.

Wouk, Herman. *This Is My God: The Jewish Way of Life*. New York, 1959.

Wyden, Peter. *Stella: One Woman's True Tale of Evil, Betrayal, and Survival in Hitler's Germany*. New York, 1993.

Wyman, David S. *The Abandonment of the Jews: America and the Holocaust, 1941–1945*. New York, 1984.

———. *Paper Walls: America and the Refugee Crisis, 1938–1941*. New York, 1985.

Zaklikovsky, Eliezer. *America Is No Different*. New York, 1999.

Zalman, Schneur. *Tanya*. New York, 1969.

———. *Torah or Parshas Toldos*.

———. *Torah or Parshas Vayeishev*.

Zuroff, Ephraim. "Orthodox Rescue Revisited." *Jewish Action* 63, no. 3 (Spring 2003).

———. "*Out of the Inferno.*" *Jerusalem Post*, 15 December 2002. Review of Rachel Altein and Eliezer Zaklikovsky, eds., *Out of the Inferno.*

———. *Response of Orthodox Jewry in the United States: The Activities of the Vaad Ha-Hatzala Rescue Committee, 1939–1945.* New York, 2000.

ACKNOWLEDGMENTS

I have so many people to thank for their contribution to this work that it would be difficult to name them all, yet there are several who deserve special mention. Foremost on the list is Jonathan Steinberg, my Cambridge adviser. The foundation for this book was written for my master's degree at Cambridge University in 1997 under his guidance. It could not have been written without his support and encouragement, which helped me through some of the most challenging experiences of my academic career. He has done the further service of reading this manuscript twice. I thank him from the bottom of my heart.

I would like also to mention my professor at Yale University, Paula Hyman, for whom I wrote a short essay about the rescue in a course on the Holocaust in the spring of 1996. At that time, she encouraged me to continue to research the subject and explore the larger issues surrounding this event. Her insightful comments have been incredibly helpful.

Over the past three years, historian Michael Berenbaum of the University of Judaism honored me by reading my work several times, giving invaluable advice and criticism. I am grateful to my editor at Yale University Press, Larisa Heimert, for her dedication and her attention to detail. Keith Condon and the rest of the Yale team have been incredibly professional and a pleasure to work with.

David Kranzler, director of the Holocaust Archives at Queensborough Community College, read my work meticulously and gave me cogent feedback. He has a wealth of knowledge and, besides that, he is a real mensch.

Martin Bloch, the son of the man primarily responsible for the rescue, entrusted me with hundreds of documents about his family. I spent time at his home discussing his father and the documents on various occasions between 1996 and 2002. Indeed, without his assistance, I would have had a difficult time reconstructing his father's history. Bloch was also responsible for putting me in touch with Ursula Cadenbach, Bloch's secretary, who in turn put me in touch with Klaus Schenk. Both of these people helped me tremendously. Bloch's other children, Cornelia Shonkwiler, Maria Obenaus, and Christian Bloch also supported this project with encouragement and information. Along with Bloch's grandson Felix Bloch and his daughter-in-law Maria Bloch, these family members have been incredible in their enthusiasm and interest, not to mention diligent in their hours of proofreading.

Milton Gustafson assisted me in the search for documents in the National Archives. Though a high-ranking civil servant, he personally went into the stacks and retrieved documents that had proved difficult to procure. For his insights into Jewish and Lubavitch history, I thank Arthur Green of Brandeis University. Milton Kramer, the son of the former president of Chabad, Hyman Kramer, and a former Chabad president himself, and Debby Kramer Neumark, the daughter of Chabad's legal counsel, Samuel Kramer, were invaluable in helping me reconstruct the history of their family. Milton Kramer's dedication to and support of this work have strengthened and encouraged me more than he knows.

Many Lubavitchers were more than willing to meet with me and discuss the rescue, in particular, Leib Altein, Mordechai Dov Altein, Rachel Altein, Shmuel Fox, Zalman Gurari, Meir Greenberg, Hirsch Kotlarsky, Shalom Dovber Levine, Eli Shmotkin, Zalman Shmotkin, and Joseph Wineberg. My special thanks go to David Edelman, Manis Friedman, Heschel Greenberg, Simon Jacobson, Yoseph Yitzchak Jacobson, Avraham Laber, Zalman Posner, Immanuel Schochet, and Eliezer Zaklikovsky. These men are resident experts on Lubavitch history and philosophy, and their thoughtful suggestions and feedback enabled me to piece together the story of the Rebbe's background and escape. In addition to their guidance, Yosef Jacobson, Laber, and Zaklikovsky provided me with hundreds of pages of invaluable documents that helped reconstruct the roles the U.S. government and the Lubavitchers played. They went beyond the call of duty in sharing their time and advice. Although they have not always agreed with my conclusions, they have remained open to discussion and debate. Their dedication is a testimony to their sincere generosity and their devotion to Chabad and their Rebbe, Menachem Mendel Schneerson.

My special thanks go also to the grandson of Rebbe Joseph Isaac Schneersohn, Barry Gourary, who allowed me to interview him and who proofread my manuscript. Although old and sick, he gave generously of his time and knowledge. He is the only living eyewitness to many of the events in this book, and he provides a counterhistory to the formal history of Chabad. Since he is no longer part of the Lubavitch movement as a result of a fallout with the Chabad leadership soon after his grandfather's death, he has shown much courage in coming forward and talking about these events. For his continued support and guidance the past several years, I thank Rabbi Dovid Gottlieb of Ohr Somayach Yeshiva in Jerusalem. I appreciate the interview Karin Falencki, a survivor of the attack on Poland in 1939, granted me. Her insights were truly helpful.

Winfried Meyer provided an important perspective on the story, which he briefly discusses in his excellent book *Unternehmen Sieben*. Without David Wyman, whose scholarship is unmatched on the subject of United States immigration policy during the Holocaust, I could not have reconstructed much of the historical background. For insights into Hasidic life, I would like to thank Agudah leader Rabbi Chaskel Besser of New York. For their advice on theological issues, my thanks to Eva Fleischner of Montclair State University and Joe Errington, a Methodist minister who was the chaplain supervisor of the Program Review Division in the Federal Bureau of Prisons. James Leonard Abrahamson of American Military University and Evan Bukey of the University of Arkansas offered detailed comments and criticism about the content and structure of this book. For their knowledge of Jewish history, I am grateful to Rabbi Kenneth Roseman, David Lyon, Kip Lombardo, Hillel program director at Boston University, and Bernhard Klein, chair of the History Department of Kingsborough College, as well as Lawrence Burian, David Berger, and Avrum Ehrlich. During a conference in California in February 2004, distinguished Holocaust scholar Raul Hilberg discussed possible titles with me and his advice was greatly appreciated. Donald Niewyk at Southern Methodist University provided tough criticism and helpful suggestions. And Henry Feingold, director of the Jewish Resource Center of Baruch College in New York, did me a great favor in reading through my manuscript and offering excellent advice.

The editorial comments of Peter Schliesser, who suffered under the Nazis as a "half Jew," enriched my research tremendously. For her insight into Judaism and her careful proofreading, I am grateful to Roseanne Schnoll of Brooklyn College. Alex Rossino of the U.S. Holocaust Memorial Museum also commented very helpfully on my work. I thank Jim Wood, a highly decorated Loach pilot (three Distinguished Flying Crosses) and Vietnam veteran for his comments as well. For their constructive criticism and advice, I also thank former Yale professor Mark Shulman and the president of the Cordell Hull Institute, Hugh Corbet. My agent, Rob McQuilkin, has gone beyond the call of duty and read my work with the utmost care. Rabbi Moshe Kolodny, director of the Agudath Israel of America Archives, not only helped me find documents but gave me crucial feedback. I also appreciate Grace Roosevelt, whose suggestions have strengthened it.

Sam Anthony, special program director at the National Archives in Washington; Kate Flaherty, specialist in still pictures at the National Archives in College Park, Maryland; Robert Clark, archivist at the Franklin D. Roosevelt Library in Hyde Park, New York; Shulamith Berger, curator of Special Collections at Yeshiva University; and Michael Smith at the Fretz Park Library in Dallas all deserve deepest thanks for their professionalism and their assistance locating materials for this book.

I would also like to tell my mother-in-law, Mary Delle Stelzer, and my aunt Mary Rigg-Dalbey how much I appreciate their editing and advice, as well as the support of my brother, David Rigg. And in conclusion, I wish particularly to thank my patient wife, Stephanie, for her incomparable help over the past several years. This book is dedicated to her.

INDEX

Page numbers in italics refer to illustrations